Memoir Of Eliza S. M. Quincy

Eliza Susan Quincy

MEMOIR

OF THE

LIFE OF ELIZA S. M. QUINCY.

BOSTON,

MASSACHUSETTS:

1861.

BOSTON:

PRINTED BY JOHN WILSON AND SON,

22, SCHOOL STREET.

MEMOIR.

PART I.

IN compliance with the request of my children, I have written from memory, and from the recollections of my mother, now residing in our family, and eighty-three years of age, the following narrative of some events in the lives of my maternal ancestors and of my own early life.

ELIZA SUSAN MORTON QUINCY.

QUINCY, MASSACHUSETTS,
JULY 12, 1821.

NOTE.

In 1878, the Editor accidentally received a copy of a letter from JOHN KEMPER, the youngest brother of Mrs. MORTON (see page 259), to PETER H. KEMPER of Virginia, dated at Hudson, New York, in which he states that "his father, JACOB KEMPER, was born at Bacharach, a fortified town on the Rhine, of which his father, Colonel KEMPER, was the military commander or governor, the office being hereditary in the male line of the family." He died in 1712, having been a Colonel in the service of Frederick William the Great Elector, and of his son Frederick the First of Prussia; and, as all the officers in these armies were noblemen, he must have been a man of rank. Bacharach is situated a mile above Kaub. From the time of the Romans, it has been celebrated for its wines, and derives its name from an altar to Bacchus in the Rhine, visible at low water. It was fortified with walls and twelve towers. On a huge cone of rock above it stood the Castle of Stahleck, connected with Bacharach by two fortified walls, and for centuries the residence of the family of the Hohenstauffens, and of the Counts Palatine. It was besieged, taken, and rebuilt eight times, and blown up and destroyed by the French in 1689. JACOB KEMPER sold his hereditary rights in the commission of Governor of Bacharach for 600 rix-dollars, and with that money came to America.

CHAPTER I.

M^Y maternal grandfather, Jacob Kemper, was born in Germany, in the city of Caub, on the river Rhine, A.D. 1706. His father, an officer in the Prince Palatine's army, was so severely wounded, that he was obliged to retire upon a pension. He survived many years, and died, after a lingering illness, in his easy-chair, — a circumstance to which his children used often to advert as a singular termination of the life of a military man who had received fourteen wounds in battle. His pension was continued, and his widow was thus enabled to give each of her three sons a liberal education. The eldest, a physician, went to the East Indies; returned, after many years, a man of large property; and settled in Holland. The profession of the second son is not remembered.

Jacob Kemper, the youngest son, was six years of age when his father died. He refused to finish his studies at the university, for which he was prepared; and insisted upon entering on some active employment. His mother yielded to his wishes, and purchased a vessel for him; as master of which, he took freight on his own account at the cities on the Rhine. In 1736, he married Maria Regina Ernest, of Manheim. Her father was a minister of the Reformed Church in that city. Her mother, a woman of rank and fortune, had offended her parents by her marriage with Mr. Ernest, who had been her tutor. They never forgave him; but, once a year, sent for their daughter and her children to visit them at their splendid mansion : and, when her father died, his grandchildren in America shared in her portion of his property. In 1737, Mrs. Kemper accompanied her husband to Coblentz, where her first child was born. She received great kindness from the ladies of that city ; and one of the principal stood godmother to the infant, and named it, after herself, Anna Gertrude. As Coblentz was a Roman-Catholic city, Mrs. Kemper was not allowed to depart until her child was baptized with the ceremonies of that church. Her second daughter, Maria Sophia, my mother, was born at Kaub in 1739, and named after her two grandmothers, Mrs. Ernest and Mrs. Kemper.

In 1741, a company of men called Newlanders were employed by ship-owners in Holland to persuade the Germans to emigrate to America, which they described as a perfect Arcadia, — a land flowing with milk and honey, and enriched with mines of gold and silver. They thus induced persons well situated in their native country to rend asunder the ties of kindred and affection, and to go three thousand miles across an ocean to an unknown land, where the language, habits, and customs were entirely foreign to their own. Mr. Kemper was so infatuated by these representations, that, contrary to the entreaties of his mother and friends, he converted all his possessions into money, and prepared for his voyage.

From the number and value of the articles Mr. and Mrs. Kemper brought with them, they must have been people of property and cultivation in their own country. They had a folio Bible in the German language, and many books, fine editions for that day, handsomely bound, and ornamented with prints, which I remember to have often seen and looked over. They also brought trunks and chests of household linen and clothing ; many articles of furniture, which I also recollect ; and stores of tapes, needles, pins, thread, silk, &c. ; which were not exhausted for six or eight years, and which marked great care, foresight, and ability to spend on their outfit.

Mr. Kemper's mother — when she found he was determined to leave her, and to take his wife, to whom she was attached as to a daughter, with their two children, one born and both reared in her house — supplied them with every accommodation in her power. Her only daughter was married, and settled at a distance. She was left alone, and never ceased to grieve for the loss of her children, like that of death to her. They heard from her occasionally; but, in those times, communication with Europe was rare and difficult.

Mr. and Mrs. Kemper embarked from Amsterdam in 1741. Their voyage was lengthened by touching at a port in England, and was not performed under many months. During the passage, my mother was seized with symptoms of the small-pox; and the captain, who had never had that disease, then so dreaded and often so fatal, though a humane man, at first insisted that she should be immediately thrown overboard. He said, that, if he died, the passengers would be left in the midst of the ocean, with no one capable of commanding the ship, and of conducting them to the land to which they were destined; and what was the value of the life of a child of two years old, compared with those of all on board? But the parents successfully combated these arguments. Mrs. Kemper shut herself up with her child in her cabin: the disease proved of a mild type, and did not affect another person on board. The vessel was large, and well fitted up for the better class of passengers. They consisted chiefly of young married people, with their children. Each family had separate accommodations, and were supplied from their own sea-stores.

Mrs. Kemper was accompanied by her younger sister, Christina Ernest. Her only brother, Matthew Ernest, had many years previous left Manheim, without the knowledge of his parents. After a long time, he wrote word that he had gone to America, had married a widow of fortune, and was established as a merchant at a place called Rhinebeck, from the settlers having come from the river Rhine, and from the name of the proprietor Beekman.

To Mr. Ernest Mr. and Mrs. Kemper wished to direct their steps; but they were landed at Philadelphia, two hundred miles from his residence, — ignorant of the language, of the country, and of every thing which might help them on their way. A German agent induced Mr. Kemper to exchange his gold and silver for depreciated paper money, which he represented as of equal value, and more convenient, as it was the currency of the country. When Mr. Kemper reached New Brunswick, he met with an honest German resident, — whose name was Dillidine, — to whom he exhibited his funds, and who told him he had been defrauded by a sharper. His journey of eighty miles from Philadelphia had exceeded all his other expenses since he left Germany, from the use of the depreciated paper money. From Brunswick Mr. and Mrs. Kemper took passage in a sloop to New York, and thence up the Hudson to Rhinebeck, where they were received with great kindness by their brother, and passed the ensuing winter in his hospitable abode.

In the spring of 1742, Mr. Ernest advised Mr. Kemper to take the command of a sloop which he owned, or to buy one for himself, and ply up and down the Hudson, between Rhinebeck and New York, — a profitable business, in which he had been employed in Germany. His family could then remain near Mr. Ernest, and have the advantage of a church and school in their own language. But by a singular fatality, as it appears to us, Mr. Kemper insisted on going back in the country, on the "New-land" he had heard so much of, to become a farmer. He had left Germany with this project, and nothing could divert him from it; and his ignorance of the English tongue probably made him diffident of engaging in business carried on in that language. Finding Mr. Kemper obstinately bent upon his purpose, Mr. Ernest yielded, and purchased for him a farm on "the patent" of Robert R. Livingston, on a lease of three lives, in that part of Dutchess County, now the town of Beekman, — sixty miles below Rhinebeck, and twenty from the Hudson. On this farm there was a small house and barn, and land cleared for a garden; and the rest was as wild and uncultivated as could be desired: and there this family, brought up in cities and used to all the accommodations of life, were set down in a wilderness, ignorant of the best modes of clearing and cultivating the ground, and of obtaining daily comforts. Christina Ernest remained with her brother, who continued to assist Mr. and Mrs. Kemper by every means in his power. He visited them several times a year, and sent or brought them coffee, tea, sugar, &c., sixty miles over roads almost impassable, — equal to hundreds at the present day. Mr. Ernest always travelled on horseback; and my mother remembers how his saddle-bags used to be loaded for the family, and the joy his arrival occasioned.

In this wild country an incident happened to my mother, which she has often related. When a child of six years of age, she was accustomed to eat her bowl of rice and milk, after dinner, seated on the sill of the house-door; and was heard to speak of "die schöne Schlange,"* who came and ate her rice. Her mother watched to see what these words meant; and, to her surprise and consternation, saw a large rattlesnake, with its head in the bowl, eating with the child, who, when her visitor took more than its share, tapped it on the head with her spoon. It went quietly away when the meal was finished. But this intimacy was too dangerous to be allowed, and Mr. Kemper killed the snake. The rattle, a very large one, with eleven or twelve rings, was preserved for some years, but was lost when the family removed from the Livingston Patent.†

Soon after this occurrence, the women and children were secured in a stockade from an alarm from the Indians, which happily proved groundless. The next year, my mother broke her arm in jumping

---

* "The beautiful snake."

† This incident is the origin of an anecdote related with some variations by Priscilla Wakefield, in a work entitled "Instinct Displayed." It has also been made the subject of an engraving executed in Germany, entitled "Das Kind mit der Milch und der Schlange."

from a chest in play. A young neighbor, Zacharias Flagler, went on horseback twenty miles for the nearest surgeon. He did not arrive for twenty-four hours, and was obliged to wait a day and night to reduce the arm before he could set it. Philip Solomon Flagler, the father of the young man just mentioned, Mr. Kemper's nearest neighbor, instructed him in the management of his farm. His kindness and that of Mr. Brill and Mr. Wiltzie was gratefully acknowledged. Mr. Kemper cleared many acres of land; planted an orchard; raised wheat, corn, &c.; owned cattle and other stock; and his situation became more eligible. But cares of another kind began to press upon him. His children, three daughters and two sons, were growing up without schools. Mrs. Kemper taught them the Catechism and Psalms, and to read the Bible; and continued an observance of the sabbath by regular devotional exercises, as they were twenty miles from the nearest church.

In 1748, Christina Ernest married Mr. Wetzel, and went to reside in New York; and Mr. Ernest also removed to that city. These changes increased Mrs. Kemper's desire to leave their secluded situation; and her brother, Mr. Ernest, on his last visit, in the autumn, proposed that they should sell their lease, quit their farm, and remove to a place he would provide for them.

Mr..Kemper, therefore, sold the property of his lease, which was on three lives, — one of them my mother's. A few years since, in 1816, an inquiry was made whether she was yet living, as the estate was still held by that tenure.

Early in the spring of 1749, Mr. and Mrs. Kemper left their farm, and the improvements of six years, to the great regret of their kind neighbors, who assisted to convey the family to Rhinebeck; thence they went down the Hudson in a sloop to Mr. Ernest in New York.

In 1749, Mr. Kemper, by the sale of his lease, farm, and improvements, repaid Mr. Ernest for an excellent stone house in Albany Street, New Brunswick, N. J.; and engaged in a profitable business as a merchant. Here his family had the advantage of good schools; and my mother, for the first time within her remembrance, entered a church, — an interesting occasion she has often described. As Mr. and Mrs. Kemper had hitherto resided in a settlement where German was alone spoken, their children knew only their mother-tongue; but by attending a church where the services were in Low Dutch, the prevalent language of the town, and an English Presbyterian church, and by going to schools, they soon acquired both languages.

They experienced great hospitality and kindness from their neighbors; for, in those days of primitive simplicity, there existed apparently more warm-heartedness than in these of more cultivation and refinement. Each member of a small society had an individual sympathy for the others, since all were in some degree subject to the same wants. Interests and affections were stronger when thus concentrated, than when divided, and spread abroad. There was then danger from contracted views, and means of information. In our times, we experience the comparative heartlessness of an extended circle, where there is less equality, and greater division of interest. But these changes are the results of the improvements of society, and are no more to be complained of than the advantages of a cultivated mind and a refined taste, which open new avenues to both pleasure and pain.

The defeat of Gen. Braddock took place at this period, and my mother remembers seeing the remains of his unfortunate army pass through the town. Two German grenadiers, by the names of Burns and Kaun, were quartered in her father's house; and she often heard them describe that dreadful scene.

When the first Episcopal church was built in New Brunswick, a young man named William Voorhies, the son of one of Mr. Kemper's friends, employed in the erection, fell from the steeple. Although severely injured, he entirely recovered; but was ever afterwards distinguished by the name of "Steeple Voorhies."

After Mr. Kemper had resided ten years in New Brunswick, trade was suddenly turned into new channels; the town declined, and he was obliged to seek a new abode. He sold a vessel he had built to ply between Brunswick and New York, and all the property he could dispose of without sacrifice. His real estate was retained two years, when it was sold at a reduced price. With the proceeds he entered into business in New York, where Mr. Ernest was an affluent merchant.

This removal from New Brunswick in 1759 was very painful to Mr. and Mrs. Kemper, and especially to their children. Their hearts were grieved at leaving friends, who lamented their departure with tears, and whose kindness they took every opportunity to return.

Mr. Kemper's affairs continued prosperous; and his family, which now consisted of five sons and four daughters, improved in their education.

In 1761, his eldest daughter Gertrude, born at Coblentz on the river Rhine, married Dr. Miller, a young German physician, who, like many others, had been induced to come to America, and was successfully practising his profession in New York. In 1765, he visited Germany; and as he was an only son, and heir to a large property, his father forbade his return. He therefore requested his wife and their two children to follow him under the care of her brothers Matthew and Daniel Kemper. Dr. Miller received them in Holland, and conducted them to the city of Königsberg, in the King of Prussia's dominions, where they remained on his father's estate. Daniel Kemper returned; but his eldest brother Matthew married, and settled near Mrs. Miller. Their relatives in New York received frequent letters until 1774, when intelligence arrived of the death of Matthew Kemper, leaving a widow and children. Mrs. Miller, in her last letter, expressed great anxiety to revisit her friends in America, but it was impossible; and the war of the Revolution terminated all communication.

Six weeks after the marriage of Mrs. Miller, in 1761, Mr. Kemper's second daughter, Maria Sophia, married John Morton, a young man employed in the British Army in the commissary department. He was of an amiable and cheerful disposition. Descriptive cognomens were the usage of that day, and his personal advantages obtained for him that of " Handsome Johnny." His family were of Scottish descent, and liberal Protestants. His father resided near Dawson's Bridge, in the north of Ireland. He was an elder in the Rev. Mr. Henry's church for thirty years, and died in that office. He gave his children a good English education, and instruction in all branches requisite to render them capable men of business; and their excellent mother early taught them to seek success by the efforts of virtuous industry. Two of their younger sons, Clarke and James Morton, also came to New York, but died early in life.

Catherine, the third daughter of Mr. Kemper, married Capt. Dawson, of the British Army, — a man of amiable character and manners, to whom she was warmly attached. Their happy union was severed by her death in the first year of her marriage, and her husband did not long survive. Her parents transferred to her infant son the tender affection of which she had long been the object. He lived to be seven years of age, and was long remembered in the family by the endearing name of " Little Harry."

The sons of Mr. Kemper were successful in different pursuits; but the war of the Revolution broke up their establishments. Exiled from their happy homes, they were subjected to danger and anxiety in the theatre of actual warfare.

" What was the situation of Mr. Ernest during all these changes ?" will naturally be asked by all who read this narrative, and remember his unwearied kindness towards his sister. After Mr. and Mrs. Kemper had removed to New York, Mr. Ernest, who had acquired a large fortune, resolved to visit Germany, in the hope of seeing his father once more. But the good minister of Manheim had died one month before his arrival. This disappointment was very affecting to Mr. Ernest, who, many years before, had left his father's house without the knowledge of his parents.

He then heard of the fate of his sister Susan Ernest, who was married, and resided on the banks of the Rhine. By the sudden bursting of a water-spout against a mountain in her neighborhood, a tremendous flood descended to the river, carrying death and destruction to all within its course. Her house was washed into the Rhine. She was last seen standing at her door, with an infant in her arms. No help could be afforded her, and she perished with all her family.

Mr. Ernest had the consolation of seeing his mother, and his surviving sister Catherine, who had married Christian Hoffman, and who, with her husband and two sons, returned with him to America. He brought workmen from Germany, and established a glass-house six miles from New York; but this undertaking failed from the incompetency of the chief person employed, and Mr. Ernest consequently lost a great part of his fortune.

When the Revolution began, he entered into business in Philadelphia; and, when the British troops came there, he put all his property and furniture on board a sloop, to be taken up the Delaware to Trenton, while he went to that place by land with his wife. Instead of going to Trenton, the captain of the vessel went over to the British; and Mr. Ernest again lost all his possessions, except the money he had with him. He afterwards came to his friends in Morristown, where he resided until his death, — three years before peace was proclaimed.

Previous to Mr. Ernest's visit to Germany, his only son, John Ernest, a promising and excellent young man, married, and settled in New York as a merchant. Both he and his wife died early in life, leaving two sons, Antony and Matthew. The youngest, Matthew Ernest, was employed during the residence of his grandparents, Mr.

and Mrs. Ernest, at Morristown, in iron-works in that place, and, by his industry and his affectionate conduct, contributed to their support and comfort. After the peace, the widow of Mr. Ernest returned to New York, and found a home in the house of Jacob Sharpe, her son by her first marriage.

CHAPTER II.

Soon after the marriage of Mr. Morton with Maria Sophia Kemper, he relinquished his place in the commissary department, entered into business as a merchant, and soon acquired a large property. He made two voyages to England, or "Home" as it was always termed by the colonists, to arrange correspondences with merchants and with manufacturing establishments. He owned a large brick house in Water Street, New York, in which he resided; and also a wharf behind it, which extended below low water mark. His ships used to unlade into his spacious warehouse situated on the wharf, which also served as a flaxseed store, — a branch of trade in which my father was largely engaged. The demand for Irish linen was so great, that the flax was not allowed to ripen in Ireland. It was there immediately worked up at the manufactories, and the seed for the next year imported from America, where it was then raised in immense quantities on the borders of the Hudson. This lucrative business was destroyed by the Revolution. From the introduction of cotton fabrics, it never subsequently revived; and trade found new channels.

At that period, the importations of merchants comprehended a great variety of articles. Mr. Morton's large establishment was filled with every description of English manufactures, from the finest laces to broadcloth and blankets, and also those of other countries, — superb mirrors, engravings, china, glass, &c., — often sent directly from the manufacturers, on the most advantageous terms; and his commercial relations were, therefore, very prosperous.

In 1774, the family of my parents consisted of four children, — two sons, and my sister Margaret and myself, then an infant.

From the commencement of the Revolution, my father and all the connections of our family took the side of liberty and the Colonies, and became what were called warm Whigs. After the scenes attendant on the Stamp Act and the Tea Tax, when war seemed inevitable, and when the "Asia," a British man-of-war, came into the East River, opposite Mr. Morton's house, and threatened to fire upon the city, he determined to leave New York. He was promised protection and security if he would remain a loyal and quiet subject; but he did not hesitate to abandon his property, rather than submit to the unjust measures of a government which had become tyrannical and oppressive to his country.

A vessel belonging to him had arrived from England, laden with valuable merchandise. All the goods in the warehouse were hastily packed and sent on board this ship, which, with its cargo, was ordered round to Philadelphia, — a place then considered out of reach of the British, — under the care of Mr. Gallaudet, the confidential clerk of Mr. Morton; where they were sold at high prices, and the money deposited in the Loan Office.

The amount thus devoted to the use of the American Army by John Morton caused him to be denominated by the British "the Rebel Banker." As he was not able, and his sons were not old enough, to fight the battles of his country, he said he would pay those who could, to the last farthing he possessed.

Mr. and Mrs. Morton sent over their furniture, and all their effects which could be removed, to Elizabethtown in New Jersey, and hastily followed with their family; abandoning their excellent house and all their real estate to their enemies, who soon took possession of their pleasant dwelling, and appropriated every thing to their own use during the seven succeeding years. My father's property was also diminished by the depreciation of the paper money issued by Congress, in which currency he was obliged to receive all debts due to him. The partial interest allowed by Congress for the money deposited in the Loan Office, after the French Loan was negotiated, was paid in specie; and this, together with merchandise taken out of New York and sold or exchanged for articles requisite for the family, furnished their means of support during the war.

In 1775, Mr. and Mrs. Kemper also removed to Elizabethtown. Two of their sons entered the American Army. Jacob Kemper rose to be a captain; Daniel served as a quarter-master. Their youngest daughter, Susan Kemper, resided with my mother. My father purchased a house, with a large garden adjacent, at Elizabethtown. As my eldest brother had been there prepared for college, my parents were previously acquainted with several of the inhabitants. They were intimate in the family of Elias Boudinot, and attended the church of the Rev. Mr. Caldwell, a Presbyterian minister, who joined the ranks of the American Army with his parishioners, and served as a volunteer. His profession, his zeal and patriotism, rendered him peculiarly obnoxious to the British.

While Mr. and Mrs. Morton resided in Elizabethtown, their cares were increased by the birth of another son, whom they named Washington; a proof of their confidence in that great man at the time he was appointed Commander-in-chief of the American Army. My brother was certainly the first child ever named in honor of him.

Alarmed by the approach of the British Army, our family fled to Springfield, seven miles distant, where they remained several weeks in a house with five other families, who were also fugitives. My father then sought a safer situation, and purchased a house and farm at Baskinridge, fifteen or twenty miles from Elizabethtown; and conveyed thither all the furniture and effects brought from

New York. Mr. and Mrs. Kemper removed to Germantown, fourteen miles farther inland, in the neighborhood of many of their countrymen.

Baskinridge was in a retired, pleasant situation, enclosed by some high land called " the Long Hills." It was a secure place from the British, and at times in the centre of the American Army. The head-quarters of Washington were at Morristown, only seven miles distant. The hospital was located on Mr. Morton's estate. It was a long, low log building, situated on a rising ground in a meadow: a brook ran in front of it, and supplied the inmates with water for cooking and washing. Dr. Tilton, the director of the medical department, with Dr. Stevenson, Dr. Coventry, and other physicians, had rooms in my father's house ; and a small school-house was converted into an apothecary's shop. This arrangement continued more than two years, and the society of these gentlemen was very agreeable.

Across the high road was a fine spring, — excavated, and lined with boards, — making a kind of cistern four or five feet square. Over a small brook which ran from it was what was called a " spring-house," for milk and butter, under the shade of some large trees. The barns were also on that side of the road, farther up the hill ; on the top of which, the church, the burial-ground, and a school-house, were situated near a wood of oak trees. At the foot of the hill, below the garden, another brook flowed through a meadow ; and beyond it was a grove of trees, not thick, but shady. In this brook, and about it, my sister and I often played, building dams across it to have the pleasure of seeing the water fall over them.

There were several women employed as domestics in our family, and a negro man — Belfast — who deserves a particular notice. He was a boy of nine years old when my father purchased him ; a mode of securing service then considered as proper as by wages.

There is no subject on which the opinions of society have undergone so great a change as upon that of slavery. The iniquity of the cruel treatment of field slaves, on plantations in the Southern States, was at that period acknowledged; but in the Middle and New-England States, where they were domesticated and kindly treated, slavery seemed to have lost its horrors. The owners of negroes appeared entirely unconscious of the guilt of bringing them forcibly from their own country to one where they were better off in some respects; and thought it was doing them a service, though against their will. The fact was, their minds had never been turned to reason on the subject. I remember the great surprise I felt, the first time I heard an intimation that it was wrong to hold a slave, although the truth of the proposition was so self-evident that it needed only to be stated to be allowed by an unprejudiced mind.

Belfast was so named from the port to which the captain belonged who sold him to my father. He was kindly brought up, instructed in reading and writing; was faithful, honest, and cheerful, and gratefully attached to his master and the family. We children were very fond of him. I was his great favorite; and he often carried me up and down the hill, and from school, in his arms. He used to sing and dance for our amusement, and to play on the comb, for us to dance; in which accomplishment he was also our instructor. Yet such was his respectful familiarity, that he never offended in either word or action. He was an excellent cook, and ready at all kinds of work within and without the house.

At a period and in a situation when assistance was difficult to obtain, Belfast was an invaluable domestic. After our family returned to New York, he married, and asked and obtained his freedom. He always sustained a good character, but did not long survive leaving his old home. The change probably was not for the better, — for his comfort and happiness; but he enjoyed the gratification of being a free man. A good man he certainly was, to the best of his knowledge and ability; and I never think of him, even at this period of my life, but with respect and affection.

Soon after the removal of our family to Baskinridge, my father's brother, James Morton, who was established at Hartford in Connecticut, died at the age of thirty. On his way to Baskinridge, he was attacked by a fever at the house of his friend Mr. Wilson, a few miles from our residence, whence he could not be removed. My parents were with him during his illness; and his remains were brought to Baskinridge, and interred in the burial-ground on the hill. An amiable man and an affectionate brother, he was much lamented by my parents, who soon afterwards went to Hartford to settle his affairs. They travelled in a phaeton, which I remember, and also the large black coach horses. Taking the road on the Jersey side of the Hudson, they crossed that river where the banks were in the possession of the American Army.

The country people near Baskinridge were not generally kind or hospitable to the exiles from New York; but there were many honorable exceptions. Among these were our excellent neighbors, the families of Mr. Lewis and Mr. Southard. The lower classes in New Jersey did not enjoy the advantage of the common schools of New England; and they were too ignorant and selfish even to understand the peculiar hardships endured by those who were driven from their homes, and exposed to severe suffering for the same cause in which they were also engaged. Jealousy is often excited in ordinary minds by any degree of superiority. It was a common taunt among the most ignorant and uncivilized, that any article complained of was good enough for " the Yorkers," or for " the Quality," as they termed the exiles, whom they envied, even in their unhappy circumstances, for their superior advantages of education and manners.

It was supposed they had brought a great deal of money and property with them from New York. Their clothes were their most coveted possessions. My mother was often obliged to part with any article of dress fancied, and enormous prices were asked for all provisions. As the war lasted seven years, even the most common implements of convenience and industry, such as needles, pins, &c., became extremely scarce and valuable. There was, for instance, only one darning-needle of the size to carry yarn among the families in our neighborhood; and it was sent from house to house, and valued as a treasure. One day, my mother imprudently intrusted it to my little brother Washington to carry to a friend, with many charges to go straight and be careful. These were soon forgotten, and the precious darning-needle was lost. After the dismay at such an accident had subsided, a strict search was made along the path taken by the delinquent; and the darning-needle was at length discovered, sticking in a stump by the side of the road where he had placed it while he stopped to play. Great were the rejoicings at its recovery, and it was never again intrusted to such a youthful messenger.

The house at Baskinridge was of two stories, situated on the high road, about half way down a hill. On one side, therefore, the parlor windows were even with the ground: on the other, was a high porch with seats, the steps of which led to the second story. I remember seeing " the Doctors," as we used to call them, sitting in the porch through which they entered their apartments, without incommoding the family. In front was a small court-yard, enclosed by pales; and on the side down the hill, an excellent garden. It was a comfortable, convenient house; and the furniture, plate, books, pictures, and mirrors brought from New York, gave it the appearance of a gentleman's residence. The " View near Naples," by Claude, engraved by Vivares; the " View of the Seat of the Duke of Argyle at Whitton," drawn and engraved by W. Woollett; an engraved likeness of Maria, Countess of Coventry, and of her sister the Duchess of Argyle, — were among the ornaments of the walls, and, with the exception of the latter, are now in my possession.

At the distance of half a mile from my father's residence, in two farm-houses lived the family of Elias Boudinot, who had retired there from his elegant seat in Elizabethtown. He had an only daughter, about seventeen; and his sister Mrs. Hetfield, and her family, resided near him.

Dr. Kennedy, the clergyman of Baskinridge, was educated as a physician; and, having afterwards studied divinity, he skilfully practised both professions. He was a Scotchman; a man of uncommon good sense; "an Israelite indeed, in whom there was no guile;" and, being one of our nearest neighbors, his society and ministry were considered a great privilege.

The seat of Lord Stirling, called by the country people "the Buildings," was two miles distant. Designed to imitate the residence of an English nobleman, it was unfinished when the war began. The stables, coach-houses, and other offices, ornamented with cupolas and gilded vanes, were built round a large paved court behind the mansion. The front, with piazzas, opened on a fine lawn, descending to a considerable stream called "the Black River." A large hall extended through the centre of the house. On one side was a drawing-room, with painted walls and a stuccoed ceiling. Being taken there when a child, my imagination was struck with a style and splendor so different from all around. The daughters of Lord Stirling, called Lady Mary and Lady Kitty, afterwards Mrs. Watts and Mrs. Duer, the Miss Livingstons, afterwards Mrs. Kane and Mrs. Otto, and other cultivated and elegant women domesticated in the family, made an impression I can never forget, for they were all very pleasing and kind to me.

Lord Stirling's family was of Scotch origin. His mother, Madam Alexander, owned a large establishment in New York, acquired property by trade, and sent her son to Scotland for his education. He returned, married Miss Livingston, and, when he inherited his fortune, claimed a Scotch title, and affected the style of life of a nobleman. When the Revolution began, he took the side of the Colonies, held the commission of a general in the American Army under Washington, and died in 1783. He left no son to inherit his title and estates; and thus ended his plans and prospects.

Ten years afterwards, I again visited " the Buildings; " but what a change had taken place! The family had removed, the house was tenanted by a farmer, and the hall and elegant drawing-room, converted into granaries, were filled with corn and wheat, and the paved court-yard with pigs and poultry. The stables and coach-house were going to ruin; and through the door of the latter, which was falling off the hinges, I saw the state-coach of the fashion of Sir Charles Grandison's day. It was ornamented with gilded coronets, and coats-of-arms blazoned on the panels, and the fowls were perching and roosting upon it.

The families I have enumerated, and visitors from Morristown and the neighborhood, formed a delightful society, and much was enjoyed in the midst of exile, anxiety, and alarm. The constant excitement of their situation made up for inconvenience and distress. They lived every moment, " and snatched a fearful joy." Still it was enjoyment, perhaps much greater and more exquisite than that afforded by more tranquil scenes and peaceful times; and here, as everywhere, we recognize the doctrine of balances and compensations, — giving to every lot peculiar pleasures and sufferings.

Being myself, during the war, a child under nine years of age, my impressions, although lively, are unconnected. I shall state the events I remember, in precise terms, and describe the rest from the recollections of my mother, corroborated by other relatives.

The American troops were constantly passing and repassing, and the house frequently full of officers, who were always received and treated with hospitality and kindness. All was freely given, — shelter, food, forage for their horses, relief for the sick and wounded.

The residence of Mr. Morton's family upon the high road, and near head-quarters, exposed them to great expense, fatigue, and labor. They were frequently obliged to bake three or four times in one day;

for, as soon as one batch of bread was taken from the oven, a party of hungry soldiers would pass by, to whom it would be given, and another and another prepared. These also would be called for, and bestowed in the same manner, together with beer, cider, and whatever provisions the house afforded. But it was all generously given; the owner thinking himself amply repaid by the information he received of passing events, in which he took so deep an interest. General Washington and his suite were often my father's guests. Among the stores brought from New York were two pipes of Madeira wine, which often contributed to the refreshment of the beloved chief.

The capture of General Lee on the 13th of December, 1776, occurred soon after the settlement of our family at Baskinridge. He had come from the American camp at Morristown to reconnoitre; and put up for the night at Mr. White's tavern, not half a mile from our house, — up the hill beyond the church. My father, who was always attentive to every officer of the army, called on General Lee, and invited him to breakfast the next day. He accepted; but, as he did not appear at the appointed time, Mr. Morton became impatient, and walked up the hill to meet his expected guest. On his way, he encountered many of the country people running in great consternation, exclaiming, "The British have come to take General Lee!" My father hurried on, and saw Lee, without hat or cloak, forcibly mounted, and carried off by a troop of horse; and, as he had but few attendants, little resistance was attempted. One of his men, who offered to defend him, was cut down and wounded by the sabres of the horsemen. He was brought down to our house, where he was taken care of until he was carried on a litter to a surgeon at Mendon; and after three months he recovered, and came to thank my mother for her kindness to him.

Information of the unguarded situation of General Lee at Baskinridge was given by a countryman to Colonel Harcourt of the British

Army, who, with a body of cavalry, had been sent from New Brunswick to watch his movements. A detachment of seventy light horse surrounded the house where Lee staid, before he had any intimation of their approach, and carried him off in triumph. The terror of the inhabitants of Baskinridge was very great : they feared the army of the enemy was upon them, and could hardly believe the troops were gone as soon as they heard they had come. At that time, however, they remained undisturbed, except by their own apprehensions.

The British Army never penetrated to Baskinridge : but there were repeated alarms of their approach with fire and sword; and the children were often sent in wagons to cottages among the hills, several miles distant, — considered places of safety. On one of these occasions, I was sent at night, with my sister and my brother Washington, to a Mr. Gobles, in the woods. We were placed on our beds in the wagon; and well covered up, as it was very cold, were driven by Belfast, who cheered and encouraged us in our darksome expedition. At our place of refuge we were received very kindly by the good woman of the cottage, who gave us some bread and milk, and spread our beds on the floor. But great was my astonishment at her arrangements for her own children : she raised some boards in the corner of the only room in the house, under which there was a bed of dried leaves, where they were placed, and covered with their clothes and a blanket. I was very much afraid I was to be put in there too; but Belfast comforted me by saying he would take care of me, and sit up all night by the fire, which he did, with the hospitable owners of this humble roof.

This alarm proved groundless; and when my parents, who had remained at home, came for us the next morning, and beheld the steep and dangerous road we had passed over in the night at the risk of our lives, they rejoiced to find us in safety, and our hosts were liberally rewarded.

By another of these reports that the British were advancing, which caused our family to disperse, one of our servants was much alarmed; and, her thoughts being equally divided between terror at the approach of the enemy and the care of her clothes, she put on so many gowns and petticoats, and so loaded herself with the remainder, that her flight could be neither fast nor far. She only reached the middle of the burial-ground on the hill, where she sank down, overcome with apprehension and the weight of her apparel; and mistaking one of the family, who was passing quickly, for a British soldier, she called out, " O sir ! take all I have, but spare my life." She was soon happily undeceived, and assisted home again with her property unharmed; and great was the amusement her adventure excited in all who heard it, after their own fears were dissipated.

CHAPTER III.

In 1779, Susan Kemper was married to Dr. Jackson of Philadelphia, and went to reside in that city. Her uncommon vivacity, cheerful temper, and great capability had rendered her a most useful and delightful inmate in our family. I had been named after her, and was grieved at her departure. My sister Margaret was afterwards sent to stay with her aunt, and attend school, in Philadelphia. As we had no advantages of the kind at Baskinridge, my mother wished me to go there also; and she proposed to visit my aunt, and take me with her. I was pleased with the plan, as the intention of leaving me at school was not mentioned. This was the first journey I had ever made; and the mere motion of the chaise in which I was seated between my mother and my eldest brother, as we moved on through roads and places I had never seen before, was delightful. But, when I reached Philadelphia, I was disappointed. I did not know what to expect; but something beautiful, new, and strange was connected in my imagination with the city where my aunt Susan had gone to live. The image I had formed in my mind was very different from the reality. The houses crowded together; the streets full of people, hurrying to and fro; the throng of carriages, carts, and wagons, — impressed me very disagreeably. I was stunned with the noise, and terrified by the confusion and danger which seemed to threaten me if I moved out of the house. My aunt was as kind as ever; but she had the cares of a family, and could not be as attentive to me as she had been at Baskinridge. I soon discovered that my mother intended to leave me in Philadelphia, and this completed my discontent. I cried to go home; and nothing would pacify me, till my mother promised I should be sent there with Mr. Martin, without waiting for her return.

Mr. Martin was an old man who carried the mail between Phila·delphia and Morristown, and was called "the Post." He used to wear a blue coat with yellow buttons, a scarlet waistcoat, leathern small-clothes, blue yarn stockings, and a red wig and cocked hat, which gave him a sort of military appearance. He usually travelled in a sulky, but sometimes in a chaise or on horseback, according to the season of the year or the size and weight of the mail-bag. Mr. Martin also contrived to employ himself in knitting coarse yarn stockings while driving or rather jogging along the road, or when seated on his saddle-bags on horseback. He certainly did not ride *post*, according to the present meaning of that term.

Between Baskinridge and Philadelphia and Princeton, he was the constant medium of communication; and always stopped at our house to refresh himself and his horse, tell the news, and bring packets. He was an excellent, honest old man; and I was secure of a good reception at any of the private houses to which he chose to take me. I shall never forget the delight I felt when I found myself seated beside Mr. Martin in his chaise, and going away from Phila·delphia; nor the surprise of our family at Baskinridge, when they saw me driving down the hill with him. They all ran to the door; when Belfast exclaimed, "Well, if here isn't our Susan coming, riding home with the Post!"

When my mother returned, I was sent with my brother Washington to stay with Mrs. Kemper at Germantown, to attend the school ot Master Leslie, who, though a good man, was very severe in his discipline. His modes of punishment would astonish the children of the present day. One of them was "to hold the blocks." They were of two sizes. The large one was a heavy block of wood, with a ring in the centre, by which it was to be held a definite number of minutes by his watch, according to the magnitude of the offence. The small block was for the younger children. Another punishment was by a number of leathern straps, about an inch wide and a finger long, fastened to a handle of wood, with which he used to strap the hands of the larger boys. To the girls he was more lenient.

Master Leslie was particularly anxious to instruct us in the Scriptures; and, according to the custom of that day, we stood up in classes, each child with a Bible in hand, and read a verse in turn. We constantly came to unintelligible passages, and fatigue and disgust were the consequence. Lists of texts of Scripture beginning with the same letter, written upon paper and pasted upon boards, were also hung round the schoolroom. These alphabets, as they were called, were given to the scholars to take home, and commit to memory on Sunday, with catechism and hymns. By early painful associations, the subject of religion was thus rendered tedious and repulsive to many persons in after life.

To give us some idea of geography and astronomy, Master Leslie used to employ his snuff-box, and sundry little balls of yarn, to represent the solar system; and thus completely puzzled and confused my brain. I knew he would not tell a falsehood; but to make me believe that the sun stood still, and we whirled round it, required a clearer explanation. He succeeded, however, in elevating himself in our opinion.

> " And still he taught; and still our wonder grew,
> That one small head could carry all he knew."

The British made a descent upon Elizabethtown on the 7th of June, 1780, where they observed great decorum and discipline. They then advanced five miles to Connecticut Farms. To that place Mr. Caldwell, the Presbyterian clergyman of Elizabethtown, had removed. His zeal and activity against the British had excited their keenest resentment, and had rendered it insecure for him to remain at home. From this retreat, on the approach of the British, he withdrew a few miles to join the Americans at Springfield. He left his wife and children, supposing they could not be objects of cruelty. The militia of "the Farms" had all marched to Springfield by the command of Colonel Dayton, so that there was no cause for firing a gun.

Soon after the royal forces came to "the Farms," a soldier who had been a servant in the family of Dr. Chandler, the Episcopal clergyman of Elizabethtown, and who had there seen Mrs. Caldwell, came to her house, put his gun into the window of the room where she was sitting with her children, her infant in her arms, took deliberate aim at her, and discharged his musket. She received the ball in her bosom, and instantly expired. At the earnest request of Captain Chandler, a son of the Episcopal clergyman of Elizabethtown, in the British service, the body of Mrs. Caldwell was protected, and carried with her children to a house at some distance, while her own was set on fire, and consumed, with all the property it contained. The enemy burnt about twelve other houses and the Presbyterian Church, and then marched back to Elizabethtown.

The murder of Mrs. Caldwell renewed the spirit and enthusiasm of the troops. She was considered as a martyr in their cause, and they swore to revenge her death. The army was suffering from desertion, and from want of money, provisions, and clothes; and the people were dispirited by the defeat of General Lincoln at Charleston, South Carolina. Two regiments had mutinied; but, in deference to their commander, had returned to their duty, although in the greatest distress for pay and food. But, at that moment, this event inspired the Americans with new courage.

The British remained at Elizabethtown Point till the 23d of June, when they advanced to Springfield. General Greene, of the American Army, — who, upon the first alarm, was detached to defend that place, — posted his troops on the hills, hoping the enemy would attack him there; but they declined the action, and set fire to Springfield. Fifty dwelling-houses and the church were burnt; and, except four houses, the whole village was reduced to ashes. The strength of General Greene's position prevented the enemy from penetrating to Morristown to destroy the magazines and stores of the American Army in that vicinity. The British, pursued by the militia enraged by the conflagration they had just witnessed, again retreated to Elizabethtown Point, and crossed the same night to Staten Island.*

A few days after the burning of Springfield, my father and mother collected all the clothing and every article which could be spared from their own stores or those of their neighbors, and went to offer relief to the sufferers. The inhabitants of that ill-fated town, although in such distressed circumstances, were in good spirits. They were already beginning to collect materials for temporary shelter, and were raking out of the ashes of their former dwellings nails, hinges, and other iron work, for the erection of new habitations. Many anecdotes of courage and magnanimity were related to my parents.

Upon the approach of the British, the women and children fled from the town, and were collected together on the brow of a hill, about a mile distant, in full view of the conflagration. As one house after another caught fire, they would call out, "There goes your house!" and "There goes yours!" One woman, whose husband had just built a fine large house, and shop adjacent, was among them; and, as she seemed to have the most to lose, was observed in proportion. One of her companions called out to her, "There goes your

---

* "The British advanced with five thousand infantry, a large body of cavalry, and fifteen or twenty pieces of artillery. I lament our force was too small to save the town. I wish every American could have been a spectator: he would have felt for the sufferers, and joined to revenge the injury." — *Letter of General Greene, Springfield, 24th June,* 1780: Sparks' "*Washington's Writings,*" vol. vii. pp. 506–8.

beautiful new house!"—"Well, let it go," said she: "we can live in the shop." In a few moments after,—"There goes the shop too!" "Well, let it go: they can't burn the ground it stands on; and here's wood enough to build another, when they are all beaten and driven away." Such was the spirit that animated the women of that day; among whom it was a common saying, that, "if the men became tired of fighting, the women would turn out, and take their places."

The death of Mrs. Caldwell has been the subject of history; but the fate of Mr. Caldwell is not so generally known. My parents had been his parishioners in Elizabethtown, and were strongly attached to them both; and, as this appears an appropriate place, I shall here conclude their sad story.

Two years after the burning of Springfield, when negotiations for peace were pending, the inhabitants of Elizabethtown began to return to their deserted homes. Mr. Boudinot and his family left Baskinridge, and Mr. Caldwell resumed his pastoral charge. At this time it was known that Mrs. and Miss Murray, ladies of a Quaker family, had made great exertions for the relief of American prisoners in New York; and when a boat with a flag of truce came thence to Elizabethtown, and it was understood that Miss Murray was among the passengers, her name was universally hailed with gratitude and respect. There was a contest among the inhabitants, who should go down to the landing to do her honor and service.

Mr. Caldwell, with that zeal which marked his character, insisted on being one of the number; although his friends suggested he might incur danger. A flag of truce rendering the perpetration of violence incredible, he went to the boat; but found the lady had already landed, and gone to the house of her friend Mr. Ricketts. He put out his hand to take a packet, accidentally left by Miss Murray, from the captain, when he was shot by a man concealed on board, who confessed he had vowed to kill Mr. Caldwell, and had waited for an opportunity many years. Every one was struck with horror at this violation of the laws of civilized warfare. The inhabitants of Elizabethtown, at first, would not believe that this act of treachery had not been perpetrated by design; but the captain of the boat, and all on board, disclaimed any knowledge of the man's intentions. The truth of their assertion was confirmed by their delivering the assassin up to the punishment he deserved, and by the man himself, who gloried in the deed he had committed.

This event produced a great sensation. My mother and my brothers went down to Elizabethtown to the funeral of Mr. Caldwell; which took place from the house of his friend Mr. Boudinot, and was attended by all the people in the country far and near. A funeral sermon was preached by the Rev. Dr. MacWhorter, of Newark, from the appropriate text in Ecclesiastes, "But there is no discharge in this war."

Public and private sympathy was greatly excited for the children of Mr. and Mrs. Caldwell, deprived by such calamitous events of both their parents. I was acquainted with each of them, as they were adopted into different families among the friends of my mother. Mr. Boudinot was their chief patron. By his care, the certificates for payments due to Mr. Caldwell for service in the American Army were preserved and put out at interest until the youngest child, the infant Mrs. Caldwell held when she received the fatal shot, came of age; and a considerable sum was then divided among them. Such was the general interest in this family, that the eldest son was adopted, and taken to France for his education, by the Marquis de Lafayette. At the commencement of the French Revolution, he was sent back to America; and, to the great distress of his friends, returned a Roman Catholic. But, at his age, there was little difficulty in reconverting him to the religious opinions of his father. Another of these children, Elias B. Caldwell, is now (1821) Attorney for the District of Columbia.

The revolt of the Pennsylvania line occurred in January, 1781. The soldiers, driven to desperation for want of food, clothes, and pay, determined to march to Philadelphia, and force Congress to redress their grievances. One of the officers, in attempting to suppress the mutiny, was killed, and others wounded. Obliged to fly from their camp at Morristown, several took refuge at my father's residence in Baskinridge. Captain Christie was the first who rushed into the house, gave intelligence of the revolt, and begged to be secreted from the soldiers he feared were on his track. He was accordingly concealed till the danger was past. My parents were terrified, and it was apprehended that the troops would go over to the British ; but this fear proved groundless, and the termination of this rebellion is recorded in history.

In February, 1781, the several States agreed to Articles of Confederation. The completion of this important compact, which it was hoped would preserve the Union until a more efficient system could be adopted, was the last event in favor of American independence which my father was destined to witness. In the final success of the cause of his country, for which he had undergone many sufferings and sacrifices, he did not live to rejoice.

CHAPTER IV.

In the spring of 1781, my brother John Morton, with a classmate from Princeton, was passing a college vacation at Baskinridge with his parents, whose family then consisted of their youngest son Clarke Morton, and their domestics. All had retired for the night, when they were aroused by a number of armed men forcibly breaking open the front door of the house.

Their chief, whose face was blackened, and disguised by a handkerchief tied round the head and brought down to the eyes, first demanded all their keys and gold watches. A bayonet was presented at every window or door, when escape was attempted; and, thus surrounded, submission was unavoidable. My father was much indisposed; and into his apartment, all the family, with the exception of his son John Morton, were thrust, and a sentinel placed at the door. They soon perceived a stranger was among them, and at first supposed him to be one of the robbers; but his terror and exclamations soon proved he was a prisoner like themselves. He said he was a militia-man who had been out on duty. As he was returning home, he met the party then in the house, who had captured him, and put him under guard to prevent him from giving an alarm.

From the conduct of the intruders, there was cause to suppose that among them were persons well acquainted with the arrangements of Mr. Morton. They first went to a closet where his money and valuable papers were deposited in an iron chest, as was the custom at that period. It contained thirty pounds, in gold and silver, which he had just received as part payment for his house in Elizabethtown. A report had been spread that he had also sold his estate in New York, and received a large sum for it.

Great disappointment was expressed by the robbers at not finding more money; and they swore they would kill John Morton, if he did not show them where his father had hid his treasure. They forced him to open all the drawers and chests; and then took him into the cellar, where they thought money might be concealed, and again threatened him with death. As he could tell them nothing more, they again ransacked the house. Into large sacks which they had brought for the purpose they put the wearing apparel of the family, including twelve ruffled shirts just completed, made of linen bought at a high price in Philadelphia. All the plate, a tea and coffee service, a large tankard, and every article of silver then used in a gentleman's establishment, were also taken. A silver tankard, which had been used the night previous and left at the kitchen fire, blackened with smoke and ashes, the thieves mistook for pewter; and it alone escaped. Out of the silver it contained, a bowl and two goblets, marked with the crest of the Morton arms (a lion rampant), were afterwards formed, and are now in my possession.

After remaining two hours, the robbers departed, declaring they would return and set fire to the house, if the family did not remain quiet. Exhausted by terror and fatigue, it was day-break before they alarmed the neighborhood. The traveller who had been captured said he had seen among the trees near the church a number of horses fastened, on which the robbers undoubtedly escaped with their booty. Their plan had been well laid to insure success. Contrary to the entreaties of his family, Mr. Morton, though suffering from illness, insisted on pursuing the robbers with some of his neighbors. After following several routes unsuccessfully, he at length got upon their track, and pursued them to the river-side near Newark ; where it was supposed they took boat, and went over to New York.

After my father's return from this journey, fatigue and disappointment brought on an attack of apoplexy, which, in one week, terminated his life ; and his family were plunged in deep affliction. My eldest brother, then a youth of nineteen, a student at law with Judge Patterson at Rariton, had returned to Baskinridge on hearing of the robbery. The first intelligence of it, and of the death of my father, was brought to Mrs. Kemper by the messenger sent for Washington and myself; and she immediately accompanied us home. Dr. Kennedy performed the services at the funeral; and the procession, attended by a concourse of people, proceeded to the burial-ground on the hill, near the church of Baskinridge.

Mr. Boudinot, my mother, and my eldest brother, were appointed executors by my father's will; and the two last fulfilled the trust. Mr. and Mrs. Kemper left Germantown to reside with my mother, and Dr. and Mrs. Jackson came from Philadelphia to visit her.

In September, my brother John Morton, on taking his degree at Princeton, delivered a valedictory oration; and his youth and deep mourning dress interested and affected his audience. From this time, my eldest brother resided at home ; and, by his kindness and attention, gained my affection, and led me to regard him as a father.

Among the books brought from New York by my mother were "Dodsley's Collection of Poems," the "Wonders of Nature and Art," and the "Vicar of Wakefield." These I read and re-read, until I almost committed them to memory.

In "Dodsley's Collection of Poems," I first read Gray's "Elegy in a Country Churchyard;" and my fancy was struck with its beauties, although many of the ideas and images were to me obscure. Yet others were made plain and familiar by my spelling out the inscriptions and texts on the "frail memorials" erected on the hill, in the churchyard, in which I often wandered. The "uncouth rhymes and shapeless sculpture" I there beheld exactly answered the description of the poet.

"Paradise Lost" and "Paradise Regained" were also among our books; but I cannot boast, with Mrs. Grant of Laggan, that I understood them, with the exception of a few passages. I was touched by the allusion to Milton's blindness, because it reminded me of the situation of my grandfather Mr. Kemper, who, during his residence at Germantown, had become suddenly blind; and also by the lamentation of Eve on leaving Paradise and her flowers. The rest of the poem was dark and unintelligible.

"Pilgrim's Progress" was a great favorite. The Celestial City, and the Shining Ones who welcomed Christian and Christiana with their children, I preferred to Milton's sublime descriptions of heaven, and the angels Michael and Gabriel. Mr. Greatheart was, in my opinion, a hero, well able to help us all on our way; and I trusted to his good assistance. I also read the "Holy War," and was much interested in the good town of Mansoul.

The works of Shenstone, Thomson, and Lyttelton, I admired; but those of Goldsmith were my chief delight, especially "The Vicar of Wakefield," which continues to justify the choice of my early years by the pleasure which the exquisite sweetness, simplicity, and pathos of the style still afford me. My taste was thus formed by the best authors, and I learned to appreciate their works before I was aware of their comparative value; and, when my reading became afterwards more extensive, I instinctively disliked the extravagant fictions which often injure the youthful mind.

In August, 1781, the French Army passed through Baskinridge, on their way to Yorktown in Virginia. They halted opposite our house to refresh the soldiers at the spring, while the officers were entertained within. Our family were all in raptures at the sight of their new allies coming to fight their battles and insure victory. Every one ran to the doors and windows, except Mrs. Kemper, who retired to her apartment with my grandfather. The cruel conduct of the French soldiers in Germany could not be forgotten by these emigrants from their " father-land." They refused to be comforted, and bewailed with tears the introduction of these allies.

In 1783, peace was concluded, and our family removed to Elizabethtown. Friendly intercourse between families of different politics was now renewed. The Rev. Mr. Chandler, the Episcopal minister, and his son, had served in the British Army, and were obliged to go away; but my mother was intimate with his wife and daughters.

At this time, my mother went to New York with a pass from the Commander-in-Chief, Sir Guy Carleton, obtained by her friend Mrs. Smith, whose husband was Chief Justice under the Crown. We passed a fortnight with my mother's aunt Mrs. Hoffman (Catherine Ernest). With her husband and her youngest children, she was accidentally detained in New York, in 1775, until the time of departure was gone by; and was not allowed by the British authorities to follow her eldest son and daughter, who had gone to Elizabethtown to prepare for the reception of their family. Mr. Hoffman was accused of being favorable to the American cause, and was imprisoned as a rebel by the Hessian officers. An illness, caused by his sufferings, ended in his death; and he never saw his family united again. His widow remained in New York: her daughter was married in Morristown; her eldest son had entered the American Army; and, at the time of our visit, she resided alone with her youngest son, Christian Hoffman. Her house stood in Broadway, (how different from the Broadway of the present day!) nearly opposite the City Tavern, which was a two-story house, plastered over and whitewashed, but dingy and dilapidated. The street was only half built up, the houses of every shape and size. Trinity Church, and a church where Grace Church now stands, were heaps of ruins. The British never injured Episcopal churches; but these had been accidentally burnt during the war. There was but one good house above St. Paul's: all beyond was a square open space, called "the Fields," built round with low, wooden, ordinary houses,— the resort of the negroes and soldiers. The Jail, Workhouse, and Alms-house were in this vicinity. These are now superseded by the City Hall, of white marble; and "the Fields" are converted into the Park, and are ornamented with trees.

Sir Guy Carleton and his aids passed our house every day. Many of his officers were quartered opposite, at the City Tavern; and their evolutions, and those of the British troops, were a source of great amusement to me. My cousin, Christian Hoffman, often took me to see the parade on the Battery,— then literally a battery; the sides towards the Bay broken into ramparts, with cannon and their carriages. The view was thus excluded, except from the ramparts. The interior was a parade-ground, with barracks for the soldiers. A military funeral which passed our house made a deep impression on my memory. The full band playing the "Dead March in Saul;" the funereal pomp; the slow and measured step of the soldiers; the commander-in-chief and his officers in full uniform; the coffin of the deceased, with his hat, gloves, and sword; his horse, completely accoutred, led by his servant, his boots thrown across the saddle,— all seemed to speak of the departed, and point to his vacant place with a solemnity I had never felt before. My cousin gratified my wish to follow the procession to St. Paul's Churchyard. We passed through the crowd to the open railing, and he lifted me up in his arms to see the ceremony. I saw the chaplain in his gown and bands open the book, and read the service; after which, the troops fired over the grave.

The city looked ruinous. My mother took me to our house in Water Street, still inhabited by British officers; and I saw Mr. Pitt's statue, at the corner of Wall and William Street. It had lost an arm, and was taken down by the citizens on their return. I accompanied my mother to visit Mrs. Smith, the wife of Chief-Justice Smith, who received us very kindly, and brought in her daughter Harriet Smith, a few years younger than myself. "This child," said Mrs. Smith, "has been born since the *Rebellion*." — "Since the *Revolution*," replied my mother. The lady smiled, and said, "Well, well, Mrs. Morton, this is only a truce, not a peace; and we shall all be back again, in full possession, in two years." This prophecy happily did not prove true.

A few months afterwards, on the evacuation of New York by the British, Mrs. Smith accompanied her husband to Quebec; and he became Chief-Justice of Lower Canada. His daughter, Harriet Smith, married his successor in office, Chief-Justice Sewall, an exile from Massachusetts, and a grandson of Edmund Quincy; and in 1797 I met her again in Boston, at the house of his aunt, Mrs. Hancock.

After my return to Elizabethtown, I visited my friend Miss Mason, whose father, Rev. Dr. Mason, had taken our house at Baskinridge until he could return to New York. With her I revisited the scenes of my childhood, and "the Buildings," where I saw the Miss Livingstons and other members of Lord Stirling's family. In December, 1783, we removed to New York. The weather was so remarkably mild, that we dined and sat upon deck. I shall never forget the delight and transport, even to tears, with which my mother and her friends returned to their recovered abodes, whence they had been driven seven years before. Yet their joy was chastened by many sorrowful recollections of those who had gone out with them, but who did not return. As Mr. Seaton, who resided in our house, could not leave it immediately, we hired one in William Street for a year. My eldest brother opened an office as a lawyer; John Morton went into a merchant's counting-house; and Washington, Clarke, and myself were sent to school. As all the Presbyterian churches had been converted by the British into barracks, riding-schools, or stables, the congregation of Dr. Rogers, to which my mother belonged, assembled in the French church in Cedar Street until their church in Wall Street was finished; when the re-opening of their old place of worship was a day of thanksgiving, almost as great as that of their first return to New York.

Mr. Wetzell, the husband of Christina Ernest, took no part in politics; and, being in good business, acquired property during the war. Their eldest daughter had married Sebastian Bowman, a Prussian officer in the British service, under General Gage. On his marriage, he left the army, and entered into business as a wine merchant. He afterwards espoused the American cause, and received a colonel's commission. His military knowledge, and his skill as an engineer, made him very important; and he was employed on the works at West Point, and at the siege of Yorktown. In 1784, when we had returned to my father's house in Water Street, his daughter, Maria Bowman, came to visit us. She was a lovely young woman, engaged to Major Shaw, who had served for seven years in the American Army as aid to General Knox. During her visit, he embarked from New York to open commercial relations between the United States and China. They were to be married on his return; and I remember their parting at my mother's house. Maria remained with us; but her health declined, and her life was soon terminated.

Colonel Bowman had returned to the city; and her funeral from his residence, through the streets of New York, was the only one I ever saw conducted in the same style. The pall was supported by six young ladies, dressed in white, with white hoods, scarfs, and gloves, — emblematic of the character of the young friend they were attending for the last time.

The grief of Major Shaw, on his return, I shall not attempt to describe. By devoted attentions to Mrs. Bowman and her family, he gave convincing proofs of his attachment.

On the adoption of the Federal Constitution, Colonel Bowman received from General Washington, as a reward for his faithful services during the war, the office of Postmaster of New York, which he held till his death. His other daughters were estimable women; but none of them equalled the lamented Maria.

Mrs. Wetzell (Christina Ernest) survived her husband and all her children, but was left with considerable property. She died at the house of her grand-daughter, Mrs. Dalle, who resided on the Hudson. Her sister, Mrs. Hoffman, sustained with Christian resignation a series of trials and the loss of sight. She was supported by an annuity, and cheered by the kind attention of my mother and other friends.

In 1785, Mr. and Mrs. Kemper returned to New York, to a convenient house near my mother; who, with their other children, contributed every thing requisite to their comfort. A long life of exertion was now drawing to a close, without an adequate reward for their industry and perseverance; but they never regretted their emigration to America, where they left their children in the possession of civil and religious liberty.

My grandmother was an excellent woman, and deserves a tribute from one she always distinguished by partial kindness. From my earliest recollection, her attention to all my wants and wishes was a source of my happiness, and her entertaining and instructive conversation my delight. She often gratified me by describing the cities, rivers, mountains, and people of the Old World, beyond the great sea over which she had come through so many dangers and with so many sacrifices. Often have I shed tears in sympathy with her, at the sad story of her separation from all her dear friends, never to see them again in this world. She had a fine voice, and sang the German hymns with a pathos which early charmed my ear with " the music of sweet sounds." But her strains were always mournful. The songs of Zion, in her native language, carried back her thoughts from a foreign land to scenes beyond the world of waters, to which her heart always turned with fond affection. Maria Regina Ernest Kemper died in New York, in her seventy-eighth year, Nov. 6, 1789.

During the five years Mr. Kemper survived his wife, his privations were alleviated by the attentions of his children and grandchildren. My mother removed him to her house, and was devoted to his comfort and amusement. She read his German books, and I the newspapers, to him daily. He had his national love of music; and my piano was placed in an apartment adjacent to his own, that he might hear me play and sing as often as he wished. To the last days of his life, he was patient, sensible, and resigned; and, after a short illness, departed, in 1794, at the age of eighty-seven years.

Thus closed the lives of all the first emigrants of our family who came from Germany to America.

CHAPTER V.

In 1784, I was sent with my sister to a school kept by Miss Dodsworth, an Englishwoman. We staid through the week, and came home to pass Sunday. There was no discipline. Two daughters of a British officer who had gone away with the troops were the tyrants of the school. At length, their father sent for them. Miss Dodsworth went also; and with her successor — Miss Ledyard of New London, sister of the celebrated traveller — we were happy, and improved. At the close of the year, we had what was called "a breaking-up." A stage was erected at the end of a large room, covered with a carpet, ornamented with evergreens, and lighted by candles in gilt branches. Two window curtains were drawn aside from the centre before it, and the audience were seated on the benches of the schoolroom. The "Search after Happiness," by Miss More; "The Milliner" and "The Dove," by Madame Genlis, — were performed. The characters were cast by Miss Ledyard. In the "Search after Happiness," I acted Euphelia, one of the court-ladies, and also sang a song intended in the play for one of the daughters of Urania; but, as I had the best voice, it was given to me. My dress was a pink and green striped silk; feathers and flowers decorated my head; and with bracelets on my arms, and paste buckles in my shoes, I thought I made a splendid appearance. The only time I ever rode in a sedan chair was on this occasion, when, after being dressed at home, I was conveyed in one to Miss Ledyard's residence. Hackney carriages were then unknown in New York. My friend Miss Mason, and the other girls, were all well dressed in character. In the second piece, I acted the Milliner; and, by some strange notion of Miss Ledyard's or my own, was dressed in a gown, cap, handkerchief, and apron of my mother's, with a pair of spectacles, to look like an *elderly woman*, — a proof how little we understood the character of a French milliner. When the curtain was drawn, many of the audience declared " it must be Mrs. Morton herself on the stage." How my mother, with her strict notions and prejudices against the theatre, ever consented to such proceedings, is still a surprise to me. In " The Dove," I appeared as a young girl in a garden. Among our auditors were Governor Clinton and his lady, whose daughters were among us. There were also several clergymen, and many of the friends of the children; and these performances were received " with unbounded applause."

At this time our estate in Water Street was sold, and we removed to a more eligible situation in Broadway. Madam Dwight of Stockbridge, a friend who had passed many weeks at our house before the war, came in 1786 to revisit us. The daughter of Colonel Williams of Williamstown, she married Mr. Sergeant of Stockbridge, who died in early life, leaving one son; and his widow became the wife of Colonel Dwight, one of the leading men of Massachusetts in his day. Their children were Henry Dwight, and Pamela, afterwards Mrs. Theodore Sedgwick. Madam Dwight was again left a widow, and in 1786 was upwards of sixty years of age, tall and erect, dignified, precise in manner, yet benevolent and pleasing. Her dress, of rich silk; a high-crowned cap, with plaited border; and a watch, then so seldom worn as to be a distinction, — all marked the gentlewoman, and inspired respect. She was a new study to me, and realized my ideas of Mrs. Shirley in " Sir Charles Grandison " and other characters I had read of in works of fiction. When she returned home, she asked me to accompany her; and, to my great joy, her request was complied with. We went up the Hudson in a sloop, in which we were the only passengers. The vessel, the noble river, and, above all, the High-lands, excited my wonder and delight. Our captain had a legend for every scene, either supernatural or traditional, or of actual occurrence during the war; and not a mountain reared its head, unconnected with some marvellous story. The hills reverberated the sound of the guns he fired; and one of his men played on the flute, and awoke the gentle echoes.

All this was enchanting to me. We were nearly a week on the Hudson before we arrived at Kinderhook, twenty miles below Albany; where we visited the family of Mr. Van Schaick, a house of good old-fashioned Dutch hospitality and wealth. There I saw the modes, life, and manner of treating domestic slaves, described by Mrs. Grant of Laggan, in her "Memoir of an American Lady." The elderly men and women were very familiar, and exercised as much influence over the children of the family as their parents; yet they were respectful and affectionate toward them and their master and mistress.

Three brothers of the name of Van Schaick resided near each other. Two of them, having no children, had adopted those of their brother and of their sisters, and were regarded by them with filial affection.

We staid at Mr. Van Schaick's till the wagon came for us from Stockbridge. I was seated by Madam Dwight; and we were driven by her grandson, a son of Dr. Sergeant. The distance was thirty or forty miles, — a day's journey. It was twilight when we reached Stockbridge. The first thing that attracted my attention was a fish, for a vane, on the steeple of the church. I said to Madam Dwight, "How could they put up a poor fish, so much out of its own element? It ought, at least, to have been a flying fish." She seemed much diverted at my remark; and repeated it to her friends, confessing that she had never thought of this absurdity herself, or heard it observed by others. Dr. Sergeant, Madam Dwight's son by her first marriage, resided in her mansion-house; where she retained the best parlor and chamber for her own use. He was an excellent man, and the most distinguished physician in that part of the country. We were joyfully received by him and his family. As I was fatigued, Madam Dwight took me to her room, and again expressed her pleasure at having me with her. I can never forget her affection and kindness. Her precepts and example made an indelible impression in favor of virtue and true piety. Her temper and character formed a living mirror, which reflected an image of such loveliness that my heart was firmly bound to her. She made me her companion, read to me, and talked to me with the confidence of a friend.

When, on the morning after our arrival, the window-shutters were opened, the Valley of the Housatonic, softened by wreaths of vapor rising over the mountains under the beams of the rising sun, seemed to my enchanted vision like fairy land. I exclaimed, "O Madam Dwight! it looks like the Happy Valley of Abyssinia. There is the river, and there are the mountains on every side. Why did you never tell me of this beautiful view?" My friend seemed surprised at my enthusiasm. Long familiar with the scene, she hardly realized its beauty. I became attached to her grandchildren, and passed several months in Stockbridge. Her daughter, Mrs. Sedgwick, lived upon "the Plain," as it was called, in distinction to "the Hill," where Dr. Sergeant resided. The church with the fish-vane was a mile from both, — half way up the hill, to reconcile contending parties that divided the town, but without accommodating either. It was, however, in a very pretty situation, — in a grove of pine trees. On Sunday, I rode to church on a pillion, behind Patty Sergeant. The family went in a wagon, except Madam Dwight, who had her chaise.

Dr. Partridge, a very singular character, resided with his sister, Mrs. Sergeant. He used to ride about the country on an old pacing horse to visit his patients, with his saddle-bags full of medicines. In dress and appearance, he resembled a Quaker. Possessing some

property, and being a very humane man, he often gave advice without fee or reward. Like Johnson's friend Dr. Levett, —

> " His useful care was ever nigh,
> Where hopeless Anguish poured his groan,
> And lonely Want retired to die."

Their spheres of action were widely different, — one relieving suffering in the dark abodes of London; the other, among the mountains
and valleys of a beautiful country: but simplicity, benevolence, and
industry marked them both. To keep aloof from every one at the
church, Dr. Partridge constructed a pew in one corner, near the ceiling, to which he ascended by steps from the gallery; and so great
was the respect in which he was held, that this singular arrangement
excited neither observation nor ridicule.

When I was recalled home, I parted from Madam Dwight with
great reluctance, and she expressed equal sensibility. She endeavored to comfort me by saying that she would visit New York the
next spring, and that I should return with her. But she was prevented from executing this intention; and when I revisited Stockbridge, in 1792, my friend was no more.

I could not consent to stay at Dr. Sergeant's, where every thing
reminded me of the loss I had sustained; but I passed several months
at Mrs. Sedgwick's, whose daughters often staid at our house in
New York. The remembrance of Madam Dwight yet awakens feelings of deep interest and gratitude; and her letters, which I have
carefully preserved, confirm my youthful impressions of her affection
and excellence.

After the Federal Constitution was adopted, I remember seeing
General Washington land on the 23d of April, 1789, and make his
entrance into New York, when he came to take the office of President
of the United States. I was at a window in a store on the wharf
where he was received. Carpets were spread to the carriage prepared for him; but he preferred walking through the crowded streets,

and was attended by Governor Clinton and many officers and gentlemen. He frequently bowed to the multitude, and took off his hat to the ladies at the windows, who waved their handkerchiefs, threw flowers before him, and shed tears of joy and congratulation. The whole city was one scene of triumphal rejoicing. His name, in every form of decoration, appeared on the fronts of the houses; and the streets through which he passed to the Governor's mansion were ornamented with flags, silk banners of various colors, wreaths of flowers, and branches of evergreen. Never did any one enjoy such a triumph as Washington, who, indeed, "read his history in a nation's eyes."

On the 30th of April, when Washington took the oath of office as President of the United States, the ceremony took place in the balcony of the old Federal Hall, as it was afterwards named, which stood in the centre of four streets. I was on the roof of the first house in Broad Street, which belonged to Captain Prince, the father of one of my school companions; and so near to Washington that I could almost hear him speak. The windows and roofs of the houses were crowded; and in the streets the throng was so dense, that it seemed as if one might literally walk on the heads of the people. The balcony of the hall was in full view of this assembled multitude. In the centre of it was placed a table, with a rich covering of red velvet; and upon this, on a crimson velvet cushion, lay a large and elegant Bible. This was all the paraphernalia for the august scene. All eyes were fixed upon the balcony; where, at the appointed hour, Washington entered, accompanied by the Chancellor of the State of New York, who was to administer the oath; by John Adams, the Vice-President; Governor Clinton; and many other distinguished men.

By the great body of the people, he had probably never been seen, except as a military hero. The first in war was now to be the first in peace. His entrance on the balcony was announced by universal shouts of joy and welcome. His appearance was most solemn and dignified. Advancing to the front of the balcony, he laid his hand on his heart, bowed several times, and then retired to an arm-chair near the table. The populace appeared to understand that the scene had overcome him, and were at once hushed in profound silence. After a few moments, Washington arose, and came forward. Chancellor Livingston read the oath according to the form prescribed by the Constitution; and Washington repeated it, resting his hand upon the Bible. Mr. Otis, the Secretary of the Senate, then took the Bible to raise it to the lips of Washington; who stooped, and kissed the book. At this moment, a signal was given, by raising a flag upon the cupola of the Hall, for a general discharge of the artillery of the Battery. All the bells in the city rang out a peal of joy, and the assembled multitude sent forth a universal shout. The President again bowed to the people, and then retired from a scene such as the proudest monarch never enjoyed. Many entertainments were given, both public and private; and the city was illuminated in the evening.*

From this time, President Washington resided in New York as long as Congress continued to hold its sessions in that city. He lived in a large house in Cherry Street, and always received the highest proofs of affection from the citizens. On one occasion, when he was ill, I remember seeing straw laid down in the adjacent streets, and chains drawn across those nearest his house, to prevent his being disturbed by carts and carriages. I have often seen him ride through the streets of New York on horseback, followed by a single attendant. The people always regarded him with attention and great respect. What must have been his feelings of delight and gratification on such surveys of the city and the country which he had so

---

* The preceding pages, which describe the entrance and inauguration of Washington, were sent to Mr. Irving, in 1856, at his request, by the Editor; and are inserted in his " Life of Washington," vol. iv. pp. 510, 513, 514, but without reference to their source.

largely contributed to preserve! Reviving commerce, busy streets, freedom and safety, now marked the places where ruin and distress had been inflicted by hostile armies.

All the ladies in the city visited Mrs. Washington. My mother did not take me with her on this occasion, as I was thought too young. Within a few weeks, Mrs. Washington returned these visits; and I remember her coming to our house in Broadway, attended by Colonel Humphreys, one of General Washington's aids, who resided in his family. I was then introduced, and kindly noticed by Mrs. Washington. Her portrait by Stuart is a good likeness. I do not remember having seen General Washington in private during his residence in New York. My mother did not repeat her visit to Mrs. Washington, and I was too young to attend her levees.

At this time, Oliver Wolcott was appointed Auditor of the Treasury, under Hamilton; whom he afterwards succeeded as Secretary of that department. He therefore removed from Litchfield in Connecticut to New York, and hired in Broadway the house which we had quitted for the one adjoining. Mrs. Wolcott was very lovely and amiable, and I soon became attached to her and her infant. Being engaged in important public affairs, Mr. Wolcott often appeared reserved and abstracted. I thought him cold and unsocial, till, by degrees, he took more notice of me. When their child was to be christened, I wished him to receive some pretty, romantic name. They talked of Oliver, which I disapproved. One day, as I entered her apartment, Mrs. Wolcott said, "Well, Susan, Mr. Wolcott insists the baby's name shall be Oliver." When he came in, I said indignantly, "So you will make a Roundhead of my little boy, after all?"—"What do you know about Roundheads, my little saucy girl?" said the grave Mr. Wolcott; and from that time he was very kind to me. He directed my reading, cultivated my taste, and, by his conversation, excited me to render myself a companion to him and Mrs. Wolcott.

Mrs. Hazard, who resided in the house opposite ours, was also a valuable friend. She was distinguished for the exquisite neatness of her establishment, and for capability in every branch of domestic economy. She had many and excellent servants; but, in those days, it was usual for ladies to attend to housewifery, and she kindly gave me much useful instruction. Mr. Hazard was an antiquarian, and the author of a collection of documents entitled "Hazard's Collection." He also held the office of Postmaster-General.

While Congress remained in New York, its sessions were held in the Federal Hall. I was taken there, and heard a debate on the propriety of their removal to Philadelphia. Some of the members who spoke in favor of it made very gallant speeches, intended for the ladies in the gallery. Though they saw many fair reasons for remaining in New York, the public good required the change. When this measure was carried into effect, we were deprived of both our valuable neighbors; and the loss of Mr. and Mrs. Wolcott sensibly affected my happiness.

My views of life and manners were, at this time, extended by an excursion, with my eldest brother and a large party, to Bethlehem in Pennsylvania; and afterwards to Rockaway, on Long Island, where the chief amusements were riding on horseback, and bathing in the surf, as is now the custom at Newport. One morning, I was thrown down by a high wave. The shock rendered me insensible; and the next would have ended my life, had not Mr. Pintard, one of our party, come to my assistance, and carried me beyond its reach.

On an excursion on horseback, I also escaped great danger. I was mounted on a gay horse, which took fright, and ran away in a narrow lane, bordered on each side by a Virginia fence. Probably from instinct, the horse ran in the middle of the road. I kept my seat, and had the presence of mind to turn him into a farm-yard; stopped him, and sat still until the gentlemen of the party came up, pale and terrified, expecting to find me dashed on the ground.

At Rockaway I formed many new acquaintances, and my voice and musical talents made me popular. There I met Mrs. Atkinson; and, after our return to New York, I was introduced to her sister, Mary Storer, — my first Boston acquaintance.

In September, 1790, Washington Morton entered Princeton College; and I went to the Commencement of that year with my eldest brother.

On board the Elizabethtown packet we met Mr. Paul Trapier and Mr. Withers of Charleston, South Carolina, who had just graduated at Harvard. We had a stormy passage across the bay, and I was excessively frightened. Having arrived at the ferry-house, we were shown into a room, where a venerable old man was waiting to go over to the city. The moment I entered, he took off his great-coat, and said to his wife, "My dear, I do not go to New York to-day: the looks of that young lady are enough to deter me." This was the celebrated General Gates. We passed two hours with him and Mrs. Gates, and commenced an acquaintance, which was afterwards continued in New York. We then proceeded in our phaeton, accompanied on horseback by Mr. Withers and Mr. Trapier, to Princeton; where we staid at the house of Mr. Stockton, a friend of our family.

We attended Commencement; and in the evening I went to the ball, where the two gentlemen from Charleston, and Mr. W. Gaston of North Carolina, were among my partners. The next morning, we rode on horseback; and, in the afternoon, went on to Philadelphia. We passed a week with Mrs. Jackson. I went to many places with my brother, and visited Mrs. Wolcott every day.

In 1787, the property of our family consisted of estates in the city of New York, the farm at Baskinridge, many outstanding debts, and the certificates from the Loan Office. A question arose as to the expediency of selling either the real estate, which was rising in value; or the certificates, which it was the general opinion might become as worthless as the Continental paper-money, by which great losses had been sustained by my father. My eldest brother took the responsibility of retaining the certificates. The result proved his sagacity, and was of great advantage to his family. Soon after the adoption of the Federal Constitution, this confidence was rewarded by the full payment of all claims on the United States.

The sale of the real estate in New York had been previously effected, and the proceeds devoted to liquidate the claims of the foreign correspondents of my father. In 1775, no remuneration could be made for the merchandise then received by Mr. Morton; but, after the restoration of peace, full payment was made of the principal of all demands. The interest during the seven years of the war was, of course, willingly abandoned. Great satisfaction was expressed with the honorable conduct of the family of Mr. Morton, and his former correspondents offered to sustain mercantile relations with either of his sons.

This was thought an auspicious opening for my second brother, John Morton, who had served an apprenticeship with an eminent merchant of New York; and, in 1791, he went to England with the final remittances to close the former concern, and commence a new establishment for the benefit of himself and his family. He carried excellent letters, and his reception equalled all expectations; but, instead of availing himself of these advantages, he spent his time in travelling. He was amiable and affectionate, but deficient in energy of character. On his return in 1793, he relinquished business as a merchant, and became the editor of a newspaper which had a wide circulation. We removed, in 1794, from Broadway to a house at the corner of Pine and Water Streets, near his printing office; but this undertaking was also unsuccessful.

The succeeding winter, my brother often accompanied my sisters and myself to evening parties. Among the French exiles from St. Domingo, then in New York, there were very cultivated and accomplished persons, — the Viscount Malartie, the Chevalier d'Olie, M. de la Roche, and many others, with whom we became acquainted.

At a concert and ball given by these French gentlemen, and by Mr. Joseph Smith and Mr. Middleton of South Carolina, I saw a young Indian, whom the Marquis de Lafayette had caused to be educated in Paris. He played on several musical instruments; danced, fenced, and rode with uncommon elegance; and was a very handsome man. That evening I heard him sing and play, and the most fashionable ladies were his partners in the dance. One month afterwards, he went to visit his Indian relatives, returned to all the habits of his tribe, and became as true a son of the forest as if he had never left the woods.

It was on this occasion that I first saw Miss Catherine Ludlow. She was very lovely in person and character, and my eldest brother became her avowed admirer. In June, 1791, they were married at the house of her father, Mr. Carey Ludlow, in Front Street, New York; and, some days afterwards, saw company much in the present style. Mr. Ludlow's mansion was spacious, new, and elegant, with doors of mahogany, — the first I had ever seen. My sister and myself were bridesmaids, and the scene was gay and splendid. Afterwards, I accompanied Mr. and Mrs. Morton on a journey to the eastern end of Long Island. At Montauk Point, I stood on the last stone on the shore, looking towards New England; little thinking I should ever become one of her adopted daughters.

On our return, my brother took a house in Broadway, near the Battery; where I passed much of my time, becoming attached to my new sister, who was very amiable. During the same summer, I accompanied Mrs. Morton to visit her aunt, Mrs. Smith, at Haverstraw, — a beautiful situation on the Hudson, among the Highlands. Among other excursions in that vicinity, we went to Grassy Point, afterwards the seat of Mr. Denning, who married the daughter of Mrs. Smith.

At Haverstraw I saw the desolate mansion of Mr. Chief-Justice Smith, which adjoined the estate of his brother. It was finely situated, and built in handsome style; but, the owner being a royalist, his property had been confiscated, and his mansion was falling to ruin.

During these years, I passed part of every summer at Princeton, in the family of President Smith; and his daughter Frances returned my visits in the winter. From his society and conversation, and from the friendship of Mr. William Johnson and Dr. Elihu Smith of Connecticut, — all distinguished for literature and accomplishments, — I derived great advantages. By the advice of Mr. Johnson, I read a course of history. His brother, Mr. Seth Johnson, was engaged to Mary Storer of Boston, the sister of Mrs. Atkinson. Miss Mason continued my most intimate friend, and I have ever cherished for her the warmest affection. She had great beauty, an amiable temper, and fine talents. Her letters and her poetical effusions I yet preserve with care.

In the autumn of 1794, I went to Philadelphia, and passed the ensuing winter with Mrs. Jackson. Mr. Wolcott succeeded Hamilton as Secretary of the Treasury in February, 1795; and at his house I saw all the eminent men then in public life, — Hamilton, Ellsworth, Pickering, General Knox, and others too numerous to mention.

One evening I accompanied Mrs. Wolcott to Mrs. Washington's drawing-room, where I was introduced to General Washington, and kindly noticed by him. The ladies were seated in a circle; Mrs. Adams, as lady of the Vice-President, next Mrs. Washington; and the rest according to rank: while the President and the gentlemen walked about, and conversed with each other or with the ladies. Mrs. Peter of Georgetown, a grand-daughter of Mrs. Washington, had just arrived in Philadelphia as a bride; and her sister Miss Custis, afterward Mrs. Lewis, was also present.* In a former visit to Philadelphia, in 1789, I saw Dr. Franklin in the street, in a sedan-chair.

---

* See Appendix I.

At Mr. Wolcott's I became acquainted with Mr. and Mrs. George Cabot of Boston; and when Congress rose, and they passed through New York on their return, they were visited by my brother and sister, and every one was much pleased with them. They spoke to me of their niece, Anna Cabot Lowell; showed me her letters; and expressed a wish that I would come to Boston, and become acquainted with her.

CHAPTER VI.

In July, 1795, I went to Princeton to stay at President Smith's until the autumn; but in August I was recalled home to accompany my brother John Morton to Boston. The recovery of a debt due on his former mercantile concerns was the object of his journey. I obeyed the summons with great regret; being agreeably established at Princeton with plans for the summer, which I relinquished with reluctance to go to Boston.

Having arrived at home, I found my brother had already engaged our passage to Providence, Rhode Island, on board a packet, for the next day. We had a pleasant sail through the Sound; touched at Newport; and, attended by our servant, proceeded to Boston in the stage. The chief pleasure I anticipated from this excursion was that of visiting Mr. and Mrs. George Cabot, who, I had been informed, resided in the environs of that town; and, passing through Roxbury, I selected the mansion of Judge Lowell as probably theirs. As we drove over the Neck, and through the Main Street of Boston, I little imagined I was entering the place of my future residence. The ranges of wooden houses, all situated with one end toward the street, and the numerous chaises we met, drawn by one horse, the driver being placed on a low seat in front, appeared to me very singular.

At that time, Boston, compared with New York, was a small town.

There were no brick sidewalks, except in a part of the Main Street, near the Old South, then called Cornhill. The streets were paved with pebbles ; and, except when driven on one side by carts and carriages, every one walked in the middle of the street, where the pavement was the smoothest. We drove to Mrs. Archibald's boarding-house, in Bowdoin Square ; where we were well accommodated. My brother engaged Mr. H. G. Otis as his lawyer. We sent our letters ; and Mr. Storer and his sister, and many other persons, called on us. Mary Storer was very attentive ; and I was with her every day, either at her father's house in Sudbury Street, or at that of her brother, Mr. George Storer, near Bowdoin Square. The boarders at Mrs. Archibald's were chiefly gentlemen, who vied with each other in their civilities. Mr. and Mrs. Craigie soon called, and invited me to pass the rest of my visit with them at Cambridge ; and I accepted the invitation for the next week.

On Sunday morning, I went with Miss Storer to Brattle-street Church ; and was there reminded of descriptions of a former day in England. The broad aisle was lined by gentlemen in the costume of the last century, — in wigs, with cocked hats and scarlet cloaks. Many peculiarities in dress, character, and manners, differing from those of New York and Philadelphia, were very striking to me. In the afternoon, Mr. and Miss Storer proposed to take me to hear Mr. Kirkland, a popular young clergyman. They consulted where we should sit, and decided to go to Mr. Quincy's pew. This was the first time I heard the name. We proceeded to the New South Church ; and, after the service, Mr. Quincy was introduced to me, and, in the evening, came to Mr. Storer's. The next morning he called on me and my brother ; and I heard the gentlemen at our lodgings speak in high terms of his character, talents, and family.

The day following, apparently to the disappointment of my friends in Boston, I accompanied Mrs. Craigie to Cambridge, and was cordially welcomed to her delightful residence.

Mr. Craigie was a native of Boston. During the war, he was attached to the medical staff of the American Army; and thus formed a friendship with Dr. Jackson of Philadelphia, who introduced him to our family, in which he became as intimate as a brother. After the peace, he opened a large store, as a druggist, in New York; and, by successful speculations in United-States certificates, accumulated a large fortune. He then returned to Boston, and purchased the house and estate of John Vassal — the head-quarters of Washington — in Cambridge. He had recently married a beautiful woman. His establishment was complete and elegant, and he lived in a style of splendor and hospitality. Every day there was a party to dine, and pass the evening. He expressed gratitude for the attentions he had received from my family, and was happy to return them.

Mrs. Craigie evinced great interest in me, and gave me her opinions of her guests. Of Mr. Quincy she spoke in the highest terms, and said his name was one she had always been taught to honor and respect.

When Mr. Craigie heard me say that I wished to visit Mr. and Mrs. Cabot, he ordered his carriage to convey me to their residence in Brookline; and their pleasure at this unexpected meeting was equal to my own. The next day they came to Mr. Craigie's, and invited us to dine. My brother accompanied me to Brookline on the day appointed, and there I was introduced to Miss Lowell and others of the Higginson and Lowell families. Every affectionate attention was lavished on me by Mr. and Mrs. Cabot; and, had my engagements permitted, I would have gladly passed some days with them.

Miss Lowell soon called at Mr. Craigie's, and engaged me to visit her; and I met her and other ladies at Fresh Pond, at a party given by Mr. William Sullivan and Mr. Quincy. With Mr. and Mrs. Craigie I passed a day at the seat of Mr. Barrell, whose establishment exceeded in elegance even that of Mr. Craigie. At his table I saw Mr. Balch, a man celebrated for his wit and humor; and heard him tell some comic anecdotes and stories. We also dined at Charlestown with Dr. and Mrs. Morse and their family. With Mrs. Morse I was previously acquainted, as she was a niece of Mrs. Hazard. I passed some days with Miss Binney,* who resided at Watertown with her step-father, Dr. Spring; and was taken by her to see Mr. Lyman's seat at Waltham.

The time I spent with my friends at Cambridge was as delightful as novelty and kind attention could render it. I took leave of them with sincere regret; and Mrs. Craigie conveyed me in her carriage to Boston, where we parted with mutual affection. I passed the last week in Boston with Mary Storer, at the house of her brother, Mr. George Storer; and was taken to see the new State House, then just completed, the cupola of which I ascended. We also viewed the house of Mr. D. D. Rogers near it, then unfinished. The mansions of Governor Hancock and Mr. Joy, and a few old-fashioned wooden houses, were the only edifices beyond the State House. I went up on Beacon Hill, read the inscription on the Monument, and walked in "the Mall," which at that time I could not think equal to "the Battery." In all these excursions, Mr. Quincy was our constant attendant.

The afternoon we visited Miss Lowell at Roxbury, Mr. and Mrs. Cabot made me repeat every song I had ever sung to them; and insisted on my commencing a correspondence with Miss Lowell, and forming a friendship on their account. The proposal was accepted; and, during her life, the friendship thus begun remained unaltered. Judge and Mrs. Lowell, with their children and their nephews and nieces, formed a very interesting family-group.

In 1792, eight years after the death of my cousin Maria Bowman, Major Shaw married Miss Phillips of Boston. As his friends, our

---

* Afterwards Mrs. Wallace of Philadelphia. Her son, Horace Binney Wallace, was highly distinguished for talent and intellectual power.

family visited his wife in New York, whence he sailed in 1793 on a last voyage to China; and we paid her every attention in our power until she returned home. An elegant house near Bowdoin Square had been built and furnished for their residence; but Major Shaw died on the homeward voyage, and his widow and friends suffered the loss of one of the most excellent of men.

In 1795, Mrs. Shaw was passing the summer in Dedham, at the residence of Mr. and Mrs. Dowse, who were then in England. Her nephew Mr. Quincy, having discovered the intimate friendship which had existed between my family and Major Shaw, informed her I was in Boston, and brought Miss Storer and myself a pressing invitation to visit her at Dedham, where she gave us an affectionate welcome. Mr. Quincy, who accompanied us in a post-chaise, insisted on returning over Milton Hill to show me the prospect. The view of his house and estate at Quincy from thence was probably his real object, as I remember he said that there he placed all his plans of happiness. During these excursions, I became much acquainted with Mr. Quincy. All I heard of his character tended to raise him in my estimation; and I left Boston with very different views and sentiments from those with which I had entered it.

We returned to New York by land, then a journey of eight or ten days. At New Haven, a letter directed me to repair to Long Island, as an alarm from the yellow-fever had dispersed our family. Accordingly, we crossed the ferry above New York to Brooklyn, where I was welcomed by Mr. and Mrs. Morton, who had taken a house directly opposite the city; and here I had time for recollection and thought after the fatigue of the journey, and the scenes of interest through which I had lately passed. I could hardly determine how to read the page of futurity, which seemed to open before me.

Our situation on the heights of Brooklyn, commanding a view of the entire eastern side of New York, was delightful. I often spent whole afternoons sitting with my little nephews on the banks of the

East River, among the trees, looking over to New York, which was as still as a city of the dead. Not a sound, not a motion, could be observed; no smoke from a single chimney, nor even a boat moving near one of the wharves, where all used to be noise, bustle, and animation. After many weeks of suspense and anxiety, the city was declared safe, and the inhabitants returned. My mother was soon re-established in our house in Water Street. I went home, and my brother's family returned to Broadway.

In December, Mr. Sullivan and Mr. Quincy arrived, on their way to Philadelphia. They received every attention from my brothers, and were much admired in society. Mr. Quincy brought me letters from Miss Lowell and Miss Storer. They went on to Philadelphia, Mr. Quincy intending to go to South Carolina: but he soon re-appeared in New York, being called home by the failure of a man to whom part of his property had been intrusted; and, with the probability that our meeting again would be deferred for a long time, I consented to a correspondence.

In the summer of 1796, I went to Princeton, as my brother Clark Morton was to take his degree. Mr. Quincy came to Princeton at Commencement, and we met frequently in society there and in Philadelphia. I visited Mrs. Jackson, and accompanied her to Easton; where we passed a fortnight in the family of Mr. Sitgreaves, who had married my cousin Mary Kemper; a man of fine talents, polished manners, and commanding personal appearance. He resided many years at Easton, in a beautiful situation at the confluence of the Delaware, the Lehigh, and the Bushkill, commanding a view of three chasms in the Alleghany Ridge, called the Delaware Gap, the Lehigh Gap, and the Wind Gap; through which also a river had evidently once forced its way. We visited Bethlehem, Nazareth, and other places of interest.

[The letters from which extracts are here inserted were written at this period.]

Miss E. S. Morton to Mrs. Jackson, Philadelphia.

NEW YORK, Dec. 27, 1795.

Mr. Quincy and Mr. Sullivan of Boston, who offer to convey this letter to you, my dear aunt, are both generally admired in society. Mr. Sullivan brought me a letter from our friend Susan Binney, who expresses a grateful remembrance of your kind attentions to her.

My affection for you (one of the first attachments of my childhood) remains so intimately interwoven with my happiness, that it will be, I trust, one of the last I shall lose. I delight to indulge in recollections of the time I passed with you last winter, — our morning conversations in the nursery, our evening excursions to the theatre, and our discussions of what we saw and heard. Though usually of the same way of thinking, we had great pleasure in comparing our opinions. . . .

NEW YORK, Jan. 21, 1796.

Your letter by Mr. Johnson, my dear aunt, is flattering to my pride, and grateful to my better feelings. The chief wish of my heart has ever been to gain the affection of the good. It is too proud to be gratified by compliment, and can be satisfied only with esteem and love. . . . You have pleased me by approving my friends, — a kind of flattery to which we are all open. I am ever disposed to like those who praise what I admire.

That you have discovered and distinguished the merits of Mr. Quincy is not surprising; for I believe penetration and justice to be equally leading features of your character.

Tell Mr. Sullivan that we are to have a party at my brother's house to-morrow evening, and that we have been wishing he could be one of the company. I shall have my despatches for Boston in readiness; for I apprehend New York will not long detain him after dazzling and being dazzled in the meridian of Philadelphia.

NEW YORK, April 18, 1796.

I cannot withhold from you, my dear aunt, so great a pleasure as that of forming an acquaintance with the gentleman who will give you this letter. He is a son of Mr. Copley, the celebrated painter in London, who is an American. If he should hand you this letter himself, and if you have an opportunity of conversing with him, a highly cultivated mind and polished manners will gain your approbation.

Will you do me the favor to introduce Mr. Copley* to Mrs. Wolcott, and ask her to like him for my sake? . . .

Your affectionate

E. S. MORTON.

President Smith to Miss E. S. Morton.

PRINCETON, Feb. 27, 1796.

You think, perhaps, my dear Susan, that I have forgotten my promise of another letter; but I have been assiduously attending our Legislature to gain from them a small pittance, which will not answer half the purpose for which they granted it. It is appropriated, in the law, to repair the college-buildings, replenish the library, and purchase a philosophical apparatus. But that apparatus alone would require a thousand dollars more than they have been pleased to assign. To make up this sum, I wish to write to all those who have graduated here since I came, to request them to beg a few dollars each in his

---

* Afterwards Lord Lyndhurst, and Lord High-Chancellor of England.

neighborhood, and send them to me for this purpose. If I live, I am resolved, if possible, to have in future one of the best apparatuses on the continent.

But why all this detail to you? Because I know you are so good, that you feel a sympathy with me in every object which interests me. . . .

Alas the insult that a forward spark has committed on my paper! If I were like Cowley, or some modern wits, I would say it is an emblem of the ardor with which sparkish beaux fly to the paper which bears your name. I might say, if I were a younger man, that it is consumed only by the warmth of my sentiments. That poet has many conceits as forced as these; and I have heard some young and flippant gentlemen playing the gallant, very charmingly as they believed, with wit quite as strained. Your good sense, I am convinced, always knows how to estimate the exuberances of a fancy much more pleased with itself than with the lady to which it pretends to be paying homage.

I will not say that the ardor of my sentiments burns my paper, but assure you and Frances of the affection of a father.

SAMUEL S. SMITH.

Letter from Hon. S. Sitgreaves.

EASTON, PENNSYLVANIA, Oct. 30, 1796.

MISS SUSAN MORTON, — I cannot resist the desire I feel to offer you the assurance of a friendship, which, though of recent growth, has nevertheless arrived at full maturity. Prepared as I was to feel a lively interest in those dear to my wife, you have inspired me with an esteem which nothing could have created but a personal knowledge of the engaging qualities which have fascinated all who have had the pleasure of your society.

Although there are many who have earlier pretensions, I delight to believe that your heart is sufficiently capacious to admit me to a participation in affections which none can appreciate more highly. The cold and sordid regards of the world are but little estimable to a discriminating mind; but life would be deprived of its principal charm, if it did not offer us the means of cultivating the good opinion of the few whose virtues and accomplishments give value to their esteem. Suffer me, therefore, to persuade myself that I am among the number of your friends, and I shall harmonize in perfect good humor with all the letters of the alphabet from C to Q; or, if this selection is without a reason, with the whole series from A to Z.

We prolong the pleasure you permitted us to enjoy, by renewing the walks we took together, by conversing of you round our evening fire, and by anticipating the time when we hope you will again wind with us the meanders of the Bushkill, or climb the steeps which impend over its margin; and we trim the vine that it may yield the wild grapes in perfection, while you shall repose under its shade, and read your favorite poet on the banks of the Delaware. . . .

Believe me, with true attachment, your friend,

S. SITGREAVES.

Miss Lowell to Miss E. S. Morton, New York.

BOSTON, Jan. 6, 1797.

MY DEAR FRIEND, — The promise your last letter contained, of writing another by Mr. Copley, was not the least pleasing of its contents; but the society of New York and Philadelphia have charms so seductive, that I fear it will be long before he returns to us. The quickness of feeling, and susceptibility of pleasure, which are striking traits in that gentleman's character, are the occasion of his forming frequent and warm prepossessions; and, wherever he goes, will create him friends he will find it hard to leave. Regret, however, in such minds, is seldom a lasting sentiment; since new objects of interest easily supply the place of those separated by absence. Of Mr. Quincy I should say much: for he has won me by entreaty, and bribed me by flattery and attention; and all this that I may say handsome things of him to you. But Mr. Quincy is so much better qualified to recommend himself, that I enter upon my office with real diffidence. Indeed, of all his excellences, I shall only at this time notice one: it is a just and delicate taste in the selection of his female friends. I am aware of the apparent vanity of the last remark; but it will be softened when I add, that Mr. Quincy never distinguished me as a favorite until he knew me as your friend. Since I returned, I have met him only twice in public, and then we had but one subject. I cannot do justice to his manner of treating that. By the ladies here, he is charged with coldness and indifference; but certainly I sometimes touch a string which vibrates to sensations very opposite to those of apathy. Last evening, he was unusually animated; and, indeed, a very brilliant assembly, where every face wore a smile of satisfaction, was sufficient to inspire every one.* . . .

Your friend,   A. C. LOWELL.

Letter from Mrs. Wolcott to Miss E. S. Morton.

PHILADELPHIA, April 18, 1797.

After so long a silence, how shall I make my dear Susan sensible of the pleasure her last charming letter gave me? Until you become a wife and the mistress of a family, you cannot sufficiently realize

---

* Mr. Copley (Lord Lyndhurst) and Mr. Quincy, mentioned in the preceding letters, were both born in Boston, Massachusetts, in 1772. After holding various high offices, they survive in 1861, in full possession of their mental powers, and correspond with each other across the Atlantic.

why I do not oftener employ my pen in testimonies of regard to my absent friends. . . . I hope to be one day a witness of a scene of domestic felicity which I have planned for you, which I think you in every respect qualified to adorn, to render happy, and to enjoy; and, were it to be measured by my wishes, would be all that is truly good in this world, joined to the most well-founded hopes of a happy hereafter. I fear I am growing too serious, and will only add that your image ever presents itself to my mind among those who share my most tender love and solicitude for their happiness. . . .

Mr. Wolcott requests me to offer to you the continuance of his highest esteem. Congress will soon meet, which will increase his burthens, and my cares and solicitude.

Your affectionate   ELIZA WOLCOTT.

CHAPTER VII.

In May, 1797, Mr. Quincy came again to New York. His mother, who had a large and elegant house in Pearl Street, Boston, proposed that our engagement should be fulfilled, and that we should reside with her; and this offer was gratefully accepted.

The regret of my family at the prospect of my removal to a distance was tempered by the confidence with which they intrusted my happiness to such a friend. When our arrangements were completed, President Smith came from Princeton to perform the ceremony of our marriage; which took place at my mother's house in Water Street, New York, on the 6th of June, 1797. The only persons present on that occasion, besides my own family, were my uncle Daniel Kemper, Mr. and Mrs. Dowse of Boston, and the Rev. Dr. Rogers of New York.

Mr. and Mrs. Morton, Mr. and Mrs. Dowse, and Washington Morton, accompanied us to Haerlem, where we dined; and there I parted with my eldest brother, whom I had long regarded as my chief protector, and entered on untried scenes of life with another guardian. Every thing was new to me in prospect. I had never seen Mr. Quincy's mother or any of his relatives, except Mr. and Mrs. Storer, Mrs. Shaw, and Mr. and Mrs. Dowse; but, secure in the worth and disinterested attachment of him to whom I was now united, I felt no fears, no apprehensions.

We travelled pleasantly in a private carriage and four; and reached Marlborough, Massachusetts, on the evening of the eighth day of our journey. The next morning, Mr. Quincy went to inform Mrs. Ann Quincy, the widow of his grandfather,* of our arrival. Our reception from her, and from her son-in-law and daughter, the Rev. Mr. Packard and his wife, with whom she resided, was all that affection could dictate. At noon, we saw a carriage approach, which brought Mr. Quincy's mother, accompanied by his cousins, Miriam Phillips and Hannah Storer, whom she had selected as appropriate attendants on her new daughter.

Mrs. Quincy was then fifty-three years of age, still retaining traces of great personal beauty, with a fine expression of countenance, and cordial and graceful manners. Her dress united richness and elegance with propriety and taste. I was much agitated at the thought of this meeting; but from the moment I saw her, and received her first welcome and embrace, I felt at ease, and sure that we should promote each other's happiness. Mr. Quincy's satisfaction was complete when he beheld me with his mother, and surrounded by approving friends.

The next day, we had a very gay journey to Boston in the carriage with Mrs. Quincy and her companions; sending our luggage by the one which had brought us from New York. We drove over Cambridge Bridge, and through Boston to the residence of Mrs. Quincy in Pearl Street, where she again welcomed me to her home. In the afternoon, Miss Lowell came, delighted to receive me as an inhabitant of Boston; and, with Miss Storer and Miss Phillips, remained several days. These ladies acted as bridesmaids, though we did not receive company in formal style. The nearest relatives of Mr. Quincy had been invited for the evening. They were Mr. and Mrs. Storer; Mr. and Mrs. Phillips, with their families; Mr. and Mrs. Jona-

---

* Josiah Quincy of Braintree, Massachusetts.

than Mason and their parents; Mr. and Mrs. William Powell and Miss Anna Powell; Mr. and Mrs. Daniel D. Rogers; Mrs. J. Powell and Miss Bromfield; Mr. John Phillips; and many others, whose names I cannot enumerate.

The next day we saw company, morning and evening; and Mrs. Quincy and Miss Lowell were much amused by my observations on the characters, manners, and dress of the variety of persons who visited us. Some of the old gentlemen especially, when introduced for the first time, appeared to me very singular.

For several weeks we were continually engaged, as many parties were made for us. We frequently visited Mr. and Mrs. Cabot, and Mr. and Mrs. Craigie; were invited to their houses: and they were entertained in return, in the most elegant style, by Mrs. Quincy. The whole summer passed in agreeable excursions and engagements.

At the Commencement of 1797, the first I ever attended at Harvard College, we dined at Mr. Craigie's, in Cambridge, with more than a hundred guests. I corresponded constantly with my own family; and Miss Lowell, who visited New York in the autumn, gratified them highly with an account of my reception and situation in Boston.

Mary Storer, who had married Mr. S. Johnson of New York the year previous, often adverted to our unexpected change of residence. Accompanied by my sister, she came to Boston in September. Mrs. Quincy spent several weeks with Mrs. Dowse, at Dedham, at this time, to leave us in full possession of her establishment. Miss Binney and Miss Foster, the niece of Mr. Craigie, passed some days with us; and our engagements were constant during my sister's visit. After her return to New York, Mrs. Quincy came home; and we were constant companions during the winter. I learned from her all the circumstances of her past life; her attachment and marriage to her husband; his character, his rank in his profession, and his devoted patriotism; all that she had suffered during his illness and absence, and by his death on his voyage from England, within sight of the American shore. After this irreparable loss, it had been the object of her life to render their son worthy of his name and family.

We read together, and found a coincidence, as delightful as it was uncommon, in our views on every subject. By nature, and habits of thought and action, we seemed formed for each other. I felt myself appreciated by a woman who deserved all my respect and admiration; and we drew many plans for the future, in which we were always to be united. Her son contemplated with delight our affection and friendship; but a cloud arose over this fair prospect. The health of Mrs. Quincy gradually declined. She at length consented to consult a physician, and every effort was made for her restoration.

In the spring of 1798, we were made happy by the birth of an infant; and our mother was as much interested in the event as ourselves. Three days afterwards, my physician informed me imprudently that the malady from which she suffered would prove fatal. I consequently became dangerously ill; and, when my child was ten days old, she expired.

In consequence of my illness, I was kept in ignorance of this event. The friends and relatives of Mrs. Quincy assembled at the house of her brother, William Phillips, in Tremont Street. Her son attended her remains to Quincy, and placed them beside those of his father, in obedience to the wishes of both parents; and thus fulfilled the last filial duty. "To those who conversed with Mrs. Quincy only as a general acquaintance, she was the object of warm regard; and by her more intimate connections she was loved as a friend, trusted as a guide, prized as a companion, and revered as a pattern. Correctness and vivacity of thought marked her understanding; the heart of sensibility was joined to firmness; and sweetness mingled with dignity in her manners. Adversity brightened her virtues, and prosperity could not corrupt them. None better knew both how to enjoy and to improve life, — equally alive to every innocent gratification, and ready to every serious duty." *

Several weeks elapsed before I became aware of the loss I had sustained; my physician, alarmed at the effect of his own imprudence, being anxious to postpone the agitation and grief such intelligence would occasion. After I had recovered sufficient strength to bear the excitement of the meeting, our friends and relatives gathered round me; and my own mother came on from New York. New duties and engagements claimed our attention. We found ourselves in possession of the house and property of our beloved parent; and it seemed to me as if her benign spirit presided over the scene of her former presence, to bless her children in the home she had prepared for them. To the present day, the thought of her opinions has influenced my conduct; and this is the tribute to her memory she would have most valued.

Mr. Quincy gave me a diamond ring, — the gift of his father to his mother on their engagement. I also retained her watch, a present from her sisters Mrs. Dowse and Mrs. Shaw; to whom we gave the rest of her immediate personal property. Our first visit, after my recovery, was to them and to Mr. Dowse. They received us with sympathy and affection, and from this time held a parental relation toward us and our children. From Mrs. Shaw I learned, that, retaining her consciousness to the last moment, our mother had endeavored to calm the intense grief of her sisters by reminding them how short would be the separation. Her last expressions of affection were for me. She charged Mrs. Shaw to be a mother to me, in her place; and to convey to me the assurance of her love, of her perfect approbation, and her last blessing.

---

* Obituary Notice of Mrs. Abigail Quincy, by Rev. J. T. Kirkland. — *Columbian Centinel*, March, 1798.

After the decease of Major Shaw, his widow was accustomed to pass the winter months with her sister, in Boston; and this arrangement was continued with us for several years.

The first occurrence which turned the course of our thoughts was the appointment of Mr. Quincy, by the authorities of the town of Boston, to deliver the oration on the 4th of July, 1798; when I heard him speak in public for the first time. His audience in the Old South were excited by the aspect of political affairs; and I observed that Colonel T. H. Perkins (the commander of the Cadets) and other gentlemen were affected to tears by his impassioned address.

Our residence in the family mansion at Quincy (which has been since our abode during many happy years) commenced that summer; and then began my friendship with President and Mrs. Adams.

In the spring of 1799, accompanied by Mrs. Alsop of Middletown and our cousin Susan Storer, we took the stage for our party, reached New York in eight days, and passed six weeks with our relatives. During that and the succeeding year, we had constant social meetings with many friends; and Miss Lowell continued my most intimate associate.

At this time, I formed an acquaintance with Mrs. S. Cabot, one of the friends of Mr. Quincy's mother. Her husband, Samuel Cabot, a brother of George Cabot, was then in England, commissioner, under the treaty, with Messrs. Gore and King. My attentions to Mrs. Cabot were unremitted; and, after her decease in 1809, they were continued to her children. Colonel T. H. Perkins resided near us, in Pearl Street; and with him and Mrs. Perkins we have ever since sustained an affectionate friendship.

In 1801, we made a journey to New York in our carriage, and passed some weeks with my eldest brother and his family. They then resided at Greenwich, two miles from New York, on an estate which our grandfather, Mr. Kemper, had taken, on a lease, from Trinity Church. The high bank of the Hudson, fringed with trees, on which the house was situated, commanded an extensive view of that noble river; and the grounds were ornamented with trees and shrubs, and a fine hawthorn hedge. When the lease expired, this estate was levelled, and divided into city lots; and the site of my brother's house is now marked by Morton Street, in the city of New York. My brother Washington Morton, who, in 1797, had married Cornelia Schuyler, a daughter of General Schuyler of Albany, and my uncle, Daniel Kemper, and his family, also resided at Greenwich.

Receiving intelligence that Dr. Jackson of Philadelphia was dangerously ill, we went on to that city; and, passing through Princeton, were received most affectionately by President Smith and his family. Dr. Jackson was an excellent man, extensively engaged in his profession. He survived but a short time, and his widow was left with a numerous family dependent on her care. In the autumn, her eldest daughter, afterwards Mrs. I. P. Davis of Boston, came to pass the winter with me. In New York, we selected a monument of white marble, to be erected to the memory of the parents of Mr. Quincy; as, at that period, no such memorial could be obtained in Boston. On our return through Connecticut, Mr. and Mrs. Wolcott cordially welcomed us; and we passed several days with them at Litchfield. After our return, President Smith and his daughter Frances spent several weeks at our house in Boston; and my brothers, Washington and Clarke Morton, also visited us.

In the spring of 1802, I gave a large evening party, on the return of Mr. and Mrs. John Quincy Adams from Europe. Our house in Pearl Street was thrown open to all our acquaintance, and a ball and supper arranged in the most elegant style of that period.

The following summer, Mr. and Mrs. Wolcott passed a month with us. Their numerous friends — George Cabot, Fisher Ames, the Higginson and Pomeroy families, and many others — gathered around them; and we were constantly engaged in a succession of parties and entertainments, among which were included several visits to President and Mrs. Adams at Quincy. The time passed delightfully away in the companionship of these distinguished friends.

PART II.

AFTER the preceding pages were written by Mrs. Quincy at leisure moments, they were copied into a volume by her daughter, Margaret Morton Quincy; from whose manuscript they have been prepared for the press, and the narrative concluded, by

ELIZA SUSAN QUINCY.

BOSTON, MASSACHUSETTS,
APRIL 20, 1861.

CHAPTER I.

SINCE the close of the last century, Boston has almost lost its identity by changes within its precincts. The mansion where Mrs. Quincy was received on her marriage stood on the southern slope of Fort Hill, surrounded by open fields. These are now covered by brick houses and granite stores, and its site is marked by the Quincy Block. It was a handsome edifice of three stories, the front ornamented with Corinthian pilasters; and pillars of the same order supported a porch, from which three flights of steps of red sandstone, and a broad walk of the same material, descended to Pearl Street. Honeysuckles were twined round the porch, and high damask rosebushes grew beneath the windows. The estate extended to High Street; and at the corner of Pearl Street stood the stable and coach-house. The grounds ascending toward Oliver Street were formed into glacis, and were adorned by four English elms of full size and beauty, the resort of numerous birds, especially of the oriole, or golden robin.

Mr. Merchant, a Bostonian engaged in the commerce then opening with China, erected the house on this estate, but died before its completion. In 1792, it was sold, with the land now comprehended in Quincy and Pearl Places, by his executors, William Foster and Harrison Gray Otis, for a thousand pounds, to William Phillips; who caused his daughter, Mrs. Quincy, to remove to this mansion, which she arranged with taste and elegance. The spacious hall was carpeted with straw matting, among the first imported from China; and furnished with arm-chairs and a lounge, of cane.* The dining and drawing rooms, which opened from the hall on either side, had cornices of stucco; and the walls were hung with a plain green paper, relieved by a broad, highly colored border, representing flowers and shells. The furniture of both apartments was of mahogany, carved and inlaid. Four Chinese drawings in water-colors (views of Canton and its vicinity) and an engraving of Stuart's portrait of Washington hung in the dining-room, which communicated with a china-closet, and with a clock-room, in which stood a high, old-fashioned timepiece, and a mahogany secretary and bookcase, with mirrors in the doors. With the exception of the entrance-hall, the carpets on both the lower stories were Brussels and Axminster. Graceful wreaths of flowers, on a white ground, formed the pattern in the drawing-room; in which apartment there were large mirrors and cut-glass chandeliers. Among its ornaments were several rich china vases and an ivory model of a pagoda, presented by Major Shaw in 1792 to Mrs. Abigail Quincy. A large apartment in the second story was devoted to the library, the books being arranged in mahogany cases with glazed doors.

As the situation of the house was elevated, it commanded an extensive view of the town, crowned by the State House, and by the Monument on the beautiful cone of Beacon Hill. Mr. Wolcott, in 1802, admired these structures, and said, "The Bostonians, like the Romans, may boast of their Capitol and their triumphal column." Mrs. Quincy replied, "They are more like the Athenians. A grasshopper ought to be placed on Faneuil Hall." She was not then aware, that, as a crest of the Faneuils, a grasshopper had actually long surmounted the Cradle of Liberty.

---

* A similar set was seen by Mrs. Abigail Adams, in one of the royal palaces, in the dressing-room of Queen Charlotte; and a lounge of the same pattern stood, in 1856, in one of the show-rooms of Warwick Castle.

Before the American Revolution, Governor Oliver resided in Oliver Street; and Thomas Palmer, an opulent merchant, in Hutchinson Street. Mr. Palmer's mansion was divided, and became the residence of James Lovell and Thomas Handyside Perkins; and the name of the street was changed to Pearl Street. A field extended between the houses of Mr. Quincy and Mr. Perkins; and beyond, on the north side of Pearl Street, were the residences of Chief-Justice Parsons and Mr. John Prince, whose estate bounded on Milk Street.

From the Mall, on Fort Hill, there was an uninterrupted view of the town and harbor. Summer and Winter Streets and Bowdoin Square were bordered by houses, separated by fields and gardens. Franklin Place was the most modern part of the town, and the only continuous range of brick houses. All the churches in Boston, except the Old South, the Stone Chapel, the Brattle Street, and the North Church, have been either rebuilt or founded. The only avenues to the country were the Neck, and Cambridge and Charlestown Bridges.

The places which knew the inhabitants of Boston at that period cannot be said to "know them no more;" for their mansions have vanished like themselves; and the very ground they stood on has been carried away, and cast into the sea. Sketches of those with which Mrs. Quincy was then most familiar, are, therefore, here appropriate.

William Phillips, the maternal grandfather of Mr. Quincy, resided in Beacon Street, in a house erected, in 1720, by Edward Bromfield, for many years an eminent merchant of Boston. He died in 1756; and, in 1764, his mansion * was purchased by his son-in-law, Mr. Phillips. It was of three stories, and richly furnished according to the fashion of the last century. There were large mirrors in carved

---

* See Appendix II.

mahogany frames, with gilt mouldings; and one apartment was hung with tapestry, representing a stag-hunt. Three steep flights of stone steps ascended from Beacon Street to the front of the mansion; and behind it was a paved court-yard, above which rose successive terraces filled with flowers and fruit-trees. On the summit, a summer-house, elevated higher than the roofs of the houses which, in 1861, form Ashburton Place, commanded a panoramic view of the harbor and environs. Some noble trees near it, a landmark before the Revolution for ships approaching the coast, were cut down by the British during the siege of Boston. The hill on which this mansion stood — between those of Governor Bowdoin and David Sears, both of subsequent erection — was levelled in 1845; and the site is now marked by Freeman-place Chapel, and the adjoining houses on Beacon Street.

The Faneuil Mansion in Tremont Street, opposite the Stone-Chapel Cemetery, was purchased by William Phillips, sen., after the Revolution; and became the residence of his son. The deep court-yard, ornamented by flowers and shrubs, was divided into an upper and lower platform by a high glacis, surmounted by a richly wrought iron railing decorated with gilt balls. The edifice was of brick, painted white; and over the entrance-door was a semicircular balcony. The hall and apartments were spacious, and elegantly furnished. The terraces, which rose from the paved court behind the house, were supported by massy walls of hewn granite, and were ascended by flights of steps of the same material. The crest of the former owner, — a grasshopper, — similar to the vane of Faneuil Hall, yet glittered on a summer-house in the garden, which commanded a view only inferior to that from Beacon Hill.

The house erected by Sir Henry Vane in 1636 was situated on Tremont Street, beside the court-yard of the Faneuil Mansion. It was also purchased by Mr. Phillips, and remained standing until 1820. These estates bounded on that of William Vassall, afterwards the property and residence of Gardner Greene, Esq. Comprising several acres of land, they became too valuable to be retained as private residences; and, in 1834, these ancient mansions, with their beautiful grounds and gardens, long the ornament of the town of Boston, were sold and levelled, and transformed into Pemberton Square and Tremont Row.

The mansion of Ebenezer Storer, an extensive edifice of wood three stories in height, was erected by his father in 1700. It was situated on Sudbury Street, between two trees of great size and antiquity. An old English elm of uncommon height and circumference grew in the sidewalk of the street, before the mansion; and behind it was a sycamore tree of almost equal age and dimensions. It fronted to the south, with one end toward the street. From the gate, a broad walk of red sandstone separated it from a grass-plot which formed the court-yard, and passed the front-door to the office of Mr. Storer, for many years a merchant of Boston, and the Treasurer of Harvard College from 1777 to 1807. The vestibule of the house, from which a staircase ascended, opened on either side into the dining and drawing rooms. Both had windows toward the court-yard, and also opened by glazed doors into a garden behind the house. They were long, low apartments; the walls wainscoted and panelled; the furniture of carved mahogany. The ceilings were traversed through the length of the rooms by a large beam, cased and finished like the walls; and from the centre of each depended a glass globe, which reflected, as in a convex mirror, all surrounding objects. There was a rich Persian carpet in the drawing-room, the colors crimson and green. The curtains and the cushions of the window-seats and chairs were of green damask; and oval mirrors and girandoles, and a tea-set of rich china on a carved table, completed the furniture of that apartment. The wide chimney-place in the dining-room was lined and surrounded by Dutch tiles; and on each side stood capacious arm-chairs, cushioned and covered with green damask, for the master and mistress of the family. On the walls were portraits, in crayon, by Copley; and valuable engravings, — representing Franklin with his lightning-rod, Washington, and other eminent men of the last century. Between the windows hung a long mirror in a mahogany frame; and opposite the fireplace was a buffet, ornamented with porcelain statuettes and a set of rich china. A large apartment in the second story was devoted to a valuable library, a philosophical apparatus, a collection of engravings, a solar microscope, a camera, &c.

After the death of Mr. Storer, in 1807, many of his books, engravings, and telescopes were purchased by Mr. Quincy. When President of Harvard University, he presented to that institution a comet-catcher imported by Mr. Storer, which was used to observe the great comet of 1843; being the best instrument then to be obtained at Cambridge for the purpose. Beneath the windows of Mr. Storer's library, gardens extended toward Hanover Street; but the situation was low, and commanded no view. This locality is now completely changed; stores and hotels having superseded a mansion long the abode of hospitality, and the resort of intellectual and cultivated society.

The mansion which, in 1798, became the summer residence of Mrs. Quincy, and in 1861 continues that of her family, was erected in 1770, by Josiah Quincy of Braintree, on an estate of several hundred acres purchased of the Sachem of Mos-Wechusett, in 1635, by Edmund Quincy of England, and which has remained unalienated.* It is a well-proportioned edifice of wood, two stories in height, with attics forming a half-story; the roof finished with a carved balustrade and eaves. Open fields extend around it, bounded on the north-east by that part of Massachusetts Bay which forms the outer harbor of Boston. . Although near the level of the ocean, the views from the

---

* From Mos-Wechusett, or Arrow-head Hill, which is situated on the isthmus which connects the peninsula of Squantum with the mainland, the word "Massachusetts" was derived. — *Neale's History of New England. Hutchinson's Massachusetts*, vol. i. p. 408.

windows are extensive, comprising the Blue Hills of Milton, Dorchester Heights, Boston, its harbor, and the distant Atlantic.

In the front, toward the south, a porch, supported by carved pillars, with seats on each side, shelters the entrance-door, with its heavy brass knocker, which opens into a hall lighted by narrow windows, and hung, in 1798, with paper representing columns and arches, with busts in appropriate niches. A wide staircase with carved balusters ascends to the second story. The west parlor has a high wainscot, painted walls, and a panelled chimney-piece with carved mouldings. Its fireplace is of brown stone; but those of the other apartments are surrounded by Dutch tiles, of the same colors as the rich papers which formerly decorated their walls. The cast-iron chimney-backs are stamped with the date of the erection of the house; and on one is a bust of General Wolfe, with military trophies. In 1770, it was deemed a spacious and elegant mansion; and the size of the panes of glass in the windows, fourteen inches by ten, excited the admiration and curiosity of the neighborhood.

The steps of the porch descend to a broad gravel-walk parallel with the house; from which, in 1798, three granite steps led to a court-yard, divided by gravel-walks into four grass-plots with borders of flowers, and surrounded by a Chinese fence of the same pattern as the balustrade. There were gates at each end of the broad walk before the house (that on the west opened on an orchard); and beyond were fields adorned by aged oaks and other native trees, once the shelter of Indian sachems and their subject tribes, and comprising hundreds of acres belonging to the estate and to those of other proprietors.

The gate on the east opened on the carriage-road, which separated the house from a garden, surrounded by a brick wall, raised on a high bank, and surmounted by an open fence of carved wood. Beyond were orchards, comprehending many varieties of French pear-tree. A narrow, winding road led to the highway, over Milton Hill, to Boston, then twelve miles distant.

This mansion was the residence of Josiah Quincy of Braintree during the exciting scenes of the American Revolution. Here he bade adieu to his only surviving sons, — one exiled from his country by the success of the patriotic cause, which the other sacrificed his life to promote; and here, in brighter hours, he corresponded with Washington, enjoyed the society of Bowdoin and Franklin * and their contemporaries, and watched the infancy and childhood of his grandson, to whom, in 1784, he bequeathed his portrait by Copley, and this estate.

With characteristic sensibility and enthusiasm, Mrs. Quincy appreciated the interesting associations of the place. It became her favorite abode, where she delighted to receive the children and friends of the former owner, and to make them once more at home under his roof. Her taste and judgment suggested many improvements. Obstructions to the views were removed; walls and fences levelled; lawns, with trees and shrubs judiciously disposed, replaced the court-yard and gardens; and the approach to the house was turned through an avenue of elms, a third of a mile in length, planted by Mr. Quincy in 1790.

In 1802, the town of Quincy was a retired village, twelve miles from Boston; and few changes had taken place since the American Revolution. There were only two churches, both ancient wooden edifices, — the Episcopal, erected in 1728; and the Congregational, rebuilt in 1732. The pews in the centre of the latter, having been made out of long, open seats by successive votes of the town, were of different sizes, and had no regularity of arrangement; and several were entered by narrow passages, winding between those in their neighborhood. The seats, being provided with hinges, were raised when the congregation stood during the prayer; and, at its conclusion, thrown

* Dr. Franklin passed some days with Josiah Quincy in October, 1775; and his apartment, in which these pages were written in 1860, has since been denominated in the family the Franklin Room.

down with a momentum, which, on her first attendance, alarmed Mrs. Quincy, who feared the church was falling. The deacons were ranged under the pulpit, and beside its door the sexton was seated; while, from an aperture aloft in the wall, the bell-ringer looked in from the tower to mark the arrival of the clergyman. The voices of the choir in the front gallery were assisted by a discordant assemblage of stringed and wind instruments. In 1806, when the increased population of the town required a larger edifice, the meeting-house was divided in two parts; the pulpit, and the pews in its vicinity, were moved to a convenient distance; and a new piece was inserted between the fragments. After this alteration, the spacious pew Mr. Quincy had inherited was reduced to the size of the rest, and all were arranged with uniformity. In 1803, the distance from Quincy to Boston was diminished four miles by the Neponset Bridge and Turnpike, obtained chiefly by the exertions of Mr. Quincy.

Among the elder relatives of Mr. Quincy at this period was Henry Bromfield of Harvard, Massachusetts, — the son of an eminent Boston merchant, and the descendant of an old English family. After visiting Europe, and passing his youth and manhood in mercantile pursuits, Mr. Bromfield purchased, in 1770, a mansion erected, in 1720, by Mr. Seccum of England, in a beautiful valley commanding a view of a small lake, near the retired village of Harvard. Lofty elms surrounded the house, and formed two avenues, — one leading to the high road, the other to the burial-ground and the village church. . Several family portraits hung in the hall; and in the dining-room were valuable engravings, — views of the ruins of Rome, after Panini; and the children of Charles I., engraved by Sir Robert Strange, after Vandyck. There was also a bookcase, containing one of the first editions of the " Spectator," and other contemporary volumes; and a buffet, filled with old plate and rare china. After the loss of his

---

* His son, the Rev. T. Seccum, was the first clergyman of Harvard.

wife and the marriage of his daughters, Mr. Bromfield continued to
live happily in solitude, attended by confidential domestics, and enlivened by occasional visits from his relatives and friends.   Removed
from the attrition of society, time had not obliterated the peculiarities of character acquired in the last century; and he remained, in
mind, manners, and costume, a living representative of an age which
had passed away.   In conversation, he constantly referred to "the
year fifty," — the date of his last visit to England.   The most aged
inhabitants of Boston were spoken of by him as young men ; and
State, Court, and Summer Streets were seldom recognized by his
auditors under the names of King and Queen Streets and Seven-star
Lane.

Mr. Bromfield and his surroundings vividly reminded Mrs. Quincy
of Addison's description of Sir Roger de Coverley in the "Spectator."
It seemed to her, that she must be on a visit to that worthy knight,
especially on Sunday, when, equipped with a red cloak, and a wig
surmounted by a cocked hat, and attended by his negro servant
Othello, he escorted her under the ancient avenue of elms and
through the graveyard to the village church.   Profound deference
and respect marked the passing salutations he received; and, at the
conclusion of the service, the whole congregation remained standing
in their pews, until Mr. Bromfield and his guests had walked down
the broad aisle.

Mrs. Ann Bromfield, the wife of John Bromfield, the youngest
brother of Henry Bromfield, and her daughter, — afterwards Mrs.
Ann Tracy of Newburyport, — held a pre-eminence among the friends
of Miss Lowell and Mrs. Quincy.   Mrs. Bromfield had surmounted
many severe trials; and the serene dignity of her manners and the
benevolence of her character gave a peculiar charm to her countenance.   In that of her daughter, deep sensibility, and enthusiasm
of feeling, controlled by high principles of action, rendered her
affection a most valuable possession.

William Phillips, the maternal grandfather of Mr. Quincy, died in 1804, at the age of eighty-four. He left valuable bequests to the public, and the rest of his fortune — amounting, by the rise of real estate, to upwards of a million of dollars — to his only son. All the property which his surviving daughters, Mrs. Dowse and Mrs. Shaw, received beyond small annuities, was the gift of their brother William Phillips; who also gave to his nephew Mr. Quincy the estate in Pearl Street, where he then resided.

Mrs. Ann Quincy, the widow of Josiah Quincy of Braintree, and who survived him twenty-one years, died at the age of eighty, in 1805. She had a life-estate in the farm which Mr. Quincy inherited; but, in 1797, he relieved her of the care of the property, and, giving her the incomes, enabled her to reside with her daughter at Marlborough. A strong mind, uncommon vivacity of temperament, and great benevolence and warmth of heart, rendered her generally respected and beloved. Mrs. Quincy became much attached to her, invited her annually to the mansion formerly her home, accompanied her to visit her old neighbors and friends, and enjoyed her description of past times.

CHAPTER II.

A JOURNEY to Burlington, Vermont, made in 1803 by Mr. and Mrs. Quincy, was highly enjoyed by her.

> "A lover of the woods
> And mountains, and of all that we behold
> From this green earth," —

the beautiful shores of Lake Champlain, and the wild scenery of Vermont, excited her enthusiastic admiration.

In an excursion to Nantucket at the same period, she was much interested by the primitive customs and manners then prevailing in that island. Leaving their phaeton and servant at New Bedford, Mr. and Mrs. Quincy embarked in a sloop loaded with firewood; and, after sailing through the Elizabeth Islands, were hospitably received at Nantucket. In the evening, they were invited to see the cows come in, and were conducted to a barrier without the town. A herd of upwards of six hundred cattle soon appeared in the distance. Having approached, they all paused, waiting for their leader. Presently a small cow, but undoubtedly a strong-minded individual, stepped forward, and passed the barrier. The rest followed rapidly, each one finding the way to her owner's dwelling. Mrs. Quincy was amused by this novel spectacle, and declined with regret a pressing invitation to remain to witness the sheep-shearing, — the great festival of the island.

In 1797, when Mrs. Quincy became a resident of Boston, her friend Miss Mason was married to Hon. John Browne, — a distinguished member of the Senate of the United States, from Kentucky, from 1792 to 1805.

Extracts from the letters of Mrs. Browne, at this period, are here inserted : —

To Mrs. Eliza S. Quincy.

FRANKFORT, KENTUCKY, Jan. 3, 1803.

If one of my earliest and best-beloved friends still thinks of me with that degree of affection with which I have ever remembered her, she will not think me impertinent in making some inquiry respecting her health and happiness, after a separation of nearly six years. Yes, my dear Susan, though fate has placed us at the extremities of the Union, my memory often recurs with delight to the many, many happy hours we have passed together in New York, — whether in receiving the rudiments of education, engaging in childish amusements, or reciprocating those sentiments of affection and friendship, which, to judge by my own heart, grew with our growth. Those scenes can never be re-acted by us; but they have given place to others more interesting and important. Fancy often presents you to my view as engaged in the duties and pleasures of domestic life. With the exception of the separation from my early friends, my happiness has known no change but that which arises from new objects of interest. . . .

DEC. 22, 1804.

Since I find Mr. Quincy is elected member of Congress, I regret Mr. Browne is not re-chosen; as I should have met you in Washington next winter. . . .

In compliance with your request, I will give an account of my local situation, and the state of society around me. To one who has been accustomed to a broken and picturesque country, the situation of Frankfort will be extremely pleasing ; for, though low, it is surrounded by high and beautiful hills, on whose luxuriant and varied foliage the eye is never weary of gazing, and whose summits afford interesting and delightful prospects. The Kentucky River, on which Frankfort is situated, is of greater utility than beauty. Its banks are so high, that, in the summer season, it is scarcely perceptible at a little distance ; and it is subject to such great changes, that, a few weeks ago, there was a public dinner and dance on some rocks in the bed of the river, over which two schooners had sailed in the spring.

The town contains about eight hundred inhabitants, one-third of whom are black ; and more neat and convenient dwelling-houses than could have been expected from the time the place was first settled, which is not yet ten years. It commands a very considerable trade ; and retail goods, groceries excepted, are sold as reasonably as at New York. The seat of government being established here occasions a great influx of strangers in the winter season. My own situation is very agreeable. I have a commodious, and even elegant house, and a charming garden containing four acres, bounded by the river, and planted with grapes and every kind of fruit, either natural to the soil or which can be adopted with success.

The state of society is not exactly what I could wish. The gentlemen are too much devoted to business to attend to any literary pursuits unconnected with their professions ; and that portion of learning which has been thought requisite to qualify a man for being a physician, a lawyer, or a divine, is most conscientiously devoted to professional purposes, and is considered too sacred or too hardly earned to be sported on ordinary occasions. The researches of the ladies are generally limited to the regions of romance. They marry so young, and are so soon encumbered with the cares of a family, that they have little leisure for improvement. What time they can command is usually devoted to dress, in which they display a great deal of taste.

The perfect equality which prevails, and which acknowledges no superior (however elevated by wealth or talents), diffuses a universal ease, and gracefulness of manners, over every class of citizens; and more genuine politeness and hospitality prevail in this State than in any other with which I am acquainted. One disagreeable circumstance which results from this state of society is, that poverty produces the same effect here which unprincipled wealth does in other societies: it makes men arrogant.

But the existence of slavery occasions me more melancholy sensations than any circumstance relating to this country; for though the slaves enjoy comparative happiness, are very well fed and clothed, humanely treated, and allowed greater liberties than any hired servants at the eastward, yet there is something in the idea of involuntary servitude which shocks humanity, and to which I pray I may never become reconciled. We have no slaves ourselves, but hire all our servants; and have found great advantages in being esteemed the friends of emancipation. The negroes consider us as entitled to their gratitude for our good wishes; and, while others are complaining of their depredations, our property, as far as relates to them, is as secure as if guarded by a hundred dragons.

Though furnished with a very excellent library, I have not made that use of it which those who are acquainted with my early pursuits would have expected. My time is chiefly devoted to my children; and the frequent absence of Mr. Browne, by depriving me of the advantage of his superior knowledge, and the pleasure of communicating to him any new ideas which I might acquire, has destroyed the greatest inducement to application. There is a natural propensity of the mind to assimilate itself to its situation; and frequently conversing on the trifling topics which prevail in all small towns has retarded my mental progress. But the loss of my two youngest children has destroyed the cheerfulness of my disposition; and I have returned to my books with eagerness, in the fond expectation, that, in perusing the book of knowledge, I may meet with the page of forgetfulness. If my mind possesses any latent spark of genius or refinement, a frequent intercourse with you by letter will call it forth: write to me, then; and rely on my warmest gratitude. I have been imperceptibly led to write more than I intended. The stillness of the hour, which is interrupted only by the gentle breathing of my sleeping children, seemed peculiarly favorable to my employment; and I never reflected, that, while gratifying myself, I was perhaps trespassing on your patience. . . .

Affectionately yours,

MARGARET BROWNE.

Although Mrs. Quincy, as the correspondent and associate of her husband, was long conversant with political life, her character and views were feminine and retired. Her admiration was excited by "the charming Memoir of Mrs. Hutchinson,"* long before it was pronounced by Macaulay "the best book on the side of the Roundheads, in the great battle fought for no single land," — in the civil wars of England.

The great questions of religious faith had early touched and excited her sensitive and reflective mind; but to the doctrines of Calvin reverenced by her mother, a convert to the eloquence of Whitefield, she could not assent. Among the advantages incident to her change of residence, she most highly valued the views of Christianity given by Kirkland and Freeman, and other clergymen of Boston. In early life, she had derived satisfaction from the writings of Paley; and afterwards yet greater advantage from those of Butler, Taylor, Barrow, Farmer, and Cappe. Locke's "Reasonableness of Christianity," and his "Essay for the Understanding St. Paul's Epistles by consulting St. Paul himself," were among the works she highly

---

* "Life of Colonel Hutchinson," by his widow. London, 1806.

valued. The result was an animated practical faith in the leading doctrines of liberal Christianity, and the benevolence of a superintending Power. These proved to her an unfailing support amid the mysteries surrounding human existence, and the anxieties and cares from which this life, under the happiest auspices, is never wholly exempt.

Her children soon directed her thoughts to the subject of education. The works of Mrs. Barbauld and Miss Edgeworth obtained a decided preference; but from those of Mrs. Trimmer, Hannah More, and Mrs. Chapone, useful information was derived. For her sons, after the first years of childhood, public schools were deemed essential; but her early experience led her to prefer, for her daughters, instruction at home.

To bestow the inexhaustible treasures of a literary taste, no one was better qualified than herself. The genius of the poet and the novelist shone with peculiar effect, when she lent to their pages the beauty of her voice. Those of Shakspeare and Milton; of Addison, Goldsmith, Cowper, Thomson; of Burney, Scott, Edgeworth, and Austen, — are indissolubly associated by her children with her expressive tones.

In May, 1805, after the election of Mr. Quincy as representative in Congress from the county of Suffolk, he leased his mansion in Pearl Street to Hon. Christopher Gore, and removed part of the furniture and his library to Quincy. It was not without reluctance that Mrs. Quincy relinquished this residence, associated with the interesting events of the first years of her life in Boston; and the prospect of a separation from a part of her family caused great anxiety: but she determined, without hesitation, to accompany Mr. Quincy to Washington. Their youngest children were left at board with confidential friends and domestics; and accompanied by the eldest, and attended by two servants, they left Boston in November, 1805. They travelled in their carriage, with imperials on its roof; sending most of the luggage by water to Georgetown. On the third day, by a route then termed the Middle Road, through Worcester and Stafford, they reached Hartford; where they were immediately visited at the hotel by Governor Trumbull, his son-in-law Daniel Wadsworth, and many of the leading politicians of Connecticut. Invited by Mr. Wadsworth to his mansion the next morning, they were received by Governor Trumbull with that urbanity which distinguished his manners. As it was Election Day, the members of the Legislature came with a military escort to attend him to the State House. After accompanying Mr. Wadsworth to his mother's house on the Main Street to see the procession pass, Mr. and Mrs. Quincy resumed their journey.

At New Haven they were visited by Mr. and Mrs. Chauncey and by President Dwight, who accompanied them to visit the college edifices and the library. After passing several days in New York, Princeton, and Philadelphia, they reached Washington the fourth week after leaving Boston. At this period, there were no bridges; and the ferries, especially those of the Hudson and the Susquehannah, were often dangerous. In Maryland and Delaware, streams of considerable magnitude were forded; and the traveller was often forced to wait in miserable inns until the waters subsided. At Gunpowder Falls, the high road passed over the edge of a mill-dam, down which the passengers of the stage-coach were occasionally precipitated. After rain, the horses sank deep at every step in the red clay which chiefly characterizes the soil of the Middle States, and which adhered to the wheels of the carriages until they resembled moving globes of mud.

To avoid hotel life, Mr. and Mrs. Quincy obtained lodgings in the family of Judge Cranch, who resided on Pennsylvania Avenue, toward the Eastern Branch of the Potomac. They were soon visited by the chief residents of Georgetown and Washington. Their drawing-room was often the resort of the Federal members of

Congress, — of Pickering, Upham, and Pickman, of Massachusetts; of Tallmadge, Dana, Davenport, Pitkin, Tracy, Hillhouse, and John Cotton Smith, of Connecticut; Broome of Delaware; and many others; and important political measures were there discussed.

Among anecdotes of the war of the Revolution, which often relieved gloomy political debates, the following has often recurred to recollection: —

"In December, 1777," said Colonel Tallmadge, "when Washington was encamped at Valley Forge, and Howe in winter quarters at Philadelphia, I commanded a detachment of dragoons, and was stationed by the commander-in-chief as an advanced corps of observation between our army and that of the enemy. The duty was arduous, as the British light-horse continually patrolled this intermediate ground. Indeed, it was unsafe to permit the dragoons to unsaddle their horses for an hour; and I rarely staid through a night in the same place.

"I received orders to go to a tavern near the British lines, where a country girl, who had been instructed to obtain information respecting the enemy, and who had gone to Philadelphia to sell eggs, would meet me. Accordingly, I left my corps at Germantown, and, with a small detachment, proceeded towards the British lines. The tavern stood in a valley. I left my troop on the brow of the hill, and, to escape observation, alighted at the tavern, in full view of the British outposts, with only a few horsemen whom I stationed on guard. The girl soon came; and, while she was giving me the intelligence she had acquired, one of my men dashed into the room, exclaiming, 'The British light-horse are advancing!' On going to the door, I saw them coming at full speed, chasing my patrols. I instantly mounted; but was stopped by the girl, who fell on her knees in great terror, crying, 'They will kill me! they will kill me! Don't leave me!' — 'My child, they will kill me, if I stay here; but can you ride?' — 'Yes: any thing to save my life.' — 'Then jump up behind me, and hold on to my belt.'

"I then rode off with my men, the British in full pursuit. They fired, and we wheeled and returned it. Alternately charging and retreating, we reached our detachment on the hill. The girl behaved with great courage, and never expressed any fear; though, when the bullets whistled past us, I felt her cling closer to me. I brought her off three miles to Germantown, where she dismounted, and is now (1806) a married woman, living in Philadelphia."*

The action here described was characteristic of Colonel Tallmadge, — one of Nature's noblemen in spirit, mien, and appearance; a higher patent than one he had then been informed he had a right to claim in the peerage of Great Britain.

In the following letter, the society which met during this winter at the residence of Mr. and Mrs. Quincy is alluded to by Hon. John Cotton Smith: —

To Hon. Josiah Quincy, Boston.

SHARON, CONN., Aug. 25, 1806.

I owe you an apology for the dissolution of our political communion. The threat to which you allude was not altogether serious; but, on my return home, the declining health of my father, and the entreaties of my wife, constituted a claim on my obedience I could not resist. . . .

I do feel a pang in separating from that noble band of chevaliers, who, small as their number is, have become the only depositaries of their country's honor; nor will I conceal the tender emotions which agitate my breast at the recollection of the charming hours I have passed not many miles from the Eastern Branch.

---

* This anecdote, related from recollection as told by Colonel Tallmadge, is recorded in his Autobiography (p. 26), edited by his son F. A. Tallmadge, 1856.

Imagination will long delight itself in recalling the hospitable salutation, the undissembled courtesy, " the wisdom and the wit," which
enlivened and endeared, and rendered ever memorable, those even-
ings.   But this is a theme I must not pursue : it shall be resumed
when we meet. . . .

> Affectionately your friend,
> JOHN COTTON SMITH.

The height of party politics did not prevent Mrs. Quincy from
renewing a former friendship with Miss Bayard of New York, as Mrs.
S. H. Smith, the wife of the editor of the " National Intelligencer,"
then the chief organ of the Administration ; and with Mrs. Madison
she sustained most friendly relations.   Intelligence and animation,
intuitive perception of character, and readiness and tact in conversation, made her a general favorite ; and she highly enjoyed the variety
and brilliancy of the parties given by the permanent and official
residents then at Washington.

Her costume united simplicity with elegance.   Her carriage
dress, that winter, was a short pelisse of black velvet, edged round
the skirt with deep lace, and trimmed with silk cord and jet buttons ;
and a hat of purple velvet with flowers.   A French dress and train
of rich white silk embroidered in gold, with a corresponding head-
dress ornamented with a single white ostrich feather, was said to be
the most elegant which appeared at a ball given by the British
minister.

During this winter, Mrs. Quincy formed an intimate and permanent friendship with Mrs. Martha Peter of Tudor Place, Georgetown,
— a grand-daughter of Mrs. Washington, and a woman of superior
strength of character and intellect.

On the 15th of March, 1806, Mr. and Mrs. Quincy went to Mount
Vernon, on an invitation from Judge and Mrs. Washington, accompanied by their daughter and Judge Cranch.   Crossing the Potomac

by the ferry at Georgetown, after a fatiguing day's journey in their carriage, they reached their destination at sunset, and were most hospitably received. A niece and two nephews, and their private tutor, then constituted the family of Judge and Mrs. Washington. The evening was passed in a small drawing-room between the hall and an unfurnished apartment called "the banqueting-room." A cheerful fire blazed on the hearth; and beneath the windows, which looked toward the Potomac, stood a grand piano, on which Mrs. Washington played several difficult duets, accompanied by the instructor of her nephews.

The apartment assigned to Mrs. Quincy was the one in which Washington had died. Early in the evening, when her child was sent there to sleep on a couch for the night, an old negress, formerly a slave in the family, insisted on smoking her pipe in the chimney corner, under pretence of taking care of the young stranger, who regarded her with great alarm. Her picturesque figure, illuminated by the flickering blaze of the fire, seemed to Mrs. Quincy like a personification of the dark shadow which slavery yet cast on the hearth-stone at Mount Vernon. Highly excited by the associations of the place, the imagination of Mr. Quincy, even after he sunk to slumber, faithfully depicted the apartment. He thought he heard a heavy step in the hall, and was told the spirit of Washington always visited the guests who slept in that chamber, and was then at his door. Extreme agitation caused him to awake; but the scene remained unaltered, and it was difficult for him to believe it was a dream. Had the illusion continued a few moments longer, he might have thought he actually had seen and conversed with Washington. This incident is mentioned to prove, that Walter Scott's description of the Vision of the Green Chamber at Monkbarns is not unnatural; "imagination being much akin to wonder-working faith." Mr. Quincy arose, and looked from the window. The Potomac glittered in the moonlight, and the tomb of Washington was distinctly visible.

The next morning, Judge Washington accompanied Mr. and Mrs. Quincy to visit the garden and greenhouse, and then took a path which led toward the river. Pausing before a simple wooden door in the bank of the Potomac, he gave a key to Judge Cranch, and walked away, — endeavoring to persuade his youngest visitor to accompany him. But, with the petulance of childhood, she broke from his grasp; and, forcing her way between her father and Judge Cranch, sprang through the doorway, and was surprised and solemnized to find herself surrounded by the repositories of the dead, and close beside the coffin of Washington. It was apparently of oak, raised slightly above the others, with that of Mrs. Washington beside it. Mrs. Quincy was deeply touched by the scene, and struck by the exquisite beauty of the situation. The bank descending precipitously to the Potomac, allowed every passing vessel to approach beneath the tomb of the departed hero, to pay their tributes of respect, —

> " And oft suspend the dashing oar
> To bid his gentle spirit rest."

These lines Mrs. Quincy quoted as she earnestly besought Judge Washington to remove the remains only of the other members of his family to the new mausoleum, then erecting at some distance from the river; but to leave those of his illustrious relative and of Mrs. Washington in their appropriate position; close up the tomb permanently; and erect among the crowning oaks and cedars a simple monument of white marble, with no inscription but the name of GEORGE WASHINGTON.

This visit to Mount Vernon, which ended the next morning, was always a subject of interesting retrospection; and an affectionate friendship was sustained through life with Judge and Mrs. Washington.

A protracted session of Congress detained them in Washington until the 22d of April. On reaching Boston, they re-united their family at Quincy, where they passed the ensuing months.

The chief event of the summer was a total eclipse of the sun, — a sublime spectacle, which few of the inhabitants of this planet are permitted to behold, especially under such peculiar advantages as were given by the extensive views of sea and land and the wide horizon at Quincy. The sky was without a cloud; the sun shone with intense brilliancy; until, at the instant predicted by astronomers, — by many who had died without the sight, — darkness shadowed the western horizon toward the Blue Hills. As the hours passed, and the sun became obscured, star after star, differing from each other in glory, appeared. The cattle came home; the birds ceased their warbling, and retired to their nests; and all the sounds of evening were heard. A dim twilight gleamed from the horizon, reflected from those regions whence the sun's rays were not excluded. Night closed around; the eclipse became total; and for five minutes the sun appeared like a dark globe in the firmament.

It was a solemn moment; a pause in nature, deep and awful. There was time to realize what the world would be without the sun. His first returning ray, " shooting far into the bosom of dim night a glimmering dawn," was exquisitely beautiful, and was hailed with joyful acclamations. None of the subsequent eclipses of this century could be compared in sublime effect with that which occurred on the 16th of June, 1806. It was a memory for life.

CHAPTER III.

In the autumn of 1806, Mr. and Mrs. Quincy made the same arrangements as in the preceding winter. In 1807 and 1808, Mr. Quincy went to Washington alone, having established his family in a house he owned on Oliver Street, Fort Hill, which commanded an extensive view of the harbor and environs. That vicinity then comprised many eligible situations, — the residence of Bostonians of eminence and wealth.

At this period, the political parties and commercial interests of the United States were influenced and controlled by the conflicts of the European powers.

In 1806, Bonaparte, by the Berlin decree issued from the field of Jena, declared the British islands in a state of blockade, and prohibited all intercourse with them. After the peace of Tilsit in 1807, he became, as it were, the dictator of Europe. By an extension of the Berlin decree, all merchandise derived from England or her Colonies was liable to seizure, even on board neutral vessels. The British Government retaliated, on the 11th of November, by orders in Council, prohibiting any neutral trade with France or her allies. These measures directly affected the United States, then the only neutral power. The carrying-trade between the European colonies and their mother-countries, which had been a source of immense profit, was cut off, or made to circulate through Great Britain; and American commerce became the prey of both the belligerent powers.

A treaty which Monroe and Pinkney attempted to negotiate with the British ministry, Jefferson and Madison refused to ratify; and, for the alleged protection of American property, imposed an embargo and other commercial restrictions more harassing to the merchants of the maritime cities than all the impediments placed in their way by Great Britain.*

These were the chief causes of the political excitement described in the correspondence, from which extracts are here inserted: —

To Hon. Josiah Quincy, City of Washington.

BOSTON, Thanksgiving Day, Dec. 1, 1808.

All our dear children are once more together; but you are absent. On this day of the happy meeting of families and friends, I cannot help contrasting our divided situation. On this day of thanksgiving, there is no subject which excites more in my mind than the location of our family in New England, and, above all, in Boston. Would you were here with us! But you are in the place of duty, and that is always the right and safe place. . . . Dr. Kirkland disappointed many of his audience by the moderation of his sermon. It was less political than on any former occasion; when it was expected to be the reverse, from the excited state of the public mind.

I went to the Old South in the afternoon. Dr. Eckley gave a most violent philippic against the present rulers and measures. He spoke of Jefferson, French influence, prejudice against Britain, &c.; made out the title of Bonaparte to the character of the second beast in Revelation, — Antichrist. Endeavoring to rouse the spirit of the country, he exclaimed, "Where is the warning voice of Washington? where, the spirit of our forefathers? Where is the zeal of New England?" He commanded the deepest attention. I almost expected to

---

* Hildreth's " History of the United States," second series, 2d and 3d vols.

hear the people huzza at the close. The musicians in the gallery actually struck up " Washington's March ; " to the music of which we all marched home to comment on the sermon.

DEC. 7, 1808.

I believe I must present a complaint to you, in your public capacity, upon the oppressive effects of the embargo. I commissioned S. Cabot, jun., to send me from Philadelphia half a barrel of buckwheat meal and some sweet potatoes ; but the wise and vigilant revenue-officers, with great valor, refused to allow them to be sent without a special license.

The greatest gloom and consternation prevail at the news, brought by express last evening, of the passage of the Non-intercourse Bill, &c. Every one hoped, to the last moment, that the ruling party would stop short of this full measure of folly and oppression.

DEC. 23.

Mr. Higginson asked me if I had seen your second speech, and said that it was more powerful and animated than the first, though not perhaps containing any one paragraph equal to the idea of the Goddess of Liberty as a sea-nymph, — a figure which he said Dr. Kirkland, McKean, and Lowell pronounced admirable.*

I was pleased to see so little of personality in your speech. Even Mr. Bacon seemed to be more excited by the chafing of his own conviction than by the effect of your accusation.

Your friends seem to be entirely sensible of the merit of your exertions. Mr. George Cabot said I must take out a policy of insurance upon you, if you went on at this rate ; adding, the whole town could not furnish as much as you were worth.

The people are almost up in arms about Giles's bill and Gallatin's letter.

---

* Speech on Foreign Relations, in reply to Mr. Bacon, Dec. 7.

JAN. 6, 1809.

You will probably see by the newspapers the dreadful story in circulation, that you had fallen in a duel. Though it had been the town-talk for a week, I never heard it till yesterday, when Mr. Whitney came here, and said Josiah had been greatly distressed by it. Half the people of Quincy had been to ask him if the story was true. It had been brought out there by the market-men. Although known to our family, it was never repeated to me. The messages sent to ask when I had heard from you were usually not given : the few repeated did not excite suspicion. It was not mentioned in the newspapers till to-day, when its falsehood was generally known. How or where it originated, no one knows. Thank Heaven, you are safe, and will remain so! I have no fear from *such* dangers.

Mr. Whitney said he had presented your gift of a Bible to the town of Quincy. The parish was highly gratified by your attention, and a vote of thanks was passed. He said that the former Bible was given by your great-grandfather, Edmund Quincy, — a circumstance we were before unacquainted with.

JAN. 15.

I sent your letter to Otis, as you directed. I passed last evening at Mr. Davis's. Mr. J. Lee, who was there, said Mr. Cabot had received a most gloomy letter from Mr. Wolcott upon the state and prospects of the country. The "Wasp" is lying in the harbor, watching the motions of the merchants. Mr. Lee said he should not be surprised if she was burnt before spring. The United-States officers, in general, are becoming objects of popular detestation.

You seem to be anxious to hear how the people will submit to the new enforcement of the Embargo Law. I fancy it will not be long before they give some positive proofs of their abhorrence. Mr. James Perkins said this evening, that a letter he had received from you to-day had been taken by his brother, T. H. Perkins, to Judge Parsons; and they had agreed, with other gentlemen, to meet this evening to concert measures. The merchants and other Federalists think this last act of oppressive tyranny will have a good effect, and are determined how to act, — to proceed with calmness and moderation; and, on the first occasion of a demand from the Collector "to give bonds to six times the amount of a cargo," to refuse to comply. The Collector then must apply to the District Attorney. He must, acting officially or through application to the Governor, order an *armed force*. The owners will refuse to open their vessels, or give their keys for examination. The officers of Government break open, unlade, or take into custody, the goods and property of the citizens. A suit is then to be instituted, and a town-meeting called. They are determined not to submit in a single instance, nor countenance any one who will. They only fear they shall not be able to prevent all premature violence. Mr. Perkins desired me to relate this to you on his authority.

JAN. 17, 1809.

You will see the papers of to-day dressed in mourning. The new law has been received by the Collector. This is an eventful period. Heaven will preserve us, I hope, from distress and ruin.

I am greatly encouraged by Mr. Hillhouse's message and promise to stand by you. His mode of fighting "from behind a tree, with a tomahawk," is entirely consonant to my ideas; and, in Washington, I hope neither you nor he will ever find the want of a tree to get behind on such an occasion.

JAN. 19.

Both General Lincoln and Mr. Weld have resigned their offices in the Custom House. I heard yesterday that General Lincoln had written word to the President, that he had fought for the liberties of his country, and spent his best years in her service; and that he was not, in his old age, to be made an instrument to violate what he had assisted to acquire. I am glad you keep clear of the question of "arming and equipping the frigates." As things are now managed, it is rather an equivocal policy, as they will be entirely at the disposal of the President of the United States.

JAN. 30, 1809.

Mr. Perkins showed me, yesterday, Lloyd's letter to him, written on the 20th, after your late contest. He says that you have done honor to yourself, and deserve well of your country. Such applause, from such a man as Mr. Lloyd, is worth a great deal. I agree with him, that the affair now stands in the best possible form. You have taken true and high ground. It is the triumph of principle over brutality and degrading violence.

William Shaw was here last evening. He had dined the day before at Colonel Humphries' with Gore and Otis. They had seen Lloyd's letter, and expressed warm approbation of your conduct.

This morning, a miserable account of that debate appeared in the " Gazette," copied from the " Monitor."

Shaw came to ask my permission to frame a more accurate statement from your letter to me, to be published in the " Palladium " as an " Extract from a Letter from Washington." I consented to dictate such paragraphs as seemed requisite to place your conduct in a correct light. He said it was generally wished that a copy of your first speech, which produced all this irritation and interest, should be published.

*Extract of a Letter from Washington, Jan. 20, 1809.**

Yesterday and to-day, there has been in the House of Representatives one of the warmest and most impassioned discussions ever witnessed by a legislative assembly, on the bill for the next meeting of Congress. Mr. Quincy made an attack upon the Administration,

---

* " New-England Palladium," Jan. 31, 1809.

which called forth all the virulence of the Executive phalanx; and, to-day, Campbell and Jackson went into the House with the apparent determination to reduce him to the same necessity to which Gardenier was forced last session. Irritated by his attacks, and unable to answer him, they poured out upon him a torrent of gross and illiberal abuse. Mr. Quincy, in reply, stated specifically his ground, and told them that his honor was of little worth if it lay in the mouths of *such* men, and not in his own conduct. He was no *duellist*. He had the honor to represent, not only a wise, a moral, a powerful and intelligent, but a religious people; that, among them, to avenge wrongs of words, by resorting to the course of conduct to which it was obviously intended to reduce him, was so far from being honorable, that it would be a disgrace to any man.

To gain the temporary applause of such men as his assailants, whom he could only pity and despise, he should not sacrifice his own principles, nor forfeit the respect of those whose good opinion was the highest reward of his life. If they expected by such artifices to deter him from doing his duty, they would find themselves mistaken. Where *he was known*, nothing they could say would *injure him;* and, where *they were known*, he believed the effect would *not be greater*.

JAN. 31, 1809.

You will see in the "Palladium" of to-day the notice I allowed to be inserted. I hope you will not disapprove it. I am satisfied it was requisite.

Jonathan Phillips and Dr. Kirkland called to-day, and each expressed pleasure that such a statement had superseded the one in the "Gazette."

Buckminster was here this morning. He said he had rather be the author of that retort of yours, which appeared to-day, than of all the speeches you ever made, however eloquent or elegant. He requested me to give him pencil and paper, and permission to tell you in my letter how much he felt obliged and gratified by the respect you had paid to principle, and the example you had given. I supplied the materials requested, though not the exact medium of conveyance, — my letter.

I see that General Lincoln is hardly treated in the "Intelligencer" and "Monitor" for resigning his office, and charged with a "deliberate purpose to conspire with the *disaffected;* that he is one whom the *forbearance* of Government has *retained* in office, in opposition to the wishes of a respectable class of the community!" When such charges and falsehoods are made against the venerable General Lincoln, it seems incredible that you should be left *alone* to defend him, and to expose the true motives of the Executive for keeping him in an office which he wished to resign. Your procedure strikes me as honorable and correct. Your moving these resolutions is also a proof that you are not deterred by the late occurrences from coming forward more boldly than ever.

FEB. 1, 1809.

Your resolutions appeared in the paper to-day, with compliments to you on your defence of General Lincoln.*

The temper of the people here begins to rise quite high; but I hope there will be no violent acts. In consequence of the new orders to Colonel Boyd, not to allow any vessel, upon any account whatever, to pass Fort Independence, the colors of all the vessels in the harbor were hoisted at half-mast. In the afternoon, Captain M. Joy came in with his colors flying; and upon being informed of the reason, and requested to lower *his*, he refused, and armed himself, declaring that he would shoot any one who attempted to do it. A number of men, however, jumped on board, disarmed him, and lowered the flags; after which they quietly dispersed. But there were serious apprehensions of a riot.

* See the "Columbian Centinel," Feb. 1 and 4, 1809.

Several of your friends have sent me the "Washington Federalist," which contained the tribute to you. You cannot wish for more enthusiasm in your favor than they exhibit.

FEB. 15, 1809.

Mr. William H. Sumner called to ask if I had received any particulars of the attack made upon you by Campbell; because the Legislature had appointed a committee to inquire whether attempts had been recently made in Congress to restrain freedom of debate, and whether the free investigation of the measures of Government, by any member from this State, had been made the ground of insult, &c. "This committee *had not reported*, because they had been waiting to see the debate alluded to correctly given. They had no data upon which to ground such a report as they wished to make, except verbal accounts, or anonymous paragraphs in the newspapers." I told Mr. Sumner you said, in one of your last letters, that "they would probably never see the debate in question, or not for some time, as the 'National Intelligencer' had dropped it," either with the design of injuring you, or at least keeping out of sight their attack and your reply; which placed the affair upon the true ground, and gave you the advantage in the contest, which they would willingly conceal.

The opinion of Gardenier, of the obvious intention of the opposite party to reduce you to the necessity of fighting, which he had stated on the floor of the House, had been published. The general sentiment of indignation against them, and in favor of you, was also an evidence of the fact. The only proofs to be found were in the accounts published in the papers, in detached parts of the debates, and in the letters of Mr. Lloyd and others. He begged me to urge you to obtain the minutes of the stenographers, and, from your own memory, write a satisfactory account for publication.

Mr. Davis came in with your letter, in which you tell him of the recommitment of the embargo question to the Campbell Committee.

The people, by this news, were sadly taken aback, as the sailors say. He brought also Northampton papers, containing an account of a meeting there, composed of delegates from fifty towns. They passed spirited resolutions approving your conduct, and ordered their secretary to transmit to you a vote of thanks. Such a tribute is highly gratifying, coming from a body of men so far removed from your immediate district.

FEB. 18, 1809.

My mind has been recently engrossed by the dangerous illness and death of our neighbor Mrs. S. Cabot. She was very dear to me ; and our intercourse, this winter, has been more frequent and interesting than ever. Her confidence in me was unbounded ; and the more I discovered of her mind, principles, opinions, and views, the more highly did I respect and love her. Her attachment to me rendered her very interesting ; and I have the grateful reflection to console me, that I added greatly to the enjoyment of her life ever since I have known her, but especially during the last months of it.

Ever yours,

ELIZA S. QUINCY.

An extra session of Congress caused Mr. Quincy to return to Washington, and this correspondence was recommenced.

To Mrs. Eliza S. Quincy.

WASHINGTON, 21st May, 1809.

MY DEAR WIFE, — My journey has been pleasant. From New York, Gardenier, Dana, Goodrich, and Pitkin were my companions ; and, from Philadelphia, Tallmadge, Champion, and Sturgis.

I have as yet no business to occupy my mind. To resist the current of reflections setting homeward, I walked out this morning on Capitol Hill. Had you been at my side, I should have had nothing more to desire. The verdure was most perfect; the scene, beautiful and picturesque. I had always admired this view in the dreary aspect of winter; but now the whole of the fine plain between Capitol Hill and the Potomac is covered with a dark and splendid green, interspersed with blooming shrubbery. Cattle graze over-it freely. Scarcely a fence interferes with their rambles; scarcely a tree breaks the level of the prospect. The course of the Potomac embraces this beautiful plain, which terminates at its junction with the Eastern Branch. On one side is the rising city of Alexandria: on the other, an abrupt hill juts out at the point of union. The land rises on the Virginia bank, with a gentle slope from the river to the horizon, which gives to the grasp of the eye all the intervening objects, — rich meadows, cultivated fields, noble woods; the whole forming a most delightful assemblage. At this season, Nature, joyous at her rejuvenescence, arrays herself in her most gorgeous robes, rich in every color to awaken an interest in her charms. I stood on the hill's brow for a moment: the pleasure of the prospect absorbed my soul. The effect was transient. The objects of my affections and my hopes rushed back into my memory.

Thus I strive to shorten the distance between us, but in vain. You and ours are ever in my recollection.

To Josiah Quincy.

BOSTON, May 29, 1809.

I was much pleased with your description of the prospects around you in their summer dress. I stood with you on the brow of Capitol Hill, and fancied all you described. Wherever you go, I am ever with you. I sit with you at the social board and in the great assembly, and try to lose the sense of distance and solitude by associating myself with you in all your engagements, employments, and pursuits. I hope you will call on the President, and attend Mrs. Madison's drawing-room; and that you will accompany your friends in all their excursions. It will give me pleasure to share them with you in imagination. You describe admirably. I did not give you credit for being so good a painter. . . .

The children went to Quincy yesterday, and had a very happy time. They returned with such accounts of the delightful appearance of the place, — its beauty and fragrance, and improved aspect from the growth of the trees and shrubs, — that I feel, indeed, impatient to be there. It will not be long now, I assure myself, before we may enjoy the pleasure of viewing ourselves surrounded by our children in that scene of your father's partial regard; dear to me for that recollection, and for the affection of that other parent, who distinguished you by the bequest of it. Surely, if the events and scenes of "this dim spot" can interest the spirits of another sphere, they must be gratified; and that consideration, even now, must have a salutary effect upon their descendants.

Ever yours, ELIZA S. QUINCY.

To Mrs. Eliza S. Quincy.

WASHINGTON, 4th June, 1809.

I dined yesterday at Mount Vernon. Sixteen or twenty members of Congress, all Federal, were of the party. Mrs. Washington was absent; the Judge extremely pleasant and polite.

The view from Mount Vernon appeared much more beautiful to me than when we visited it in March, 1806. The house is in good repair, the gardens well cultivated, and the whole estate in sufficient order. At this season, the scenery is indescribably interesting. There is a richness in the foliage, a fulness of flower and herbage, equal to any I ever witnessed. Nature appears in a wild bursting luxuriance, and throws an air of unaffected negligence over her drapery, that wins and fascinates. The place might be improved; but such attempts might balance the pleasure they attained.

I conversed with Washington's old servant Billy. He could not speak of his master without tears. He said that he was never out of his mind for two hours, and that he scarcely ever passed a night without dreaming of him.

On this visit, I had no cause of regret but that you were not with me. . . .

JOSIAH QUINCY.

CHAPTER IV.

DURING the summer of 1807, a notice of the "Letters from the Mountains, by Mrs. Anne Grant," in Aiken's "Annual Review," attracted the attention of Mrs. Quincy, — especially a letter describing a day at Laggan. She marked the passage, and lent the book to Miss Lowell, who coincided in her opinion, and consequently formed the design of having an American edition of the work published from a copy her brother (the Rev. Charles Lowell) had then recently brought from Edinburgh, and of sending the profits to the writer. This benevolent enterprise was accomplished in 1809; and, with a subsequent correspondence with Mrs. Grant, proved a source of great interest and pleasure to Miss Lowell.

When conversing on the subject, Mrs. Quincy remarked, that, while the ladies of Boston were kindly assisting Mrs. Grant, they ought to remember that their own country-woman, Hannah Adams, the authoress of valuable works, was braiding straw for a livelihood. Miss Lowell acknowledged the force of the appeal, and the two friends succeeded in obtaining subscribers to a life-annuity for Miss Adams. It was requisite that the subscriptions of married women should stand in the names of their husbands; but Miss Lowell's estate could be rendered liable, and her contribution was annually paid for twenty-one years after her decease. Mrs. Quincy was the friend Miss Adams mentions on the first page of her Autobiography,* at whose

---

* Edited, and concluded in 1832, by Mrs. G. G. Lee of Boston.

request it was written. Mrs. Shaw of Dedham, the widow of Major Shaw, allowed Miss Adams a hundred dollars annually for twenty-five years.

Among the elder friends of Mrs. Quincy at this period, to whom she was affectionately attached, were Jonathan Jackson, Esq., of Boston, and Richard Cranch of Quincy. Retaining the dress and manners of the last century, Mr. Jackson was a fine specimen of the gentlemen of the old school. He often described to her the exciting scenes of the American Revolution, and said, that, on any political crisis, he always drove out to Braintree to consult his relative, Colonel Josiah Quincy, who was then his Magnus Apollo. He gave Mrs. Quincy, for her youngest son, a portrait of his ancestor, Judge Edmund Quincy.

Richard Cranch, an Englishman by birth, was a man of powerful mind and scientific attainments, and had been an intimate friend of the father and grandfather of Mr. Quincy. In personal appearance, he resembled the portraits of John Locke. His wife, the sister of Mrs. Abigail Adams, was also distinguished for excellence of character, and strength of intellect. Their long and useful lives were closed within a few hours* of each other, on the 16th and 17th of October, 1811.

In the autumn of 1809, Mr. and Mrs. Quincy leased their house in Boston, made arrangements similar to those of preceding years, and pursued the same route to Washington. Passing through New Jersey, they stopped for the night at Holmesville, a town situated on the Neshaminy, four miles from its confluence with the Delaware. In the evening, Mr. Holmes, the chief proprietor of the place, a venerable man in the Quaker dress, called on Mr. Quincy, attended by his two sons, and informed him that he had often read his speeches, and came to thank him for the views and principles he supported in Congress.

---

* In the last years of his life, Mr. Cranch raised from the seed a number of elm-trees, which he bequeathed to Mr. Quincy, and which now ornament his estate.

In reply to inquiries, Mr. Holmes said, " When I purchased the site of this village, fourteen years ago, there was only one dwelling-house upon it: now there are thirty, besides stores and workshops, a valuable set of mills, and a stone bridge over the Neshaminy. Here I have established a numerous family. I might have educated

said that Mr. Holmes was one of the best men and the most practical philosopher she had ever met with; that "his virtue proved him truly wise."

In Philadelphia they passed several days with Mrs. Jackson, who resided at the corner of Arch and Fourth Street. Among their visitors were Mr. J. Dennie (the editor of the "Portfolio"), Mr. John Vaughan, and other Philadelphians. On the 22d of November, they resumed their journey. At Christiana Bridge, in Delaware, they met Mr. J. R. Poinsett of South Carolina, and Mr. T. Jones of Boston, equipped for a journey of a thousand miles, from Boston to Charleston. They travelled in an open carriage, with two horses tandem, attended by a servant on horseback. This meeting was the introduction to many others, which proved agreeable to all parties.

At the Susquehannah, boisterous weather detained the travellers half a day. After sending their carriage and four horses over the river, two miles in width, in a scow to Havre de Grace, they crossed in a row-boat. Ice, brought down by the current through which the boatmen forced a way with their oars, threatened a formidable obstacle to their passage. The scene reminded Mrs. Quincy of an interesting incident mentioned to her at Havre de Grace in 1807, and recounted at her request by Commodore Rogers, who had then recently married a lady of that place.

After a severe winter, when the river was filled with floating ice, a negro man and woman were descried on separate fragments tending toward the Chesapeake. Their fate seemed inevitable; but Rogers, who could not see human beings perish without an effort, endeavored to induce some one to follow his directions, and attempt their rescue. Finding that no reward would tempt any man to run the risk, he determined to go himself. As no boat could live, he took two planks, and alternately walking on one, and throwing the other before him over the moving ice, at length reached the woman, seized her, and returned in the same manner. His difficulties were now redoubled: for the poor creature was so benumbed by the cold, that she was utterly helpless; and he was obliged to push her before him, and to manage the plank at the same time. But his noble efforts, watched with intense interest by all the inhabitants of Havre de Grace, succeeded. Amid loud acclamations, he landed with the woman in safety. His bride witnessed the scene from a balcony, but fainted the moment he touched the shore.

The negro man, carried by the current near the bank, escaped, and came with his wife to thank Commodore Rogers. They said they were crossing the river some miles above Havre de Grace, where the ice was firm; but it suddenly broke up, and caused the peril from which they had been rescued. As they were free blacks, they begged him to allow them to prove their gratitude by becoming his slaves; but he told them to go, and be happy. He did not save the woman's life to deprive her of freedom, and wanted no reward but the consciousness of having done a good action. Mrs. Quincy often mentioned this anecdote as a proof of true courage, and heroism of character, far beyond any that could be given amid the excitement of a battle.

At Gadsby's Hotel, in Baltimore, Francis J. Jackson, Esq., the British minister recently dismissed from Washington, had apartments near those of Mr. and Mrs. Quincy. In the evening, a band of music attracted a crowd under their windows, and excited apprehensions, as it would not have been an agreeable incident to be mistaken for the English envoy and his family by a Baltimore mob. The populace began to be noisy; and the band, instead of complimenting Mr. Jackson with "God save the King," as they probably intended, obeyed loud demands for "Hail Columbia" and "Yankee Doodle," and then departed, to the great relief of Mrs. Quincy. Mr. Broome and Mr. Hanson, residents of Baltimore, afterwards said that her fears were well grounded. At that period, they never heard a drum beat after sunset, without apprehending a serious commotion.

The next day, Mr. and Mrs. Quincy gladly left Baltimore; and, on the 27th of November, arrived at the city of Washington. They had taken all the accommodations in one of the Six Buildings, then the last block in Pennsylvania Avenue, toward Georgetown. Extracts from the letters here inserted will describe the occurrences and society of the ensuing winter.

To Miss Storer, Boston.

CITY OF WASHINGTON, Dec. 4, 1809.

MY DEAR FRIEND, — With our situation here we are much pleased. Our apartments are convenient, and even elegant. The inhabitants of this vast city are scattered over such an extent of ground, that it is almost the work of a day to reach either extreme. I visited Mrs. Madison on Saturday; and, on Sunday, received a return. She is very much disposed to please, and appears lady-like and agreeable. The President's house is much improved, and is a residence worthy the head of a great nation. On Sunday, I attended service in the new Hall of Representatives, and was delighted with the style and elegance of the architecture.

Conversation here is chiefly engrossed by a late duel between Mr. Pearson, a Federalist from North Carolina, and T. G. Jackson, brother-in-law to the President, who was the aggressor, and is dangerously wounded. He was one of the bullies who attacked Mr. Quincy last winter. In another duel, fought in this vicinity a few days since, a fine young man of seventeen lost his life. There is also a dispute between the President's Secretary and another member of Congress, which will probably end in the same way. What a state of manners and morals! I turn to your quiet home and happy fireside for subjects more congenial to my feelings. Your portraits, and group of my children, are the greatest alleviations of this tedious separation. I can see them " in my mind's eye," surrounded by kind and tender friends; and have no cause for an uneasy thought about them.

DEC. 5, 1809.

We continue to like our situation; have enjoyed good health, and much domestic comfort and happiness. We see our New-England friends often, and have received many kind attentions from all around us. Several Bostonians, with whom we were not personally acquaiuted, have visited us, — to mutual satisfaction, I believe ; for, at this distance from home, interest arises from that very circumstance.

We often saw Mr. S. Jones, son of T. K. Jones of Boston, and Mr. Poinsett of South Carolina, on the journey ; and they visit us frequently here. They have lately returned from Europe together, and are on their way to Charleston. Mr. Jones seems an amiable, clever fellow. Mr. Poinsett is uncommonly interesting, polished, and well informed. He has spent many years in Europe ; moved in the highest circles of society ; and traversed the continent, from the Atlantic to the Caspian, with great observation and improvement. I have seldom met with a more accomplished and pleasing young man. Mr. and Mrs. Lloyd are a very pleasant addition to our society.

Very few subjects of interest have yet been discussed at the Capitol. I have been there once, and heard several of the best speakers.

DEC. 20.

To have heard Mr. Buckminster's sermon which you describe would have been like "manna in the wilderness." I wish he would come here as a missionary. Do you not think Dr. Morse's Missionary Society might be prevailed on to send him here ? I should be proud to offer him as a specimen of what we think worthy of admiration in New England. We have service here every Sunday morning in the Capitol. One of the chaplains is a Baptist ; the other, a Methodist. They have the peculiarities of their respective sects ; but are men of natural good sense, though uncultivated by education. That magnificent dome deserves to be consecrated by talent and eloquence of a different order. What a prodigy would our friend appear among this motley collection from all parts of the Union and the world! He would speak their confusion into order, and raise their minds by the force of truth and eloquence.

But I am talking of sermons, when I promised you an account of a dinner at the President's. The company consisted of twenty-five or thirty people ; and not a single Federalist, except Mr. Quincy. We were in the midst of the enemy's camp; but were treated with great distinction, and passed a pleasant day. I was attended by the Secretary of State, and placed next Mrs. Madison. Do you wish to hear of her costume ? She was elegantly attired in black velvet, with a very rich head-dress of coquelicot and gold, with necklace and ornaments of the same color. The President's house is handsomely furnished in general; but is not of a piece, as we ladies say. The drawing-room curtains, couches, and chairs are of the richest crimson velvet, trimmed very elegantly and suitably; but the room is hung with an ordinary green paper, which lights badly. The carpet is not handsome, and other parts of the furniture are still worse. . . .

I took my children with me to call on Mrs. Madison the other morning; and she kindly opened the doors of the dining and drawing rooms on each side of the apartment, where she receives morning visitors, and showed them herself to her young friends. After we had taken leave, Mrs. S. H. Smith, who was there, showed us a large unfinished room, extending the whole width of the house, called the Audience Chamber (now the East Room). As we returned, we met Mrs. Madison in the hall. I said, " You see, madam, we are taking the liberty to look at your house, without leave." — " It is as much your house as it is mine, ladies," was her graceful reply.

JANUARY 10, 1810.

The first day of the year was, with us as with you, one of the mildest I ever remember. Its bright sun found us in the possession of many blessings, and, I trust, grateful for them, — the frame of mind most likely to insure their continuance. The 1st of January is always a great gala-day here. The President has a levee, which every one is expected to attend. The whole house was thrown open, filled with company, and enlivened by a fine band of music. The foreign ministers, the officers of the army and navy, and numerous ladies, gave brilliancy to the scene. Mrs. Madison wore her carriage-dress,— the same in which she appears on Sunday at the Capitol, — a purple-velvet pelisse, and hat trimmed with ermine. A very elegant costume; but not, I thought, appropriate to a lady receiving company at home. We passed an hour very pleasantly; and I only regretted I had not complied with Mrs. Madison's earnest request, that I would bring the children with me. They would have remembered the occasion with pleasure.

Colonel Pickman and several of our New-England friends dined with us; and we spent the rest of the day in thinking of our own land, and sending good wishes to the dear friends and children who dwell there.

WASHINGTON, January 17, 1810.

We continue to pass our time pleasantly, and chiefly at home. I am devoted to Mr. Quincy every morning till eleven o'clock, when he goes to *school,* and I begin mine. The lessons of the children engage me until one o'clock, when I admit or return visits. We dine usually at four o'clock, when Mr. Quincy returns fatigued from the Capitol. In the evening, we always have company, as our friends often seek the solace of our fireside.

The ease with which Mr. Quincy can here give invitations to dinner is a source of pleasure. In the selection of our guests, our Yankee sympathies have considerable influence. We strengthen by mutual interest the naturally firm tie of country, and similarity of situation. We see Colonel Pickering and Mr. Hillhouse of Connecticut very often. Your account of the rigors of climate does not cool our desire to return: —

"Dear is that home to which my soul conforms,
And dear the roof that shields us from the storms."

FEBRUARY 23.

The season here begins to wear the livery and breathe the air of spring. Whenever we drive or walk, the children exclaim, " O mamma! I wish we were at Quincy. Don't you think it must be very pleasant there now?" I reason with them, more effectually, I hope, than with myself, on the duties of using every opportunity of improvement within our reach. We have had the pleasure of the society of Colonel Perkins and some other Bostonians for a few days past.

The 22d was celebrated here with uncommon festivity. There was a grand ball given in this city, to which we had invitations; and also to another at Georgetown, which we preferred. The majority of the citizens of that place are Federalists of the old Washington school. Our sympathies attracted us there, and we passed a very agreeable evening.

We enjoy much pleasure in the society of friends in Georgetown, with whom we have become acquainted this winter. The family of Mr. Teackle, a man of fortune from the Eastern Shore of Virginia, consists of his wife and three daughters, who are amiable, intelligent, and accomplished. The young ladies remind me of you and your two sisters in their industry and ingenuity in every kind of fancy and useful work. Miss Teackle would be thought a fine woman anywhere; but here she is indeed a treasure, — religious, sensible, with a mind highly cultivated, and pleasing manners; and, though not handsome, her countenance is expressive of uncommon acuteness and observation. All these good qualities have not escaped the notice of Mr. Elihu Chauncey, to whom she is engaged, and who will soon take her to Philadelphia, to the great regret of her friends here.

Mrs. Martha Peter, a grand-daughter of Mrs. Washington, and Miss Lee, daughter of Governor Lee of Maryland, are also among my favorites.* Mrs. Peter is a woman of high-toned sentiment and principles. A stanch Federalist, she manifests the energy of her character by decided expressions of political opinion. Eliza Lee, at the head of her father's establishment, has long commanded general admiration by her highly cultivated mind and graceful and attractive

---

* In 1812, Miss Lee was married to Hon. Outerbridge Horsey of Delaware.

manners. The younger Miss Teackle and the daughters of Dr. Worthington are also very lovely young women. In Washington, we have agreeable friends in Mr. and Mrs. Tayloe, Mrs. S. H. Smith and her sister Miss Bayard, and Judge and Mrs. Cranch.

At Mrs. Madison's levee last evening, Madame Bonaparte was a conspicuous figure. Her dress was a scarlet velvet robe, with white satin petticoat and sleeves. A bandeau and ear-rings of diamonds, and a watch set with diamonds, suspended by a gold chain round her neck, completed her costume. Her face and head are on too large a scale to correspond with her figure; but she is yet beautiful, and was more natural and unaffected in her manners than I expected. The Dashkoffs have left the city, and intend visiting Boston.

I have heard from Miss Lowell of the proposal to reprint the "Life of Elizabeth Smith" in Boston, and have obtained many subscriptions. I destine a copy for each of my daughters; not forgetting also you and your sisters. Miss Smith must have been indeed a prodigy of learning and talent.

Among my acquaintances in Georgetown, I ought to mention Mr. Milligan, a bookseller, and a very worthy man. I went into his store to purchase some drawing materials for Susan, and was much pleased with his excellent and judicious collection of books. He has done much good here by introducing a better taste among the inhabitants, both in a moral and literary sense. He has encouragement to reprint Miss Edgeworth's "Moral Tales," if he can obtain a copy. Will you purchase one, if the work is to be obtained at our book-stores? and, if not, borrow one from some friend, and I will replace it with a new copy. Cut the books out of the bindings, and enclose the pages, in packets not exceeding two ounces, by mail to Mr. Quincy. Be careful to send the text entire, and the titlepage. My own set are locked up at home, and you will be pleased to co-operate in a benevolent design.

We still hope Congress will adjourn the middle of April. . . .

Your friend, E. S. QUINCY.

To Miss Lowell.

Congress had resolved to rise on the 23d instant; but they have postponed adjournment until the 1st of May. The delay has enabled me to see this city and its vicinity assume its most beautiful dress. The ground is clothed in the freshest, liveliest green; the trees are in full bloom; and all nature, with a universal voice, seems to call upon us to be happy and grateful. The music of the birds, and the charms conferred by the season, give this place attractions which it never had before in my eyes. Our dear friends at Georgetown, in the families of Mr. Teackle and Mr. Lee, planned an excursion for us to the Great Falls of the Potomac on the 23d, the day we had expected to depart for home. The weather was delightful; and the scenery, which exceeded my expectations, repaid us for a drive over eighteen miles of bad road. The Potomac falls seventy feet. The banks are high, and, for half a mile, are composed of immense masses of rock in every variety of form; some towering like pyramids, others projecting rough points to the river, and others an even front like a wall of masonry. The scenery is composed only of water and rocks. Few mosses and evergreens can force an existence among such materials. Yet even here, where nature seemed to present insuperable obstacles, the ingenuity of man has triumphed; and a canal with seven locks, one of them cut in solid rock, opens the navigation of the river to an immense back country. Boats were lying in it, loaded with goods for the Indians on the Missouri and the Red River. When I looked on the river and the rocks, and heard the roaring waters, I felt as nothing amid the works of God; but, when I saw what human effort had here accomplished, I was re-animated, and felt that he had also breathed into our souls the breath of life and intelligence. The idea also, that we were viewing the scene for the only time with an interesting group of friends from whom we were soon to separate, probably never to meet again in this world, — who would certainly never assemble again on that spot, — gave a solemn impression to my mind, in which several of my companions sympathized; and all were affected by sadly pleasing sensations, suitable to the occasion and the objects around us.

In one week more, we hope we shall return to our home, our friends, and our children; and the thought of meeting you is one of the most gratifying to my heart. . . .

ELIZA S. QUINCY.

The last evening of the session, Mrs. Quincy and her children heard John Randolph and other eminent men in the House of Representatives; and, on leaving the Capitol, bade a reluctant farewell to Mrs. Peter, Miss Lee, Miss Teackle, and many other friends.

The next morning, the 2d of May, they looked back, from the heights of Georgetown, on Washington and its vicinity, with many interesting retrospections. Intending to visit Harper's Ferry, they followed a route which led near the Potomac, and through the rich lands, the property of Charles Carroll. The dogwood, the redbud, and numerous shrubs and flowers, filled the woods with beauty and fragrance. Mrs. Quincy was delighted with the scenery, especially on the Monocasy. Noble trees fringed the banks, and dipped their branches into the stream, as, swelled by heavy rains, it rushed to join the Potomac, studded with wooded islands; while, toward its source, the Sugar-loaf Mountain reared its picturesque cone in the distance. But the passage of this river was effected with difficulty. The blight of slavery rested on this fair land. Bad roads and accommodations, and the total absence of bridges, presented such obstacles, that farther progress into the mountain region was most reluctantly relinquished for the road to Frederictown. Thence they passed through Hanover and York, crossed the Susquehannah at Columbia, and traversed the fertile valley of Lancaster. From Philadelphia they pursued the usual route to Boston, where they arrived the last of May, and soon removed to their home at Quincy.

Letter from Miss Lee.

GEORGETOWN, D.C., May 30, 1810.

MY DEAR MRS. QUINCY, — I did, indeed, wish to hear of your safe arrival, and happy re-union with your friends; but to be gratified so soon, to be thought of in the midst of so many engagements of the heart, I did not anticipate. When we met of an evening, and spoke of you, I said there was no chance of a letter until you were established at Quincy. Then, indeed, I flattered myself you would cast "one longing, lingering look behind," and delight with a proof of your remembrance those friends who appreciated your worth. But this is not the first time that your kindness has far exceeded my calculations. . . .

My father, and all our family who knew you and Mr. Quincy, thank you for your kind remembrance. My sister has your best wishes, I am confident; and we Catholics have great faith in the prayers of the good of this world, as well as of the next. We heard of your disappointment with regard to Harper's Ferry, and that your lives were endangered in crossing the Monocasy. As I trust the latter was an exaggeration, I will not regret the circuitous route you were induced to take, since it afforded a view of one of our most fertile counties. Your journey occurred at a fortunate season with regard to the beauty of the country. At this time you would have found the heat intense; and instead of April's tenderest, freshest green, which you so much admired, the whole landscape looks parched and thirsty. . . .

Since I have had the pleasure of knowing you, I have felt an increased interest in all persons from New England whom I like at all. I am honored by Colonel Pickering's regard, and entreat you to present my respects to him. Little Mary * begs to be remembered to your children, and my family all unite with me in sentiments of respect and affection for you and Mr. Quincy.

Ever yours,   ELIZA D. LEE.

From Miss Teackle.

GEORGETOWN, D.C., July 16, 1810.

I cannot say, my dear Mrs. Quincy, how much I was gratified by your kind letter. I often felt tempted to solicit the favor of hearing from you; but the recollection of your various duties made me fear it would be asking too much. . . .

The disposition we evinced to be always with you renders it unnecessary to describe our regret at your departure; and our loss was more affecting, as it seemed probable that those happy hours we passed together would never be renewed. These, I trust, were the fears of clouded minds. We will yet hope that time and circum-stances will again unite us. Miss Lee informed us of your safe arrival at home. After so long an absence, I can easily imagine your happiness on returning to your own delightful habitation. Few are so pre-eminently blessed in domestic life; still fewer so well appreciate the gift. . . .

It is time I should begin to deliver the numberless expressions of regard with which I am charged by your friends here. The Lees are particular in their remembrance, and my parents and sisters not less urgent. We hope Mr. Quincy will accept his portion of our esteem, and your children also. The delightful tranquillity of your life at Quincy is truly congenial to my taste. I would sooner undergo the fatigue of travelling to participate in your enjoyments

---

* Afterwards Mrs. Charles Carroll, of Carrollton.

than any other object of my wishes; but I must only hope to see you in Philadelphia.

The Russian minister, Count Pahlen, will visit Boston this summer. The slight acquaintance I have formed with him has been highly favorable. I think I may say, you will like him very much. His brother also is greatly admired for his accomplishments and amiable manners. The whole suite appear anxious to accommodate their conduct to the American taste. . . .

I must now say farewell. Accept, my dear friend, my sincerely affectionate regard.

HENRIETTA TEACKLE.

From Miss Lee.

NEEDWOOD, MD., Oct. 17, 1810.

DEAR MRS. QUINCY, — The hope of seeing you here again this winter is too precious to be relinquished. Until you say positively, " I shall not come," I will continue firm in the faith. I almost dread to mention the removal of our excellent friends in Mr. Teackle's family, lest it should influence your decision. Miss Teackle was married on the 13th; and left Georgetown for Philadelphia, accompanied by Eliza. The rest of the family go to the Eastern Shore this week; so that I shall not have the happiness of seeing any of them again. . . . We shall not leave Needwood till late in November. My father, who farms for revenue as well as amusement, finds it requisite to remain until he disposes of the fruits of his industry; and I am not anxious to remove earlier. Our mountain scenery is finer in autumn than at any other season, and the weather more favorable for exercise. My father charges me with his respects for you and Mr. Quincy.

With my best wishes for the welfare of all dear to you,

I am ever yours,

ELIZA D. LEE.

From John Teackle, Esq., to Hon. Josiah Quincy.

ACCOMAC COUNTY, EASTERN SHORE OF VIRGINIA,
20th December, 1810.

MY DEAR SIR, — The intimate friendship which so pleasantly existed between us at Washington is often before me, and occasions much regret that our lot is cast so remote from each other. Nevertheless, we shall cherish the remembrance of you and yours with pleasing sensations, and retrospectively enjoy the happiness of your society. The cultivated mind and refined manners of Mrs. Quincy is often a subject of conversation with us ; and we all have viewed her as one whom Solomon so elegantly has styled a jewel to her husband, of high price. About the end of October, we left Georgetown ; and after an easy journey, and frequent calls on our friends and relatives in the neighboring counties, we arrived here in November, and feel much at home. It is an old family estate, and our own residence for thirty years previous to my removal to the District of Columbia. . . . We have been highly favored in our health, and no untoward circumstance has attended our removal. My household now consists of my two younger children and their mother. I have two daughters married in Philadelphia, and Eliza is with her sisters.

It will give me great pleasure to have occasional letters from you. Remote as I am from genuine information, your ideas on our relations abroad, and situation at home, will be very gratifying, and will be used with circumspection. What have we to expect from France ? Will Bonaparte's future conduct any way justify his loving promises ? And what course, under events, is it calculated Great Britain will follow toward us ? And, above all, what do you believe to be the intentions and views, of Congress and the Executive, of our distracted country ? What is to become of this nation ? . . .

I indulge a hope of visiting Washington and of seeing you in February. Mrs. Teackle requests me to offer Mrs. Quincy our united love. — With high esteem,

Yours,   JOHN TEACKLE.

From Mrs. Peter.

TUDOR PLACE, GEORGETOWN, D.C.,
Aug. 19, 1810.

MY DEAR MRS. QUINCY, — Nothing would give me more pleasure than to visit you at Quincy, beside the delight I should take in your society and in rural beauties. My feelings are particularly gratified by the manner you express yourself of those I have been taught most to respect and venerate, — General and Mrs. Washington.

It was with sincere regret I heard we were not to see our friend Mr. Hillhouse here this winter. I still hope you will disappoint the ruling party by continuing Colonel Pickering in the Senate. Several of his opponents told me the state of the elections with great joy, and that there was no chance of his being returned. My reply was, that Varnum was much better calculated to sit in the Senate with Leib; but that, in the present shattered state of the wheel of Government, I should regret losing so valuable a spoke as Colonel Pickering.

I am just returned from a visit to my friends in Virginia. While with my sister Mrs. Lewis, I took my children to Mount Vernon, which some of them had never seen, although they had often heard me speak of it as the place where I had spent the happiest years of my life. My little daughter thought it must be something more than trees and house and land, and it did not answer her expectations; but, when I asked her what she thought Mount Vernon was like, she could not express her ideas. I hope you do not venture to think of not coming to Washington next winter. . . .

MARTHA PETER.

During these years, numerous guests and distinguished foreigners were received at Quincy.

In August, 1811, Count Pahlen (the Russian minister), Count Nicholas Pahlen, and M. Poletica (an eminent statesman and diplomatist attached to that embassy), dined at the residence of Mr. Quincy with a numerous party of gentlemen. In October, Mr. Foster, the British minister, was also a guest there.* On one of his visits, a highly finished model in plaster of the Parthenon, by Fouquet, attracted his admiration.† On a close examination, he discovered that the artist had represented with faithful accuracy the sculpture on the frieze of the cell of the temple, which, concealed by the entablature of the colonnade, had previously escaped notice. Mr. Foster had visited Athens at the time the Turks were removing the marbles for Lord Elgin. They did their work so clumsily, that one morning, when he was at the Parthenon, they dropped the head of a statue from the pediment, and a masterpiece of Phidias was dashed to pieces on the pavement.

---

* Afterwards the Rt. Hon. Sir Augustus J. Foster, Bart., for many years British minister at the Court of Sardinia, resident at Turin. His last letter to Mr. Quincy was dated from thence in 1839.

† Purchased by Mr. Quincy, in 1805, of John Pickering, Esq.; by whom it was brought from Paris.

CHAPTER V.

To leave home, and separate her family, became every year more difficult; and Mrs. Quincy, therefore, did not pass any subsequent winter in Washington, but remained in Boston with her children. To gratify her preference for the talents, character, and eloquence of William Ellery Channing, Mr. Quincy, in November, 1810, after the inauguration of Dr. Kirkland at Harvard, left the New South for the Federal-street Church, — a removal which proved a source of improvement and pleasure to him and his family. Before Mr. Channing attained great general celebrity, he was their intimate friend, and often passed weeks at their residence at Quincy, to which he gave the name of Tranquilla.

The following note was written in 1811 : —

BOSTON, Thursday.

MY DEAR MRS. QUINCY, — I cannot let my sister go to Quincy without a line to express the pleasure with which I recollect my short visit at your house. I was fearful you might think my imprisonment by the weather painful; but I would that every prisoner were as happy! I indeed love trees and fields, and the delightful variety of nature; but these give me less pleasure than the view of an affectionate, peaceful, cultivated, happy family.

I hope you did not think me indolent. I did perhaps more than you imagined, though less than I might or should have done. I send to Susan a shell which I found on Chelsea Beach, — a very humble contribution to her cabinet, but not without its beauty.

To your little children you must give my love, and tell them I hope they will be less shy when we meet again.

I send you two of your books. I have glanced over "Griselda," * and hope that almost any trial of my virtues and patience will be appointed rather than such a loving wife. Have you ever known the original of this picture? It is drawn with so much life, that I presume it is taken from nature; but I have not met with it.

It is not requisite that I should express to Mr. Quincy and yourself the respect and affection which I bear you.

Affectionately yours,   W. E. CHANNING.†

The acquisition of a gifted friend was peculiarly valuable to Mrs. Quincy, at a moment when she was deprived of one who had long held the first place in her affections. The death of Anna Cabot Lowell in December, 1810, severed a long, constant, and unclouded friendship.

For intellectual gifts and exalted character, Miss Lowell held an acknowledged pre-eminence among her contemporaries in Boston. Her writings, both in prose and verse, are stamped with genius. Her letters would have ranked with those of Elizabeth Montagu and other eminent women, had they been collected and preserved. Copies of those to Mrs. Grant, though circulated in Scotland, were not obtained by her family until after her decease. In one of them, Miss Lowell paid the following tribute to her friend: —

BOSTON, Nov. 8, 1809.

Another of your warm admirers is Mrs. Quincy. This lady is a native of New York; but, marrying a gentleman of Boston, she has

---

* "The Modern Griselda," by Maria Edgeworth.

† It was at Quincy, on his return from Newport, Sept. 7, 1825, that Mr. Channing received the first intelligence of the discovery of the lost manuscript of Milton, — the subject of one of his finest Essays.

long been the ornament of our circle. Her husband is one of that band of real patriots who are now defending the cause of good government in our National Legislature. Though branded with the name of British partisan, he continues to support with firmness and eloquence what he believes to be the best interests of his country. Mrs. Quincy is one of my dearest friends: her understanding is my guide, and her virtues my model.

The following letters were written at this period : —

To Mrs. Quincy.

City of Washington, Dec. 23, 1810.

My dear Wife, — I have just received your letter announcing the departure of the most excellent and justly beloved of all your friends. How deeply I regret I should at such a moment be absent from you !

The memory of Miss Lowell is justly precious to your soul. Exemplary in life, perfect through suffering, she has left no doubt to hang upon her future fate. Rejoice for her; find consolation in her worth, in her resignation, the brightness of her hopes, and the assurances of her spirit. Guard yourself against excess of grief. . . . Be thankful for all the excellences of your friend; implant her virtues in your heart: in these she yet lives. Though absent, you possess in your own bosom an assurance, that the separation from one, whose virtues were so assimilated to your own, will not be perpetual.

Her summons was, to her mortal part, a relief; to her immortal, a joy. Her intellectual powers she yet exercises, disencumbered of the load which earth hangs about ours. If you estimate life by her attainments, she had lived long enough. The circle of her duties was complete, and the term of her fulfilling them had been lengthened out beyond our hopes. After days and years standing cheerfully at the threshold, and bidding all friends adieu, the traveller has turned, her journey has commenced, and the door is shut. You know how she was prepared. Leave her with that God into whose presence she has gone, and make yourself worthy to be a partaker of her felicity, by the dignity with which you sustain her departure, and the perfectness by which, in fulfilling your duties, you follow her example. But I forget I am uttering themes of consolation which your own spirit is so much more competent to suggest. . . .

DEC. 30, 1810.

I am entirely gratified by your views and feelings in relation to your late affliction. They are such as it is worthy in you to cherish. They elevate and strengthen the mind, and open to the intellectual eye an unbounded field of duties and of hopes.

Ever yours,   JOSIAH QUINCY.

To Mrs. Quincy.

WASHINGTON, Feb. 10, 1811.

MY DEAR WIFE, — Your affectionate and partial appeal to my heart on the occasion of my birthday has all that tenderness and encouragement which it has been so often my blessing to receive from your hand. I find in it new motives of duty and thankfulness to that Being who has planted by my side so precious and beloved a Virtue, allowed me to call her by the dearest of all names, and united me to her by the sweetest and strongest of all ties, in which I recognize not only the choicest reward of any excellence it may be in my power to attain, but a most powerful impulse to advance in whatever is wise and worthy.

The idea that our departed friends yet take an interest in those who remain in this sphere of trial and exertion, I have no question, is true. It is not an illusion. The clouds and darkness which hang over futurity, and upon the state of those who have preceded us to that region, I doubt not is a wise and paternal provision of Providence. Its tendency is to fill the thoughtful mind with awe and anxiety concerning its own destiny; to elevate it by alternate hopes and fears above the temporary pursuits of this world, and make it seek a higher standard of action and a purer rule of conduct than any terrestrial objects can enable us to form.

If my parents do indeed look down with any complacency on the conduct of their son, as you intimate, I cannot but realize with what pure and spiritual affection they must regard you; since they cannot but recognize what I love to cherish and confess, how much of whatever there is in me of mind or virtue has been the result of your influence and example. Take from one, who strives to do justice to his sense of your worth, whatever expression can give an adequate idea of mental and moral attainment. It is yours; at least, in the estimation of your devoted husband,

JOSIAH QUINCY.

Letter from Mrs. Peter to Mrs. Quincy.

TUDOR PLACE, GEORGETOWN, D.C., Feb. 15, 1812.

MY DEAR FRIEND, — Congress are so busy doing nothing, or worse than nothing, that they do not give themselves a holiday even on Saturday; and we therefore see Mr. Quincy more seldom than we wish. I assure you, it was a source of much regret to me and mine that you did not come on this winter.

The last fortnight of my mother's life was passed here with me; and the power of rendering her attentions which could not be paid elsewhere, and of being with her in her last moments, was a great source of happiness to her, and of consolation to me. Her loss deprived me of a wish to go into company. At all times, I delight in the society of a friend like yourself, to whom I can speak without reserve.

Although my life has not been a very long one, I have found that those are most likely to get well on who have the fewest confidants; and that our thoughts, except on very common subjects, are safest within our own breasts.

Persons of cold dispositions avoid a world of anxiety: but I believe the scale is equally balanced; for they know not the delights of a warm heart. Mr. Peter is at Oaklands for a week. I often think what I should do were I situated as you are; for my home seems bereft of its best half when he is absent. As you were bred in the old school, I venture to say to you, that my husband, of all mortals, is most dear to me; my children next. . . .

Your friend,   MARTHA PETER.

To Hon. Josiah Quincy.

BOSTON, February 19, 1812.

I have read your remarks critically, and give them unqualified approbation. There is not an expression or a thought that is not worthy of an American statesman, putting all party consideration out of the question. This morning I gave Dr. Pearson and Mr. Buckminster each a copy. The offering was eagerly accepted, and both desired me to present them to you in most affectionate terms. Mr. Buckminster made Josiah read Latin to him; which the boy did readily. The critic was more pleased with the pronunciation introduced at Andover than he expected to be.

Mr. Channing appeared much pleased with your letter, and expressed unqualified approbation of your remarks. He disapproved exceedingly of the tone of utter despair indulged by some of our wisest and best men here. Lately, in conversing with one of them, he said that "good seamen ought to work at the pump, and not give up the ship as long as the vessel swam." But he was answered, "What would you do if the pump pierced the bottom of the ship, and you were attempting to pump the ocean dry?"

Such is the language and the temper of some of our leading men; but not such are yours. Mr. Channing expressed himself a true convert to your opinion upon the views and character of the Administration, and admired the sagacity and firm independence with which you had formed and maintained them.

Mr. S. Higginson called here to-day. He agrees with you, that, in a political point of view, it is better the present state of things should continue till forced off by internal opposition and the proved inefficiency of our rulers. If Great Britain, by any temporary modification, should stretch a helping hand to the Administration, the system of restriction might be resorted to again and again. This, he said, is not the general opinion. The commercial world are all eagerly wishing and expecting that Great Britain will relax her orders. They look for help from no other quarter. Late letters from T. H. Perkins give his opinion, that the Orders in Council would be revoked or modified.

MARCH 16, 1812, Monday.

Your uncle, Mr. Phillips, on his way home from church yesterday, heard a report about some conspiracy by the British, and sent to know if you had mentioned it. I could not relieve his anxiety, while he excited my curiosity. In the evening, the mystery of his message was explained. Mr. James Perkins, I. P. Davis, Mr. Savage, and W. Shaw, met here. They had all read in the Washington papers, and in your letter to Otis, the wonderful ado about nothing, which the Administration are trying to excite by the correspondence of John Henry. This town has seldom been in such a state of political bustle on a Sunday as was witnessed yesterday. The mail arrived about noon: the accounts it brought, and exaggerated reports of their purport, collected a great crowd at the Exchange. Nothing in the whole business is so strange and disgraceful as the insinuation and evident design of the President's message. All the confessions of Henry only tend to the honor of the Federalists; and yet Madison talks of "the disaffected."* The gentlemen seemed to think the bubble was allowed to burst too late to affect the New-Hampshire election, and too soon to injure ours.

I told Mr. Perkins, who came first, what you said in your late letters on the subject of war. He confessed your reasonings were just as to the probable consequences, but that he was not patriotic enough to be willing to be the sacrifice; that he had nine or ten ships now afloat. A war of one month with Great Britain would sweep. our whole commerce from the ocean. The consequences to the whole community, in the effects upon insurance-offices, &c., would spread the ruin far and wide. The general result to the country at large, in a few years, might be a little favorable; but the face of society must be changed, and many reduced to poverty. He preferred the present state of things to such destruction.

I received your enclosure for Otis, and your line of apology to me in the cover. The letter was sent immediately, and delivered into his own hand. I suppose Mr. Henry has furnished your honorable body with business enough to employ them till the "Hornet" arrives, — a happy contrivance for such a purpose.

MARCH 27, 1812.

You do not return to your regular series of letters with more pleasure than I welcome you from the wilds of Democratic intrigue. I hope you convey your opinions to some of your friends who are influential in giving a tone to public sentiment and expression with regard to Henry's disclosures.

The view you propose is the vantage-ground, no doubt; but I question whether they can be prevailed upon to take it, from not understanding the designs of Madison, and his real plot to cast odium upon them by the very workings of their own honest indignation.

---

* See Appendix III.

As to Great Britain, it seems to me, they might now leave her to fight her own battles. By her long conflict, she has shown her ability; and her inexhaustible resources seem to be equal to continue her defence, even if America were added to the number of her assailants. This ought to be a comfort to those who really make a point of conscience to take part in the general question, between her and France, of right and wrong, virtue and vice. If she is proved to be safe in her own keeping, we ought to look to ourselves first, as we are not quite so well armed and prepared as she is.

BOSTON, April 2, 1812.

I have your letter re-enforcing the views and principles I have already commended. That you look on life in a different light from most men is cause of joy and pride to me, and must result in happiness and success to yourself.

To prevent the election of Strong, the opposition have made up a pamphlet of parts of Henry's disclosures, leaving out all that is honorable to the Federalists, and giving heightened representations of every thing against them. They have sent them through the Democratic post-offices, to the exclusion of Federal newspapers and statements. Mr. Davis, who called to-day, said that the news from the country was encouraging, notwithstanding their efforts; and that the general state of public opinion, with respect to the question of the British Government, was nearly what you wished to induce. The Federal party seem to have taken more just and patriotic ground than ever, and the papers have been wisely and calmly conducted; yet there are still some men who disapprove of your and yet more of Mr. Lloyd's views, as exhibited in your respective speeches. But these are few, and are daily losing their adherents.

Mr. Channing told me Mr. S. Dexter had returned from Washington, fully satisfied with the views and policy of the Federalists there, so much so as to express a willingness again to exert himself in their cause. Mr. Otis also coincides in your opinions.

BOSTON, April 4, 1812.

A rumor of embargo reached town last night, as I am informed by our servant, who says that you and Mr. Lloyd have sent on the news by express. How true this is, I know not; having seen no one to-day. The "Centinel" has just been brought, and the mystery is explained. Your letter to Mr. Otis arrived here last evening, Friday, at six o'clock, in seventy-six hours from Washington. The tidings of the impending embargo were immediately sent off in every direction by other expresses. It was to be delivered at Portland at noon to-day; so that the trick of its being suspended to so late a moment will be in a great degree counteracted. Your spirit and activity are visible in this development, and do you honor.

APRIL 6, Monday, 1812.

The intelligence communicated by your letter has excited an unprecedented sensation here. The trucks were going all Sunday; and the wharves, I am told, were as full and as busy as they were ever seen. Every ship or boat that can move is preparing to get off before they are stopped by the embargo. This effort is an important service to the merchants; and another, I hope, will be produced by the industry of the Federalists at the election to-day. The weather has been threatening, but is now clearing off. Under the present excitement, I do not think a storm would be injurious.

Few parts of the State were unacquainted with your notice of the embargo this morning. The Democrats sent off expresses also to contradict the assertion of your letter, and say it was all an electioneering trick. Never has there been such exertion before in this vicinity. There were great fears that many votes might be lost by seamen and others being hurried away; and a committee was appointed to visit the wharves, and bring up all qualified voters at the general expense. Carriage loads of seamen and others belonging to Plymouth and Salem were sent last night to those towns to vote, and to be brought back immediately to their vessels. If this day is lost, it will not be from any fault of the Federal party.

Before I close this letter, I will tell you the state of the poll here. Our servant has just come in with the annexed statement: Strong has three thousand eight hundred and thirty votes; Gerry, one thousand eight hundred and thirty-three. Strong has seven hundred more Federal votes than last year.

In Salem, at the opening of the poll, the Democrats raised a riot, forced the selectmen from their places, and declared they should not take the votes. The deputy sheriff had declined to act; and the people had sent off for the high sheriff at Ipswich, who had ordered out the militia.

APRIL 8, 1812.

The riot in Salem was owing to the selectmen having struck illegal voters from their list: it was quelled, and the election concluded within the prescribed time. Official news of the embargo has not yet arrived, though expected every hour. A signal on Fort Hill is to be hoisted, the moment it is received, to give notice to the vessels lying below to sheer off. We have heard it had been enforced in New York. Some people still pretend to doubt the account.

Dr. Eliot* came to see me yesterday: he was quaint and pleasant, as usual. Judge Davis and Mr. Channing were also among my visitors. We have a snow-storm, but do not complain, as the election is over. As far as good weather could help us, we were favored by genial skies.

To-morrow is Fast Day. Mr. Channing again declined to read the proclamation. He told me he did not think there was any reason, civil or religious, obliging him to produce in the pulpit the warrant by which he gave notice of the observance of the day according to order and usage.

---

* Rev. John Eliot, D.D., of the New North Church, Boston.

The people in this neighborhood have certainly done nobly all that could be done. Those at a distance are in some degree to be pitied. No Federal papers have been allowed to go through the post-office; while they have been deluged with those of the opposite party, and with pamphlets and agents to misrepresent the truth. The great body of the people are, therefore, probably ignorant of the real state of the country, and of the conduct of their rulers.

We have heard the embargo has passed both houses, and will be here to-day. Every vessel that could get off is gone: those that remain may go to sleep for the rest of the season.

APRIL 10, 1812.

I have received your letter of the 4th inst., and sympathize with you in head and heart. Three hours before its arrival, the flag of Embargo was hoisted on Fort Hill, — that flag which every American should blush to see thus erected to our own destruction, instead of waving to protect and extend our prosperity. You might well say, "We have no flag." Above fifty sail of vessels got out before the order came. Can there be a more evident contradiction of the pretended necessity of thus protecting a commerce only anxious to escape from its embrace?

The "Lothair," from England, arrived at six o'clock last evening, and was to have sailed again this morning; for which purpose, they were loading her all night: but she has been caught by the embargo. In the hurry to load the vessels with cotton and flour, beef, &c., the contents of those which had just arrived were scattered over the wharves. The poor people went and helped themselves unmolested; the owners saying only, "Take these things out of our way, and help us to get in the new load."

But now those walks, and scenes of activity, will be silent enough; the season most favorable to business must pass in idleness; and what misery may not be expected to follow the excision of the means of life and subsistence from so large a portion of the community! Yet thirty-five thousand men can be found in this commercial State voting to support such an Administration, — thirteen hundred in this town, — without the excuse of not knowing better. The gentlemen now seem to have no doubt of the election of Strong. There will also be a Federal House. The new division of districts prevents such a Senate as would otherwise have been secured.

Both the clergymen I heard yesterday preached very orthodox doctrine, according to your opinion. Mr. Channing's subject was the baneful effects of party-spirit. In the treatment of it, he gave much offence to some high-toned partisans. I thought it one of the most excellent and eloquent discourses I ever heard.

The people here indulge a hope that embargo and non-intercourse will be allowed to expire together; and that the last measure imposed was the only way to get rid of the Non-intercourse Act, without actually treading back their steps. Mr. Davis and Mr. Perkins were here last evening. Both were very dull at the prospect of war; and said, if you saw any light or hope, you were the only man in the country who did so. We are all disappointed that Clinton is out-generalled by Madison, who, it is intimated, has detached Governor Tompkins by proposing to make him Vice-President.

I have had some apprehensions that Calhoun might resent the use you made of his name, and the information he gave of the intended embargo. Some of the Democrats said, at first, that he deserved to be hanged; but luckily it leaked out that Seaver had written to some of his friends, several days before your letter came, that the measure could not be brought on, as they were opposed in the committee by a majority of one vote. Mr. Bridge, in consequence, made a bet with Mr. J. Coffin Jones that you were mistaken. This bet he has since paid; and, when asked why he made it, he frankly said, on the strength of Seaver's account of the committee. So, whenever any thing is said about Calhoun, they are silenced by the name of Seaver.

What do you think of the merchants here refusing to subscribe to Gallatin's loan? He will get very little.

Your views as to general policy are no doubt correct and wise; but Madison understands the nature of the people, and makes good use of the knowledge for his own purposes. I am glad you have looked with a temperate hope on the success of our election. You will be the less disappointed at the slender figure it makes.

APRIL 27, 1812.

I have just received yours of the 22d, giving hopes the question of recess would be that day decided. Mr. Channing was here this morning. He seems almost ill with anxiety about public affairs, and wearies himself to account for what is unaccountable in itself, — the motives and intentions of the dominant party. The late election in Massachusetts, he thought, must have convinced them that the system of depressing commerce could not be continued, and that the present violence was intended to ruin and destroy the merchants and the cities on the seaboard, and induce a new state and face of society more conformable to their views and policy. Everybody is coming and sending to know what you say and think. I can only reply, you know not what to say or to think, except that there is no calculation to be made about such men as lead the majority.

Have any of your friends told you of the conduct of Governor Gerry at a late meeting of the Board of Overseers of Harvard College?

When he was notified, as usual, of the meeting of the Board at the Council Chamber last week, he returned for answer, he knew of no such Board; they had no existence: and warned them, that, if they held such a meeting, it was at their peril, and the peril of the interests of the university. He also prohibited the use of the Council Chamber, and said he washed his hands of their proceedings, and of all the consequences resulting to the institution. They met, however, and immediately adjourned to the Academy Room, where they organized themselves. When Mr. Senator Dana made his appearance, Mr. Gore, who presided, immediately observed, that, as President of the Senate, he was President of the Board; and offered to resign his seat. Mr. Dana declined accepting it, saying he doubted the legality of the meeting, &c., much as the Governor had done. The gentlemen then said, that, while he was present, no other person could take the seat as President; and inferred he must withdraw, or no business could be done. Thereupon he withdrew; and they proceeded to appoint a committee to report on the real state of the question between the Board and the Legislature, and advise what steps were expedient to be taken. The committee are Dexter, Otis, Gore, civilians; Dr. Porter and Dr. Holmes, clergymen. They are to report next week; and thus the affair stands. These proceedings will interest you, and I have therefore filled my paper with them.

Ever yours, E. S. QUINCY.

A few days after the date of this letter, Mr. Quincy came home on a short visit to his family. On his return, he invited Mr. Channing to accompany him to Washington. At Havre de Grace, he formed an acquaintance with Mr. Sparks, a student, absent on leave, from Harvard College. They went together on an excursion to an island in the Susquehannah, not anticipating that they should become friends for life, or that two future Presidents of Harvard then crossed that restless wave.

The extracts from the correspondence of Mr. and Mrs. Quincy are here continued: —

To Hon. Josiah Quincy, City of Washington.

BOSTON, May 30, 1812.

This has been a proud day for Boston and Massachusetts. Mr. Strong having notified his intention of coming to Boston to-day to meet the Legislature, Mr. Gore behaved very handsomely on the occasion.* He anticipated Mr. Lyman in an invitation to Mr. Strong to pass the night at his house at Waltham; invited the Boston Hussars to breakfast there; and then accompanied him to town. The escort of private citizens assembled on Cambridge Common, in front of the Colleges. The morning being fine, we drove to Cambridge over Craigie's Bridge (the escort having preceded us by another route), took a stand in the college-yard, and had a fine view of the whole ceremony. Three sides of the Common were lined with horsemen; the fourth, by carriages. Mr. Strong came from Waltham, preceded by the Hussars, accompanied by Mr. Phillips, and in his carriage. The Hussars formed, and the carriage stopped very near us. Colonel Apthorp, on horseback, at the head of a committee of the citizens of Boston, made a very handsome address, which I heard distinctly, and also the Governor's reply. The cavalcade then formed, and passed and preceded the carriage in which Mr. Strong and Mr. Phillips were seated, the Hussars attending it: the citizens in carriages followed, and proceeded to Boston over Charlestown Bridge. There must have been several thousand people assembled; but there was not a loud word spoken. Salutes were fired from Bunker's Hill, Copp's Hill, and the Common; all the flags flying, bells chiming and ringing: in short, such a joyous reception was never, I believe, given before to any magistrate. Your uncle Mr. Phillips looked very fierce in his cocked hat and cockade.

I enclose a letter Mr. Buckminster sent here for Mr. Channing.

JUNE 6, 1812.

We were gratified to hear that Mr. Channing was able to preach the day after you arrived at Washington. The letters from Mr. Thacher are favorable; but Mr. Buckminster has had an attack of his constitutional malady.

---

* Hon. Christopher Gore, Governor of Massachusetts in 1809, and the Federal candidate the two preceding years.

I mentioned Mr. Gore's magnanimity at the accession of Governor Strong; but I think Mr. Gerry exceeded him. Mr. Davis said he deserved great credit for the manner in which he resigned the chair. All former incumbents, when superseded, abandoned the Council Chamber before the entrance of the Governor elect, leaving only some of the former Council to receive him; but last Saturday, when Mr. Strong was escorted to the State House with so much distinction, on entering the Council Chamber, there was Governor Gerry in the chair of State, with Lieutenant-Governor Gray, and his councillors. He received Mr. Strong, placed him at his right hand, Mr. Phillips at his left, and conversed politely and agreeably with them till a Committee of the Legislature came to inform the Governor and Lieutenant-Governor elect that they were ready to qualify them. Mr. Strong and Mr. Phillips then took leave of Governor Gerry, and went to be qualified, expecting he would take the opportunity to depart; but, on their return to the Council Chamber, Mr. Gerry was still there. He then rose, and with a very polite movement resigned the chair to Governor Strong; walked round the circular table, stopped opposite to him, bowed respectfully, and wished him much happiness and a prosperous administration. Mr. Gray did the same. They then left the State House. Mr. Gerry took Mr. Gray to his residence in Summer Street, and pursued his way home to Cambridge.

Now, this was doing the thing very handsomely, and does Mr. Gerry honor, whatever exertion it may have cost him.

There is no mail south of New York to-day. These failures are very tantalizing to the public.

The bells are now summoning a town-meeting for the purpose of considering and disapproving the measures of the General Government in relation to war. General Dearborn gives great offence by mounting a guard at his lodgings, and parading sentinels before the door, which are relieved with as much ceremony as if there was actual war, and a necessity for such a piece of mummery.

JUNE 10, 1812.

I have now the melancholy task to acquaint you with the death of Buckminster. That pure and elevated spirit, that mind so rich in wisdom and knowledge, the eloquent orator, the Christian minister, the ornament of society, is no longer among us. The premature brightness of his morning ray promised a meridian of uncommon splendor and usefulness. By the loss of Mr. Buckminster, at the early age of twenty-eight years, the life of Mr. Channing becomes even more valuable. His family seem to be impressed by this new proof of your kindness, and also by others, which, I believe, he has gratefully acknowledged as having received from you.

I draw great comfort from your cheerful anticipations of good from evil, and hope they will impart it to those who are less believing.

Dr. Eliot came yesterday. He truly thought I might want consolation, knowing how highly we prized Buckminster. He seemed more affected and depressed than from his cheerful temperament I should have expected him to be. The sensibility which this event excites has in a great degree superseded political anxiety.

To Mrs. Eliza S. Quincy.

WASHINGTON, June 9.

MY DEAR WIFE, — I suppose the course of our proceedings here will occasion great alarm in Massachusetts. There prevails a temper next to insanity in Congress. I shall do my duty according to my utmost talent and prudence; but little hope can be expected from exertion. All is prepared and settled in caucus, and neither argument nor passion has any influence.

Mr. Channing left me to-day for Baltimore in a coach and four, with only one gentleman, — a pleasant circumstance, as the thermometer varies from eighty-six to ninety, and the rays of the sun are like those of a furnace. He has been gratified by his journey; but our secret session precluded his attending our debates.

WASHINGTON, 13th June, 1812.

The great event pending in the Senate is in a degree uncertain; but there are ninety-nine chances to a hundred of its adoption. Its passage depends upon intrigue, upon personal and local motives. The fate of the country, so far as it rests on the proposition before the Senate, is in the hands of about five as unprincipled men, politically speaking, as there are in Congress. Should it pass, its publication will cause a great sensation. You must prepare with all your firmness to meet the worst prognostications that agitated minds can invent. Perhaps you may hear the Federalists, and even your husband, condemned by men who know nothing of the state of affairs on the floor of Congress. Undoubtedly the crisis is great; and, could it have been prevented, it would have been.

The men at the helm are determined to keep their grasp on the commercial interests at all hazards. They differ among themselves about the means.

The Southern and Western men, who want war, have seized on favorable circumstances, and are propelling the Government into it headlong. Those among the Democrats, who think that war will secure Madison's re-election, support them; while others among that party, who mean to ruin him, vote for it for the same object. The Federalists, by watching the currents, have well-nigh defeated, and may yet defeat, the project; but the chance looks hourly more hopeless, as great exertions are making by the most violent to whip in those who seem inclined to be contumacious.

WASHINGTON, June 15.

I mourn with you and the public the loss of Buckminster: —

> "He was a pearl too pure on earth to dwell,
> And waste his splendor in this mortal shell."

I cannot write all that I feel, and must dismiss this painful topic. Our business proceeds slowly, but, as I think, assuredly, to its mad end in the Senate. The first shock will be great; but afterwards, I have no doubt, good will result.

JUNE 18, 1812.

The great question of war with England was decided yesterday in the Senate, nineteen to thirteen; and yet, strange as it may appear, a majority of the Senate declare themselves opposed to the measure. The violence of the majority here is absolutely inconceivable. Since it cannot be prevented, do not allow your mind to be agitated by those around you. The memorial and petitions against war are heard with indifference; those in favor, with exultation.* My engagements are such as preclude my only assuring you of my health and devotion.

Yours,   JOSIAH QUINCY.

To Hon. Josiah Quincy.

BOSTON, June 22.

I have received to-day your final account of the decision of the Senate, and consequently the fate of the country, as far as they can implicate it by their measures. The people are stunned, and hardly know what to believe, or to expect next.

Mr. Channing reached home last evening, and called here this morning. He says he has gained health and strength, and requests me to express to you his grateful and lively sense of your unwearied kindness and liberality to him.

I gave you yesterday some political accounts. The sensation among the people is very great. I hope it may not rise to acts of absolute hostility to the Government.

It is thought Governor Strong will not consent to put the drafted militia under General Dearborn; and it is farther publicly avowed by the men, that they will not march under his command.† The ferment

---

* See Appendix IV.
† See Hildreth's "History of the United States," vol. iii. p. 378.

is greater than you probably calculate upon. Personal altercations have taken place, which had nearly proceeded to serious collisions.

Mr. Davis, last evening, seemed very melancholy. I tried to console him with some of your hopes. He allowed them no efficacy. "Where," said he, "can good come from? It is a war on Northern commerce and prosperity; and, whatever else results to the country, to us it must bring ruin and desolation. We have twenty millions of property in England; the sea covered with our ships. All this must be sacrificed; the course of trade changed; the carrying-trade superseded by other neutrals, who will come and take the produce of the Southern States, so that they will be no losers." . . .

I am sad to think what you will come home to, — no more cheerful faces or happy friends; but, if your life is preserved, we have every thing to be grateful for in that one possession.

Ever yours,   Eliza S Quincy.

CHAPTER VI.

THE political excitement and commercial distress caused by the declaration of war with Great Britain continued to increase, and every mind was agitated with solicitude and alarm. At Quincy, the ships in the harbor, especially those apparently of a warlike character, were anxiously watched. Toward evening, on the 29th of August, 1812, a frigate (recognized as the "Constitution," commanded by Captain Hull) came in under full sail, and dropped her anchor beside Rainsford Island, — then the Quarantine Ground. The next morning, a fleet of armed ships appeared off Point Alderton. As they rapidly approached, the "Constitution" was observed to raise her anchor and sails, and go boldly forth to meet the apparent enemy; but, as the frigate passed the leader of the fleet, a friendly recognition was exchanged, instead of the expected broadside. They joined company, and the "Constitution" led the way to Boston. It was the squadron of United-States ships, then commanded by Commodore Rogers, unexpectedly returning from a long cruise.

A few days afterwards, Hull, who had just taken the "Guerrière," came with Decatur to breakfast at Quincy. When this incident was mentioned, Hull said, "I must acknowledge, I participated in the apprehensions of my friends on shore. Thinking myself safe in port, I told my officers to let the men wash their clothes, and get the ship in order to go up to Boston; and, being excessively fatigued, went to my state-room. I was sound asleep, when a lieutenant rushed down, exclaiming, ' Captain, the British are upon us ! — an armed fleet is entering the harbor !' No agreeable intelligence, certainly; for I was wholly unprepared to engage with a superior force. But, determined to sell our lives as dear as I could, I gave orders to clear the decks, weigh anchor, and get ready for immediate action. I confess, I was greatly relieved when I saw the American flag, and recognized Rogers." In speaking of the conflict with the " Guerrière," he said, " I do not mind the day of battle; the excitement carries one through : but the day after is fearful; it is so dreadful to see my men wounded and suffering."

These naval officers formed a striking contrast. Hull was easy and prepossessing in his manners, but looked accustomed to face " the battle and the breeze." Decatur was uncommonly handsome, and remarkable for the delicacy and refinement of his appearance.

In the summer of 1812, Mr. Quincy invited Mr. Adams to dine at Quincy with the Massachusetts Agricultural Society, the Presidency of which he had recently resigned. When the day came, Mr. John Lowell arrived, accompanied by Colonel Pickering, with whom Mr. Adams had differed, when President, concerning an appointment, for which his son-in-law, Colonel Smith, was a candidate, and also on other subjects. Mr. Pickering resigned the office of Secretary of State, and no intercourse had been sustained between them since their parting at Washington. Mr. Quincy, after welcoming Colonel Pickering, thought it expedient to apprise him that President Adams was an expected guest. " When I accepted Mr. Lowell's invitation to accompany him," replied Colonel Pickering, " I did not anticipate meeting Mr. Adams, as I heard he had resigned his office in your society. If it will give Mrs. Quincy or yourself a moment's anxiety, I will go away immediately; but I have no objection to meet Mr. Adams as your guest, and should very much prefer to remain and pass the day here."

President Adams soon after arrived, attended by Colonel Smith. Mr. Quincy met him at the door of his carriage, and said, "On the invitation of Mr. Lowell, Colonel Pickering has come here to dine with the Agricultural Society. He says he shall be happy to meet you, Mr. Adams; and I hope it will not be disagreeable to you to see him." — "As your friend, Mr. Quincy, I am very happy to meet Colonel Pickering." After being received by Mrs. Quincy, Mr. Adams shook hands with his former associate; and they met with courtesy and apparent pleasure.

At the dinner-table, Mrs. Quincy had President Adams on her right hand, and Colonel Pickering on her left; and Colonel Smith was near the upper end of the table, which was surrounded by fourteen guests. They conversed about former times and acquaintances; took wine together; and, after a very agreeable day to all present, they parted, never to meet again in this world.

In the evening, Mrs. Quincy said to Mr. Adams, "I hope, sir, this unexpected meeting has not injured your enjoyment of to-day. It has been very interesting to us and our friends to see you and Colonel Pickering together." — "No, madam," was the reply: "I hope to meet Colonel Pickering in heaven; and, next to heaven, I certainly ought to be willing to meet him here in your house. I have had a very pleasant day; and am glad Colonel Pickering was one of your guests, and has enjoyed it with us."

The following letter from Mrs. Peter illustrates the excitement of this period: —

To Mrs. Quincy.

TUDOR PLACE, GEORGETOWN, D.C.,
July 27, 1812.

MY DEAR FRIEND, — I intended Mr. Quincy should once more have served as a penny-post to us; which you may tell him from me would be a place of distinction at this time, as he might be commissioned by worse persons. I beg you will be ready to attend him here in November, as I cannot again excuse you.

It is delightful to us to meet with those who think and dare talk as we do. I am resolved to express my sentiments till the Sedition Law is put in force; and there is not much danger of that until after the next election. Provided the present party, which Heaven forbid, are re-elected, I believe the first law they pass will be that.

We were much gratified by the respect shown at the meeting of your "Washington Benevolent Society" to the memory of General Washington. It is so seldom that I am gratified in that way in this part of the country, that I feel a great interest in the Eastern States, and think I should be more at home there than here. . . . We have read with great satisfaction an account of your last public meeting in Boston; but I beg you will not think you are the only people who dare say their souls are their own. Here, in our little village, we have dared, in the very face of the President and all the secretaries, to publish the "Federal Republican;" and not only to circulate it here, but to send it by express to Baltimore yesterday morning; first taking care to station a party of veterans of old times there to insure its success. It excited great consternation in the town, and threw every thing into confusion; but we have not heard the final result. The house from which it was issued is strongly guarded, and it is thought this will be a good trial of the strength of parties. The Federalists have slept so long, that I believe the other party thought they would never wake; and, indeed, I was very much of their opinion. But I rejoice to find there is still a little of the blood of seventy-six in our veins, and that it can become warm.

This moment, we have had information that the office in Baltimore had again been attacked last night; and that, at five o'clock this morning, the mob was not quieted. . . . Several lives were lost in the affray last night. But no more of politics. . . .

Your friend,   MARTHA PETER.

By the attack of a mob in Baltimore (as mentioned in the preceding letter) on the office of Alexander C. Hanson, Esq., editor of the "Federal Republican," he was left for dead, General Lingan killed, and several of their friends wounded.

In the midst of such excitement and alarm, Mr. Quincy would no longer consent to the separation from his family which his station in Congress involved. In 1812, he declined to be a candidate for re-election; and went to Washington for the last time in November. Extracts from the letters of Mrs. Quincy are here inserted:—

Hon. Josiah Quincy, City of Washington.

BOSTON, Nov. 23, 1812.

Your letter of the 18th gave me the great satisfaction of hearing of your safe arrival at Washington. I hope the session will prove more animated and agreeable than you expected. The good news you will hear from this part of the country, and that anticipated from others, will place you on high ground. Your prophecies are likely to be fulfilled, and you must enjoy some gratification in the present state of affairs. The gentlemen here are in high spirits, and confidently expect a change, whether Clinton is elected or not.

BOSTON, Dec. 13.

Your account of the intrigues and projects about the next Presidency, and the appointments relative to it, are disgraceful enough. The nature of our Government presents to you, and to men like you, a labor no less than that of Sisyphus, or of Hercules himself in the Augean stable. But you have always been philosopher enough to think life the sphere of exertion, and a virtuous object worth working for, even if the nature of things deny the reward of success to your efforts. Continue to think and act so, and you will attain at least the applause of your own heart, and the respect of the wise and good.

JANUARY 2, 1813.

I have received yours of the 28th, with a correct copy of your speech.* Your friends are delighted with it, and your opponents feel your weight and influence.

Speeches made on the floor of Congress may be sowing the wind; but it is those seeds which are intended by nature to be so disseminated. The whirlwind wafts them to the mountains and the vales, where they germinate and take root for the nourishment of thousands who never had an opportunity of collecting them from their original nursery. Old Massachusetts' hundred hills have, I am sure, borne fruit from some of these seeds; and I do not think you appreciate justly their importance. It is the only way by which information of this kind can reach the great body of the people. Newspaper pages are generally the production of authors without a name; they have no individual responsibility; they may be true, they may be false: but, when a man makes such statements on the floor of Congress, they can no longer be doubted. Your character as a public man, as a private individual, is pledged to the veracity of your declaration, the truth of your testimony. When such expositions are thus brought before the public, they must do good. The effect of such a speech on the House is of the least consideration; but I do not think you do justice to the situation as a *medium* through which much effect can be produced.

You complain of the apathy of some of your constituents. Most men must have the support of hope: without some prospect of success, few will be active. You, I acknowledge, are one of the few. After discouraging views, you generally go to work again with a vigor which cannot be subdued. This is noble and admirable. You must animate men, by your example, never to desist from exertion in a good cause.

---

* Speech on a report relative to relief from penalties incurred by a late importation of British manufactures ("Federal Republican," Georgetown, D.C., Dec. 28, 1812).

JANUARY 31, 1813.

You will think that I deal in superlatives when I say we have had one of the finest sermons from Mr. Channing I ever heard, on the nature of the felicity of a future state, — its progressive, active, improving character. After the views he delineated, the sublime prospects he unfolded, one might almost exclaim, "Into the heaven of heavens he has presumed, an earthly guest, and drawn empyreal air."

Mr. Shaw mentioned your speech in the highest terms, and said it was even more admired and talked of than any of the preceding. Four or five hundred copies have been sold, and they talk of a second edition.* I have read it again, and with you I say, "There is not a sentiment or a sentence which I wish to change or erase. If you are sure of your premises (as I presume you are), the conclusions are irresistible. The newspapers are now republishing it, so that its circulation will be as wide as the Federal press can extend it; and wider too, by your account of the "National Intelligencer's" ungraceful admission of it into its columns. How do you account for their publishing it at all?

BOSTON, Feb. 3.

Your friends are very anxious to know the effect of the news from Russia upon the Administration at Washington. What you say on the subject will be very grateful to them. The British do begin to work our destruction, in this part of the country, by taking all our vessels. But nothing they will do, I fear, will affect the people at the South. They will, for their own sakes, allow neutral vessels, or their own under neutral papers, to take away their products, which is continuing their harvest, while the refusal of licenses takes away every means of Northern enterprise. There are great fears that the rich

---

* Speech on an act to raise an additional military force.

men here and in New York will be tempted to loan money to Government. Your uncle, Mr. Phillips, will stand firm. He told me he had rather sink every dollar he had to the bottom of the sea.

FEBRUARY 4, 1813.

This day is not passed by me without the interesting recollection that it is the anniversary of your birth. May each future year of your life open upon you with the same increase of honor, respect, gratitude, and love, which have marked every preceding one. May your usefulness and happiness be still crowned with the approbation and blessing of Heaven, and the applause of all good men. Our children are very anxious to know how old you are; and some of them look quite distressed and apprehensive at the great age you have attained. I remember when I was as little able to calculate the real value and importance of life as they are; and thought, that, after forty, enjoyment and usefulness must cease, and life itself go out.

May the evening "lustres" of your life be still more distinguished by every good and great quality, and teach those who love you best to confess that you had taught them to give the highest value to the latest of their number.

Mr. James Perkins was here this evening. He was full of the praise of your speech, and said he had distributed copies of it through the country, on his way to Exeter.

FEBRUARY 13.

Our friend Dr. Eliot has been taken very ill suddenly. I sent to inquire about him to-day, and received word that he was not expected to survive many hours. Out of the circle of our own family, I could not have a more affecting loss. He always seemed to take a peculiar interest in you, in your success, — your happiness in every thing concerning you. He has visited me very often this winter, and talked to me confidentially of his views. Last week, he spent an hour here one morning, and mentioned some books he wished me to read: and said, when he went away, "If you want those books before Sunday, send for them; if not, I will bring them next week." I replied, "I will wait, to induce you to come again." I have been expecting him every day, little thinking of the sad intelligence I should hear. I shall never see him again. Perhaps you may be surprised at the degree of sorrow I feel at the thought; but the difference of age, and the affectionate simplicity of his manners and character, seemed to blend a parental and a friendly feeling toward us in a very endearing proportion.

FEBRUARY 14, 1813.

Dr. Eliot died this morning, — his mind perfectly clear, tranquil, and resigned; full of hope and confidence in the religion he had preached and professed. Here, then, we leave our pleasant and venerable friend. We shall no more hear his voice or see his face. We will not look at his grave, but turn our thoughts to those better mansions which are promised to the pure in heart. Judge Davis, who walked home from church with me to-day, could hardly command his voice in speaking of Dr. Eliot; and the clergy of the town and vicinity deeply regret his loss. They are all his juniors, with the exception of Dr. Lothrop; and he was very interesting to them. Your Historical Society has lost one of its most zealous members. Dr. Freeman, Judge Dawes, Mr. Gore, and all his personal friends, deeply feel this event. Dr. Kirkland told me that Mr. M'Kean had written to you immediately on its occurrence. I am pleased he remembered what was due to you on the occasion.

FEBRUARY 18.

Last evening, Colonel Pickering spent two or three hours here. He desired me to thank you for a copy of your speech; and said he admired it for many reasons, particularly for the plain speaking it contained. He was very pleasant and friendly.

Your friends will be highly gratified that you do not vote in favor of the bill about seamen. How the Federalists could allow themselves to be intrigued into a support of it, is very astonishing. This is exactly what Mr. Madison has wanted, — a relief from all responsibility, besides the advantage of the appearance of desiring peace.

Your uncle Mr. Phillips has just been here, very anxious to know what you said. I showed him your letters of the 11th, 12th, and 13th inst. After he had read them, he insisted on taking them to show to Governor Strong, as there were some accounts of affairs which he thought very important should be understood. He promised to use them with discretion, and, according to your decided wishes, not to publish any of your statements. I must have been very peremptory had I detained them.*

BOSTON, March 3, 1813.

I am at a loss whether to date your departure from Washington to-day or to-morrow; but, at any rate, it cannot be many hours now before you are actually on your way home. I see by the papers that an extra session for next May is resolved upon. How joyfully do I realize your emancipation! With what different feelings do I now look forward, assured that you are not only returning, but returning not to depart again!

I now lay down this pen, which has been the medium of so many faithful transcripts of a heart devoted to you; the soother of so many hours of solitude; the talisman, which, in imagination, has transported me to your side. I lay it down as a glass no longer requisite to help our vision of each other, which is now to be perfected face to face.

This period of our lives has not been without its pleasures and advantages, the value of which we may, if we are true to ourselves, continue to realize throughout the remainder. We ought to be

---

* It is probable that they were never returned, as they are not to be found among those of that period.

among the happiest of human beings, and urge our endeavors to become what such high privileges demand. With such feelings let us here close our correspondence, and with such resolutions let us meet. They are those which will bless us together on earth, and increase the happiness of a better world.

Here and for ever your own

ELIZA S. QUINCY.

CHAPTER VII.

THE state of apprehension and alarm which existed throughout the country, especially on the seaboard, during the war with England, is described in the following letters : —

From Mrs. Quincy to Mrs. M. S. Morton.

BOSTON, May 7, 1813.

MY DEAR MOTHER, — . . . We are very unhappy about the state of the country, and feel the effects of the war every day more and more. The distress in this and the more eastern part of the country is very great, owing to the supplies being cut off by the British squadron, and our own crop having been injured last year by unfavorable seasons. I have no doubt that this is the state of things our rulers intend to induce : they seem to wish to ruin the Northern and commercial States.

We have accounts of our army having gone into Canada, and taken York. As soon as this is known and confirmed, I have no doubt the English fleet will attack Baltimore, or one of our seaports. This war is worse, in every respect, than that of the Revolution, which you remember ; for that was a cause on which we could ask the blessing of Heaven : for the success of this, we cannot pray. But let us endeavor to look on the brightest side, and not give way to unavailing regret. What we can neither prevent nor remove, we are not responsible for. The course of Providence will proceed with the same equable progress, whether we are anxious or not. Few of us know what to wish for; and still fewer wish for what we ought, or fear what is really to be apprehended.

Letter from Mrs. Peter.

TUDOR PLACE, GEORGETOWN, D.C.,
July 13, 1813.

MY DEAR MRS. QUINCY, — Accept my thanks for the very eloquent oration of Mr. Quincy before the Washington Benevolent Society. Tell him I have received the thanks of that society for the gorget of Washington which I presented to them, and shall ever feel flattered by the approbation of so respectable a portion of your community. Mr. Quincy's friendship for the giver has caused him to represent her in too favorable a light. The remarks in the "National Intelligencer," on these proceedings in Boston, I thought too contemptible to excite displeasure, and concluded that to have *gorged* the editors was a great triumph. As I hope never to require their assistance or favor, their declaration of having no "attachment to the relics or relatives of Washington" was rather a compliment. At any rate, I should be very sorry that *my* conduct met *their* approbation.

We are all on the alert here to give the British a warm reception. An express arrived on Thursday last, saying they were in the river; and, as the wind was fair, we expected every moment to see their white sheets shivering in the breeze. The drums began to beat, the military to parade; and in a moment all was bustle and alarm. Before night, scarcely a man was to be seen in the streets: they were all posted at Fort Warburton, opposite to Alexandria. The Secretaries of War and of the Navy joined the van: and each new-made officer vied with the other who should put on most finery; expecting, no doubt, by their dazzling appearance, to strike the enemy with dismay.

I am glad Mr. Peter has no fancy for a military life; as I should much regret to have him hold a commission under our present rulers, or draw his sword in so unjust a cause. . . .

I beg you to write to me, whenever your time will admit; for, be assured, we take a sincere interest in all that concerns you. Tell Mr. Quincy, I still flatter myself I shall see him here as a senator, provided the Englishmen do not destroy our city.

Very sincerely yours, MARTHA PETER.

To Mrs. Quincy.

TUDOR PLACE, GEORGETOWN, D.C., Aug. 26, 1814.

MY DEAR FRIEND, — Having often received from you and yours flattering assurances of your regard for us, I have thought that our situation for the last three or four days must be interesting to you.

For some weeks, the citizens have expected a visit from the British, and repeatedly called upon the Secretary of the War Department and the President for protection. The first laughed at what he called their idle fears. The President said he was called on from all quarters for protection; that he could not protect every one; and the District must take care of itself. At length, he consented to abide by General Winder's opinion; and whatever he said was requisite should be provided. About three days before the British came, Armstrong acknowledged that he now believed they would be here. The Cabinet then began to make great exertions, and assured the citizens that they would have so large a force, that it would be impossible for the British to penetrate through them. Knowing our Treasury to be much in want of money, the several banks in the District loaned the Cabinet two hundred thousand dollars for their defence. On Friday last, the troops were all ordered to march, as the enemy were landing, in considerable numbers, forty-five miles from Washington. Unfortunately, we never shut the stable-door till the steed is stolen. The troops marched, but were not numerous enough to go and oblige the British to return to their vessels. They were ordered to encamp sixteen miles from the city, and there wait for re-enforcements ; during which time, the enemy landed, refreshed themselves with the fat of the land, and then proceeded twenty miles to a village called Upper Marlborough, where they staid several days longer to rest. Still our troops did not advance. On Monday, the British began their march. Some of our men had a slight skirmish, but soon retreated; and then our wise generals concluded to continue the retreat of the whole army, that they might be ready when the enemy came. They arrived near Washington on Monday night. The officers and men who had families in town came home to get something to eat; as many said they had not had a morsel for forty-eight hours, and were in no state to fight. Tuesday, they went forth to battle; and our chief, thinking his presence might occasion them great confidence, buckled on his sword, put his holsters on his saddle (pistols in, of course), and set out at five o'clock in the evening to visit the camp, attended by two of his secretaries and several private gentlemen. He returned the same night; begged the inhabitants to be composed; assured them there was no danger, as the enemy was safe at Marlborough; and that, if they had the temerity to advance, they would not proceed far before we should teach them a lesson they had yet to learn. .All this time, Mrs. Madison's horses were ordered to be in readiness, and an express was to be sent off in time for her to escape. Two cannon were placed opposite the Capitol, two at the offices, and two at the President's house.

On Wednesday, our troops received information that the enemy were at Bladensburg; and formed themselves in battle array on the ground between the city and that place. From what I can learn, nothing was ever worse ordered. For an hour before the engagement took place, the General was not to be found. The President was on the ground, who, no doubt, had some little curiosity to see what sort of beings those were who dared to approach his Capitol; but I believe he was soon satisfied, as he fled so swiftly, that he has never been heard of since. The whole Cabinet are off, no one knows where. The citizens vow they will hang Armstrong on the walls of the Capitol, when he returns.

We have been informed that there were from six to eight thousand Americans, one thousand of whom were cavalry; and yet it appears that not more than two or three hundred were engaged. The cavalry never drew a sword; and all the fighting on our side was done by the artillery, the marines, and Barney's men. The engagement lasted perhaps about an hour; when the Americans gave way, and never stopped until they got beyond Georgetown, as they were impressed with the belief that the British would pursue, and put them all to death, before they burned the public buildings; instead of which, the British returned quietly to Bladensburg, ate their dinners, and then came to Washington to begin their work of destruction. It was truly distressing to see our poor men. The day was extremely hot, and the roads ankle-deep in dust. Their officers knew so little of their duty, and were so panic-struck, that they never looked behind to see if they were pursued, but drove them on till several of them fainted; and some have died in consequence.

Although so near the scene of action, we can get no correct account of the losses on either side; some say, one hundred Americans killed, wounded, and missing, and two hundred British. You know we always kill double, although we seldom gain any thing by it.

The British were visited by our citizens under various pretences. Their officers are said to be very elegant men; their men, fine-looking fellows. Several persons who were in the battle say they appeared to approach the mouths of our cannon with as much coolness as if they expected them to be loaded with sand. They are the same men who took Bayonne, and say they have not slept under a roof for seven years.

They announced their entrance into the city on Wednesday night by the flames that ascended from the Navy Yard.* Next they blew up the magazine, and set fire to the Point, where there were a great many cannon. Then the Capitol was seen in flames; and, between eleven and twelve o'clock, the President's House and Treasury Office. They then retired to rest, I suppose; and we saw no new fires that night. Carroll's large tavern took fire from the sparks of the Capitol. The next morning, about ten o'clock, the British set fire to the War Office, saying they did not suppose it to be a public building the night before, and had overlooked it. They were proceeding to burn the Patent Office; when Dr. Thornton saw them, and begged them to spare it, saying they would injure individuals, and the world generally, by the destruction of many valuable models. They then burnt two ropewalks in the city, and, in the evening, set fire to both ends of the long bridge over the Potomac; but, not wishing to destroy the whole, they raised the draws, and the fire did not extend beyond.

The Mayor of Georgetown, and several citizens, went on Thursday to the British commander to say that we did not intend to make resistance (as well they might; for I do not believe there were twenty men in town), and they hoped that our city would be spared. Cockburn replied, that, as our President would not protect us, they would. They said it gave them pain to destroy our property; but, as long as we supported Madison, we must expect it, as their nation was resolved never to make peace with a President who was so much under the influence of Bonaparte; that they had a force on our coast of one hundred and odd thousand men; and that, as we wished for war, they would give us enough of it. This was but the beginning of trouble: they should go from here to Baltimore.

---

* The residence of Mrs. Peter, on the Heights of Georgetown, commanded an extensive view of Washington and the vicinity.

They inquired if we did not mean to displace Madison, and said that our Minister of War must be a fool to think of opposing such regulars as theirs with raw militia. They said some of our men fought well, and kept up a hot fire for a short time; but the general who commanded one wing of the army was a coward, who ran, after the first fire: and this great man, we find on inquiry, was the celebrated Stansbury of Baltimore, who was so conspicuous in the mob. They said they intended to destroy the Foundery and Parrot's ropewalk; but they left Washington on Saturday without ever coming here, after observing to some person, that the citizens of Georgetown were respectable people, and that they should do them no injury. In every instance, they respected private property; and have proved themselves, in this instance, to be a noble enemy. . . .

The public property has been most shamefully neglected. Although it was well known that the object of the British in coming was to burn the public edifices, yet not a chair, desk, or any article, was removed, except the papers. The Mayor of Washington ran off, with the rest of the dignitaries; and yesterday, after the enemy had left the place, the vagabonds were committing all sorts of depredations. It is said that the Capitol and offices may be easily repaired; and, strange to tell, much of the furniture of the Capitol is uninjured, it being in a part of the house which the wind did not set toward.

The British officers went to Gales's office with an intention to burn it; but the neighbors begged them to desist, as all the houses in the block would be destroyed also. Cockburn replied, it was not his wish to injure individuals, and that he would pull it down. After it was destroyed, he observed, "Now Madison and his friend Gales are in the same situation."

27th August, 1814.

After writing thus far, Mr. Peter and myself rode into the city to see the ruins. At the Navy Yard, we were told it was burnt by the orders of the President and Jones. The reasons assigned were, that there were vessels and stores there the British might make use of, and therefore it was best to burn it ourselves. Others say the British, on their arrival, marched directly to the Navy Yard, and set it on fire. It is very difficult to get at the truth with regard to the actions of the present Cabinet. It is said that the bridge over the Potomac would not have been injured but for the conduct of some of our wise gentry, who set fire to the end next the Virginia shore; and the British then remarked, that, as we were so-fond of fires, they would give us a little more, and burnt the end next the city.

I know not who burnt the Navy Yard; but the destruction of public property there is shameful. A great number of timbers that lay in the yard, might, no doubt, have been saved: but the fire began on Wednesday night, and has been burning ever since; and still I see the smoke.

Our Cabinet, or part of them, came to the city last evening. The President was found near Frederictown, and returned with an escort of twenty or thirty horse. The British fleet are opposite Alexandria; and, should they *presume* to come up, I hear we are to give them a *warm* reception. . . .

I fear your patience will be exhausted before you reach the end of this history. With affectionate remembrance to Mr. Quincy and your children,

Sincerely your friend,   MARTHA PETER.

During these years, the whole country was in a continual state of alarm, from the intelligence of conflicts on the Canada frontiers, and of the inroads of the British, especially on the coast of Maine. The battle between the " Chesapeake " and the " Shannon " took place within sight of the high grounds near Boston. British cruisers were often seen from the windows of Mr. Quincy's mansion, near Point Alderton.

In 1814, the vicinity of Boston assumed a military aspect. Troops from Berkshire were quartered in Dorchester, at Neponset Bridge, generally considered the last outpost toward the enemy, who, it was thought, would land on Mr. Quincy's farm. One Sunday, a report came that the British had actually landed at Scituate, and were marching up to Boston. The drums beat to arms; and the elders, who remembered the Revolution, increased the trepidation of their juniors by anecdotes of devastation. These apprehensions were much exaggerated. The extensive flats in Quincy Bay were known to be a sufficient barrier to the landing of an armed force, except at high tide; and it was not probable that an attack on Boston would be made from Scituate. But, when panic prevails among the people, reason is disregarded.

The anxiety Mrs. Quincy underwent is evinced in a letter to her mother: —

QUINCY, Sept. 30, 1814.

"We are much more easy as it respects invasion, and have at present no fears of being obliged to leave our abode here till we remove to Boston. I do not look forward to peace or rest beyond this winter, if the war continues; but we must be thankful for this respite, and try to fill it up with every good feeling, affection, and work that can be crowded into it."

Mrs. Quincy fulfilled these good intentions, and endeavored, during the ensuing winter, to give her family and friends all the pleasure and improvement in her power. An extension of hostilities was anticipated with the return of spring, and anxiety weighed heavily on every mind.

On the morning of the 14th of February, 1815, when the bells began to ring, it was supposed to be an alarm of fire. That peace was the joyful intelligence they proclaimed, was at first doubted; but inquiry soon proved that the announcement was correct. The whole

·town was soon in a tumult of rejoicing. The whole population were abroad, all classes congratulating each other on the happy tidings. Almost every house displayed a flag. Drums beat; cannon fired ; the military were in motion. Sailors in large sleds, each drawn by fifteen horses, — the word " Peace " in capitals on the hat of the foremost man, — greeted every one with loud huzzas. The joy and exultation were in proportion to the previous fear and despondency. It was a day never to be forgotten. The subsequent official celebration, of which Mr. Quincy was the chief director ; a general illumination of all the public, and many of the private, edifices ; and a public ball, — were enjoyed with enthusiasm.

In May, Mrs. Quincy returned to her favorite residence, contrasting with gratitude the tranquillity of the present with the anxiety of the past.

CHAPTER VIII.

In 1813, Mrs. Quincy formed a friendship, which continued through life, with Judge Vanderkemp of Trenton, New York, who came to Quincy on a visit to President Adams, with whom he had been acquainted in Holland.

Francis Adrian Vanderkemp was born at Campen, in the Netherlands, in 1752. After attaining eminence as a military officer, a scholar, and a theologian, his patriotic efforts in the support of the liberties of his country rendered him obnoxious to the ruling powers; and, in 1788, he emigrated to the United States of America with his family. He brought letters from Lafayette to General Washington, visited him at Mount Vernon, and was then advised to establish himself among his countrymen in New York. He resided at Trenton, Oneida County, in that State; and was employed by Governor De-Witt Clinton to translate twenty-five volumes folio of ancient Dutch records, preserved in the archives of New York. The German descent of Mrs. Quincy interested him; and he requested an account of her family, to send to Professor Kemper of Leyden, with whom he was in correspondence.*

On the 13th of September, 1815, the three daughters of Josiah Quincy of Braintree, — Mrs. Storer, Mrs. Guild, and Mrs. Packard, —

---

* See Appendix V.

each accompanied by representatives of their children and families; with his intimate friends President and Mrs. Adams, and Dr. Tufts of Weymouth, — met at the mansion formerly his residence. His portrait by Copley, which hung in the dining-room, above the head of his grandson, the heir of his estate, appeared, to the company assembled round the table, to regard them with an animated expression of benignity; and the interest of the occasion was appreciated by all present.

On the 22d of September, 1815, a classmate of Mr. Quincy, Paul Trapier, Esq., of Charleston, S. C., and a gay party of their contemporaries, dined with him. On the next day, the memorable gale of September, 1815, occurred. The force of the tempest was severely felt at Quincy. Trees were uprooted, vessels stranded on the shore, and buildings injured. The ocean resembled a boiling caldron, from which steam was escaping. The wind converted the surface of the waves into spray, which, drifting for many miles over the country, blasted vegetation and extinguished verdure during that autumn.

The previous spring, Mr. Quincy had relinquished the temporary residence of his family on Oliver Street, Fort Hill, and taken on lease the house of Gorham Parsons, Esq., in Summer Street. In November they took possession of this mansion, then one of the most eligible and well finished in Boston; and, during five successive winters, they participated in all that was valuable and interesting in the society of that period. The friendships formed during these years with John Pickering, Nathaniel Bowditch, and Washington Allston, were highly appreciated and valued through life. At this time, Mrs. Quincy also acquired another gifted friend in Eloise R. Payne. In force and beauty of diction, passages in her writings recall those of De Staël; and it is to be regretted that they have not been included in the literature of America.

The Rev. Henry Colman of Hingham was at this time a frequent visitor at the residence of Mr. Quincy, which was the constant resort of their numerous circle of relations, friends, and acquaintances. In September, 1816, Hon. N. Vandyke and Hon. James M. Broome, senators, of Delaware, with whom Mr. Quincy had been intimate at Washington, passed some days at Quincy. A party invited to meet them at dinner comprised William Sullivan, J. Callender, William Tudor, F. C. Gray, Commodore M'Donough, and other guests. In the autumn, Mrs. Quincy had the pleasure of visiting her friends Mr. and Mrs. S. Higginson and Miss Storrow at Bolton; and at Harvard she was again welcomed by Mr. Bromfield.

During the visit of President Monroe to Boston, in 1817, he dined at Quincy, on the 7th of July, with President Adams; who, in the afternoon, accompanied him to visit Mr. and Mrs. Quincy, attended by Commodore Perry and General Swift, and followed by the rest of the company, — Governor Brooks and his aids, Lieutenant-Governor Phillips, H. G. Otis, James Lloyd, President Kirkland, Commodore Bainbridge, General Sumner, Henry Colman, and many others. It was very interesting to see Mr. Adams with one of his successors in the Presidency of the United States; and, when Mr. Monroe departed, he bade him adieu with great sensibility. The weather was fine, the country beautiful. Mr. Monroe walked over the farm, and expressed an interest in agricultural improvements.

Another incident of that season was the return of John Quincy Adams, after an absence of eight years at the Russian and British courts. The day after his arrival, he came with his father to visit Mrs. Quincy. The happiness of this re-union Mr. Adams immediately wished to share with his friends. His son participated in these sentiments, and conversed with animation on the politics of Europe. From this time, through successive years, the privilege of his society and conversation was frequently enjoyed.

In September, 1818, Mrs. Quincy, accompanied by her niece Sophia Morton, and her eldest daughters, visited her sister Margaret, who, in 1815, had married D. R. Bogert, Esq., of Beekman, Dutchess

County, New York. Travelling in her carriage, after leaving Hartford, Mrs. Quincy followed the course of the beautiful Farmington River toward Litchfield. Her friend Mr. Wolcott, then Governor of Connecticut, on hearing of her arrival, urged her to leave the hotel for his mansion. His hospitality was declined, with a promise to breakfast with him the next morning. Meeting Mrs. Quincy at the door of his residence, he led her with great emotion into his library to the portrait of his wife, her early and much-loved friend. This interview was mutually interesting.

After traversing rude scenery, and crossing the Fishkill Mountain, the travellers descended into the fertile valleys of Dutchess County; and, on the fifth day of their journey, were welcomed by Mr. and Mrs. Bogert, who resided in an antique Dutch farm-house surrounded by fine trees and cultivated fields, the declivity of the neighboring mountain covered by a forest composed of large trees clear of underbrush.

Mrs. Morton, at the age of seventy-nine, had come from New York to visit Mrs. Bogert and meet Mrs. Quincy and her children. After she had arrived at Beekman, the names of Flagler and Brill among the inhabitants of the town, and of the local divisions of the county, sounded familiar; returning to her memory like a long-forgotten dream. On inquiry, she learned that, by the contingencies of life, she had accidentally returned, after an absence of sixty-nine years, to the place where her parents had resided, on the Livingston Patent, and from which they had removed to New Brunswick in 1749. Some aged descendants of the neighbors of Mr. Kemper were found, who remembered him and his family. One of them, Mr. Brill, who recollected seeing Mrs. Morton as a child riding with her father on horseback, guided her to the place where their house had stood, and showed her the spring from which they used to drink.

The country which she had left a wilderness, in which no language but the German was spoken or understood, was now covered with highly cultivated farms, excellent houses and roads, with churches, schools, and all the accommodations of civilized life. Other changes were yet more remarkable. Born in the dominions of a German prince, and having left the Livingston Patent a subject of the King of Great Britain, she returned there with her children and grandchildren, citizens of the United States of America. Mrs. Quincy enjoyed the days passed in Dutchess County. The habits, manners, and superstitions of the inhabitants, inherited from their Dutch ancestors, since delineated by Irving, were strongly contrasted with those of New England, and gave a novel and romantic character to the beautiful valleys extending among picturesque highlands tinged with autumnal hues. Her nephew, G. L. Morton, met the party at Fishkill; and, under his guidance, they passed twelve miles down the Hudson in a row-boat to West Point. There they were received by relatives among the Cadets, who escorted them to the ruins of Fort Putnam, and at midnight to the steamboat, which then, a novelty on the Hudson, touched at West Point on its voyage of twenty-four hours from Albany to New York. After remaining a week in that city, the guest of General Morton and his family (who resided in Broadway, in a spacious mansion at the corner of Leonard Street), Mrs. Quincy pursued the same route along the banks of the Hudson, and over a mountain-road, since described by Cooper in "The Spy;" and, on her return home from Beekman, visited Mr. Wadsworth's seat on Talcot Mountain.

On the 12th of September, two days before Mrs. Quincy left home to visit her sister, Mr. and Mrs. Adams and their family, Mr. and Mrs. J. Q. Adams, and many other friends, formed a gay and animated party at her house. On her return, Mrs. Adams was dangerously ill; and her death, on the 28th of October, was deeply felt by all around her. Every one had lost a most valuable friend; many, a benefactress.

After this severe deprivation, Mr. Adams sought the society of

Mrs. Quincy and her family yet more frequently. In her cultivated mind, and knowledge of public men and political affairs, he found the companionship of an associate united toward him with a filial affection.

In the autumn of 1818, Colonel Trumbull exhibited in Faneuil Hall his painting of the "Declaration of Independence," and urged Mr. Adams to visit it. This request, at first positively refused, was granted on condition that Mrs. Quincy would accompany him. Accordingly, on the 5th of November, Mr. Adams drove into Boston, and, calling for his friend, proceeded to Faneuil Hall, where many persons had assembled in the expectation of this visit. He approved the picture; and, pointing to the door next the chair of Hancock, said, "There, that is the door out of which Washington rushed when I first alluded to him as the man best qualified for Commander-in-Chief of the American Army." Mr. Adams passed the rest of the day at Mr. Quincy's residence in Summer Street, and dined with a party of friends invited to meet him.

In 1820, Mr. and Mrs. Quincy removed from Summer Street; Mr. Phillips having requested his nephew to accept of the house No. 1, Hamilton Place, for his residence. In November they took possession of this pleasant abode, which commanded a view of the malls and Common; and invited Mrs. Morton, then in her eighty-second year, to reside with them.

One morning the succeeding summer, when Mr. Adams walked from his residence to bring Mrs. Quincy the "Life of Lord Russell," the conversation turned on the American Revolution; and he was asked why so little was said of Mr. Dickenson, the author of "The Farmer's Letters," in the subsequent history of that period. Mr. Adams replied, "Dickenson became discouraged, and, at first, opposed the Declaration of Independence. He gave us a great deal of trouble. His wife and mother were Quakers; and they constantly told him that he was ruining himself and his country by the measures he was advocating. If I had had such a wife and mother, I should have been very unhappy; for I would have died rather than not have pursued the course I did. One day, in Congress, Mifflin, a relation of Mr. Dickenson, had a dispute with him. Dickenson said in the course of a speech, 'that, in a team of many horses, it was requisite to rein in the most forward and violent, and encourage the slow and cautious.' Mifflin rose, and said, 'Not so, Mr. President: you had better knock the dull and lazy horses on the head, and put them out of the team; and it will go on much better without them, even if the number is diminished.' The sentiments of the ladies of Dickenson's family were probably the cause of his indecision. He was a man of immense fortune, and founded a college in Pennsylvania." *

John Halkett, Esq., of England, a man of uncommon intelligence and cultivation, brought letters to Mr. Quincy in 1822. Mr. Halkett married a sister of the Earl of Selkirk; and was, for many years, a leading member of the Hudson-Bay Company. A promontory of America, on the shore of the Arctic Ocean, is named, in his honor, Cape Halkett. He travelled extensively in the United States and in the British Provinces; and, on his return, coasted along the shores of Lakes Huron and Superior, and crossed the wilderness to Hudson's Bay, whence he embarked for Europe.†

Chancellor Kent, John Quincy Adams, Judge Prescott, Mr. Webster, and other eminent men, dined with Mr. Quincy in August, 1823. The conversation turned on literary subjects; and the character and merits of Lord Bacon and Pope, and other celebrated authors, were discussed. In the summer of 1824, Mrs. Quincy made a tour to Niagara in her carriage, with two of her daughters; visiting Mr. and Mrs. Bogert

---

* The notices of conversations given in these pages are extracted from the diary of the Editor.

† Mr. Halkett published a work on the Indians of North America, London, 1825; and in return for the likenesses of Osage chiefs, drawn for him by the Editor, presented her with two original drawings in water-color by J. Varley, which were highly prized by Mrs. Quincy.

at Ballston, and Mr. and Mrs. Wadsworth at Geneseo. Her eldest son
met her at Buffalo to attend her to view the grand scenery around
the Falls of Niagara and to Canada.

In August, Mr. Quincy, as Mayor of Boston, had the privilege of
receiving Lafayette, and passing with him through the assembled
population. The American standard was raised for the first time
on the cupola of the State House, a royal salute was fired, and all
the bells in the city were rung. After a long progress through the
city, when the barouche paused opposite Hamilton Place, a dense
crowd extended in all directions; and the populace, climbing up on
the wheels of the carriage, obstructed its passage; until, his attendants forcing their way onwards, Lafayette passed before the children
of the public schools assembled on the Common, and arrived at the
mansion provided for his residence by the city authorities, at the corner of Park and Beacon Streets.

Lafayette asserted that the inhabitants of Boston who greeted
him on his arrival, compared with the crowds of European cities,
appeared to him like a picked population out of the whole human
race. No accident marred a day remembered with pleasure by every
individual who enjoyed it.

In the evening, Lafayette came to Mr. Quincy's residence with his
suite. His reception by Mrs. Quincy was gracefully characteristic.
Her words cannot now be recalled; but her friend Ellis Gray Loring,
after the lapse of thirty years, said he accounted it one of the felici-
ties of his life that he witnessed this interview, and heard her elegant
and appropriate welcome to Lafayette.

The scene on Commencement Day at Cambridge was also most
interesting. The church was crowded with the statesmen, politicians,
and literati of the country, and the beauty and fashion of the vicinity;
and Lafayette, standing in the centre, was hailed by reiterated shouts
of applause and welcome. The same tributes were repeated the next
day at the Phi-Beta celebration. The services, the sufferings, the

return, of Lafayette, illustrated by the eloquence of Everett, deeply affected the audience; and the enthusiasm of all present reached the culminating point.

During the whole of Lafayette's visit to Boston, public celebrations and private parties engaged every day and evening. Among the numerous foreigners and visitors from all parts of the Union were many eminent personages, whose presence gave variety and additional interest to the entertainments given in honor of Lafayette, who seemed to enjoy every moment; manifesting in his conversation and deportment characteristic tact, and presence of mind. One evening, at a party, when the conversation turned on the war of the Revolution, Mrs. Quincy said, "The American cockade was black and white; was it not, General?"—"Yes, madam," replied Lafayette: "it was black at first; but, when the French army came over and joined *us*, we added the white in compliment to *them*."

On Sunday, Aug. 29, Lafayette, accompanied by his son G. W. Lafayette and M. Levasseur, visited Mr. and Mrs. Quincy at their country residence. Among their family assembled to welcome him were Mrs. Morton, eighty-five, and Mrs. Storer, eighty-eight years of age. To them the interview was very affecting; for his presence recalled the scenes and the trials of the war of the Revolution. He dined with President Adams; and, at his residence, received the inhabitants of the vicinity in the afternoon.

After Lafayette returned to New York, he wrote to Mr. Quincy, on the 20th of September, to introduce Colonel Huger: in speaking of whom, during his visit, he had said, "I never saw Huger but for ten minutes; but, for ten years, his countenance was never absent from my mind." On the 2d of October, a party, consisting chiefly of members of the Common Council of Boston, dined with Mr. Quincy; and at the name of Colonel Huger, associated with that of Lafayette, every countenance expressed animated interest. Mrs. Quincy, on receiving him, said, "We all are under obligations to you, Colonel

Huger, for your attempt to rescue Lafayette from Olmutz."—"I only did my duty, madam," was his reply. "I considered myself the representative of the young men of America, and acted accordingly. If I have deserved their approbation, it is a full reward."

Colonel Huger, in 1824, was about fifty-one years of age, — manly and polished in his personal appearance and address, his countenance and manner indicative of self-command. His conversation marked him as a man of honor and integrity, extensive information, and knowledge of the world; evincing singular modesty respecting his own claims and opinions, and great deference for those of others. In contradicting a statement in the newspapers, that he was in early life acquainted with Lafayette in America, he said, "When Lafayette first arrived on the coast of Carolina, accompanied by the Baron de Kalb and several officers, they were pursued by British cruisers, and were very anxious to land. My father then resided on North Island; and two of his negroes, being out in a boat late in the evening, were boarded by another boat containing Lafayette and the Baron de Kalb, and were induced to pilot them to my father's house. As the depredations of British vessels caused great alarm, doors and windows were barred against these officers; but, when they succeeded in making themselves known, they were hospitably received, and the next day attended to Charleston, on their way to join the American Army. I was at that time a child of three years old, and have no recollection of these circumstances except from hearing them often mentioned by my family."

The members of the City Government present gave Colonel Huger a pressing invitation to the public dinner of the Mechanic Association; which he declined, to their great regret.

The next day, Colonel Huger came to Quincy alone, and passed the day. After dinner, when the family were seated round the table, and no one else present, he described, at the request of Mrs. Quincy, his attempt to liberate Lafayette.

"In 1794," said Colonel Huger, "Dr. Bollman was employed by the friends of Lafayette to endeavor to attempt his rescue. After a long search, he discovered that some prisoners of State were at Olmutz. He went there; introduced himself to the surgeon of the place as a physician travelling for professional improvement; inquired, as if from idle curiosity, if there were prisoners in the castle; and expressed no surprise when told that Lafayette was one of them. To avoid suspicion, he took several journeys from Olmutz, as if his design was to see the country. One day, hearing Lafayette was ill, he expressed a wish to lend him, for his amusement, some French books he had with him. The surgeon obtained permission from the commander of the garrison, provided the book was submitted to his inspection. A book was then given to Lafayette, in which Bollman had written words in the margin, which, put together, made the following sentence: 'If you will peruse this book with as much care as that lent Madame de —— at Magdeburg, you will receive equal satisfaction.' The lady referred to had received intelligence from her friends, written in lemon-juice on the blank leaves of a book. Lafayette understood the allusion, held the book to the fire, obtained information of the plans of Bollman, and, after some delay to avoid suspicion, returned it with his thanks. Bollman discerned the words 'Mettez le au feu' in the margin; and, obeying the direction, found that he was understood and answered. Lafayette could only say, that a promise had been given that he should drive every day for his health, and arranged a signal by which he would identify himself. The mode of effecting his escape was left to the ingenuity and courage of Bollman. He formed a plan, but needed an assistant. Taking leave of the surgeon as if he did not mean to return, he decided to go to Vienna. There he met me in a hotel, and communicated his design; and, as the representative of my countrymen, I felt it my duty to assist him to the utmost of my power. We hired a post-chaise and a servant, with two saddle-horses, apparently to vary our mode of travelling. Arrived at Olmutz (two hundred and fifty miles from Vienna), we sent our servant with the post-chaise on to Hoff, a town twenty-five miles distant, on the road we wished to take. After dinner, we mounted our horses as if to follow our carriage; but, in reality, to meet Lafayette. It was the hour he usually was allowed to drive. Our pistols were not loaded, and we took no other arms; as we had no intention to commit murder, even to effect our purpose.

"Near the walls of the castle, we saw in an open carriage a gentleman in a blue surtout, with an officer beside him, and an armed soldier mounted behind. Our attention was fixed upon him; and, as we approached, he gave the signal agreed on, — raising his hat, and wiping his forehead with his handkerchief. That moment, and my sensations on receiving this assurance that he was Lafayette, will never be effaced from my remembrance. We bowed slightly as we passed, in token of recognition, and rode on toward the castle; but soon turned, and followed the carriage until it reached the open country. Lafayette alighted, under pretence of walking for exercise; and drew the officer, whose arm he held, toward a wood. At some distance from the high road, he laid his hand on the hilt of the officer's sword; and, the instant he drew it, we rode up to his assistance. The officer took the alarm, called to the soldier waiting with the carriage to go for aid to the citadel, and grasped his sword with both hands. He received a slight cut in the struggle that ensued, and Lafayette's dress was stained with his blood. One of our horses, frightened at the sun gleaming on the sword, ran away. Lafayette, whom the officer succeeded in throwing down and seizing by the collar, exclaimed, 'Il m'étrangle.' We instantly rescued him, and threw the officer to the ground, who made a furious resistance. Lafayette was now free. I called to him to mount my horse, and said, 'Go to Hoff.' He rode slowly away, but soon returned to say that he could not think of leaving us in such a situation, and to ask if he could give us assistance. We replied in the negative, entreating him to depart, as the soldier had alarmed the garrison, and not a moment was to be lost. With great reluctance, he rode away. We then released the officer, and he ran to the castle. I succeeded in catching Bollman's horse, and mounted him. He got on behind me, and we attempted to follow Lafayette; but the horse not being accustomed to carry two persons, as the one had been which circumstances had obliged us to give Lafayette, soon reared, and threw Bollman. Finding it impossible to proceed in this manner, I insisted on Bollman's taking the horse to follow Lafayette. At first, he refused; but, on my urging that he could be of no use to me, and, from my ignorance of the German language, was best qualified to assist Lafayette, he very unwillingly departed.

"Left alone, with the knowledge that the whole country would be roused to pursue us, my situation was indeed rather forlorn. However, I determined to endeavor to escape, and directed my course toward a convent on a hill before me. I had a high road to cross. A loaded wagon was passing; and the wagoner paused, and looked at me suspiciously: but, as I slackened my pace and showed no alarm, he suffered me to proceed. I heard voices behind me, as I ascended the hill; and, finding it impossible to reach the convent, tried hard to gain a wood which grew half way down the hill. I succeeded just as my pursuers came up, and hid behind one of the largest trees: intending to throw the foremost horseman to the ground, by springing suddenly upon him; then to mount his horse, and endeavor to escape. At that moment, I felt as if I would give the world to be again on horseback. But my pursuers were too numerous: I was instantly surrounded, and carried to the prison of Olmutz."

With characteristic delicacy, Colonel Huger passed slightly over the sufferings he underwent; and, when closely questioned, only said, "For ten days I was treated with the utmost rigor; but afterwards had not much to complain of, except the loss of my liberty." From

• another source, his friends learned that " he was chained to the floor, in a small arched dungeon about six feet by eight, without light, and with only bread and water for food; and once in six hours, by day and by night, the guard entered, and with a lamp examined each brick in his cell and each link in his chain. His inquiries concerning Lafayette and Bollman received no answer; and his earnest request to be permitted to send to his mother in America merely the words, ' I am alive,' signed with his name, received a rude refusal." *

In continuing his narrative, Colonel Huger said, " When I was removed from the first dungeon, I discovered that Bollman was confined in the next room. We soon contrived to hold communication, and then persuaded our jailer to let us meet. From him I learned that Lafayette was also a prisoner. He misunderstood my direction to go to Hoff. As I spoke in English, he thought I merely said, ' Go off.' If I had spoken in French, and said, ' Allez à Hoff,' he probably would have understood me, and known how to direct his course. This slight mistake defeated our whole plan. Lafayette took another road; and, as his clothes were stained with blood, was arrested at the village of Jägersdorff, as a suspicious-looking person. There he was recognized, and sent back to his prison. Bollman, not finding Lafayette at Hoff, lingered about the frontier, in the hope of meeting him, till the next day, when he was also arrested, and sent to the citadel. Thus we were all three brought separately to Olmutz, and imprisoned without any knowledge of each other's fate.

" When the trial of Bollman and myself came on, a young man, employed as our interpreter, became deeply interested in our fate, and made our story known to Count Metrowsky, a nobleman living near Olmutz; who, touched by the account given of our enterprise, gave our young friend the use of his purse to any amount. He succeeded so well in bribing the judges and officers of the tribunal,

---

* Outlines of the Life of General Lafayette, by Professor Ticknor, 1825, p. 40.

that, after a confinement of eight months, we were only sentenced to a fortnight's imprisonment, and then released.

"We set off instantly for Hamburg, and had just cleared the Austrian frontier when an order arrived from Vienna for a new trial, which would probably have eventuated in a sentence of death or perpetual imprisonment. I embarked for America, and owe to Count Metrowsky and my young German friend all the happiness I have since enjoyed in my native country.

"Soon after my return, I married the daughter of T. Pinckney, Esq.; and bought an estate on the high hills of Santee, a hundred miles from Charleston. My wife, though very young, accustomed to gay society, and even to the splendor of a court, — her father having been minister to England, — cheerfully acceded to my plan, and found her happiness in the society of her family. There I have since resided; engaged in the care of my farm, and in educating a family of eleven children. These are the duties in which I have been engaged.

"Lafayette remained in the prison of Olmutz three years after the release of Bollman and myself. He was not told of our liberation, but informed that we had been taken, and sentenced to execution. For months he daily expected, every time the guard turned out, to see us shot under his windows. I never saw him again, till, after an interval of thirty years, we met the other day in New York. Determined that our first interview should be without witnesses, I repaired to his lodgings early in the morning, and was admitted before he left his apartment."

This narrative, when heard from the lips of an actor in the scenes described, excited intense interest. Every countenance expressed alternate hope, fear, anxiety, and joy.

In the evening, Mr. and Mrs. Quincy accompanied Colonel Huger to visit Mr. Adams, and then to Boston; and parted from him with

great regret, as there seemed little probability that he would ever
return to New England. In these feelings he evidently participated;
and his last words were, "Adieu for this visit! I never take a last
farewell. We shall meet again."

In 1825, the publication of a Memoir of Josiah Quincy, jun., of
1775, by his son, and the second visit of General Lafayette, were
sources of great interest to Mrs. Quincy. In June, Boston was again
crowded with distinguished foreigners and strangers from all parts of
the United States. Many of them were present at a reception Mrs.
Quincy gave, on the evening of the 16th of June, for Lafayette.

The morning of the 17th of June was bright and cloudless. The
sound of cannon recalled the day of the conflict, when, from the
precincts of Boston, the inhabitants looked forth with emotions far
different from those which in 1825 animated the multitudes throng-
ing the streets of a city established in prosperity and peace. In
Charlestown, at the base of the northern declivity of Bunker Hill, a
platform was erected for the orator and the chief personages, with
seats on each side for the ladies; those for the survivors of the battle of June 17, 1775; for Lafayette and the soldiers of the Revolution;
and, for the rest of the vast audience, rose tier above tier toward
and upon the summit of the hill. Many passages in the oration
of Mr. Webster were highly applauded, and the whole scene was
impressive.

In the evening, the houses of Mr. Webster and Mr. Thorndike in
Summer Street, thrown into one for the occasion, were crowded
with a brilliant assembly; and the scenes of the morning formed
the general theme. Mrs. Quincy, in conversation with Mr. Webster,
thanked him for the tribute he had paid to Josiah Quincy, jun.,
of 1775, in his oration. "There is no need of my help in that
cause," was his reply. "The memoir Mr. Quincy has published
will be an enduring monument. It is one of the most interesting
books I ever read, and brings me nearer than any other to the

spirit which caused the American Revolution. Josiah Quincy, jun., was a noble character. I love him because he loved the law. How zealous he was in seeking out the celebrated lawyers, in copying their reports, in studying the laws of the different Colonies! There are no such men now-a-days. Who keeps such journals?" Mrs. Quincy replied, "I hope you do, Mr. Webster."—"No: I do not. The times are far different. The members of Congress do not write such letters now." Referring to the scene of the morning, he then said, "I never desire to see again such an awful sight as so many thousand human faces all turned toward me. It was, indeed, a sea of faces I beheld at that moment." Dr. Warren informed Mrs. Quincy that he had put the Memoir of Josiah Quincy, jun., into the corner-stone of the Bunker-Hill Monument, among the memorials of the Revolution.

On the morning of the 18th of June, Mr. Quincy accompanied Lafayette to visit John Adams. A few moments after they departed, Colonel Pickering was announced at Hamilton Place. Being complimented on his good health and unchanged appearance, he told a story about some intercepted letters, written, during the Revolution, by a Frenchman, in cipher, which were thought to contain dangerous information; but all they said of him was, "As for Mr. Pickering, he is *toujours le même*." He said, "The resolutions passed in the town of Salem, on the Boston Port Bill, mentioned in Mr. Webster's oration yesterday, were written by me. At that time, every man of liberal education, except my brother and myself, were Tories; which made it the more remarkable that such resolutions should be passed. Josiah Quincy, jun., passed the night before he sailed for England, in September, 1774, at my father's house in Salem. I was not much acquainted with Mr. Quincy in college, although we were classmates: but I shall never forget his oration on Patriotism, at Commencement; and the tone of voice with which he said, 'A patriot,' and then proceeded to give the character of one."

Colonel Putnam then came, and conversed with Colonel Pickering on the times of the Revolution. He said, "I was in the American Army on the 17th of June, 1775: but my father ordered me to stay in Cambridge to guard Mrs. Inman, a Tory lady, who had placed herself under his protection; and therefore I could not go with the troops to Charlestown."

The last evening of Lafayette's visit was passed at the Boston Theatre, which was appropriately decorated. Every tribute to him was received with great applause; and on this, his last public appearance, he was followed with the same enthusiasm which greeted his entrance into Boston.

CHAPTER IX.

————

In August, 1825, the Duke Bernard of Saxe-Weimar, accompanied by Captain Ryk of the "Pallas," and Mr. Van Tromp, a descendant of the famous admiral of that name, dined at Quincy with a large party. The Duke of Saxe-Weimar was commanding in appearance, being above six feet in height; intelligent, and unassuming in conversation and manners. Unprepared for the progress of civilization in the United States, he expected to meet Indians in the streets of Boston, and was surprised that ladies should venture five hundred miles into the interior to visit Niagara. He had loaded the "Pallas" with books, articles of clothing, &c., as if he was going to a country where the accommodations of life were not to be easily obtained. Captain Ryk had raised himself by his abilities to a high rank in the navy, and subsequently commanded the Dutch fleet as admiral. He spoke the modern languages, was acquainted with their literature, and was animated in conversation. Van Tromp was studying naval tactics under Captain Ryk. Mr. Adams, when he was introduced, raised his hand above his head, and exclaimed, "Hurrah for Van Tromp!"

In the autumn, Count Charles Vidua of Turin, the son of the prime minister of the King of Sardinia, brought letters from Lafayette, to whom he had been introduced by Humboldt. He had travelled extensively in Europe, Africa, and Asia; and was remarkable for his accomplishments and acquirements, and for an insatiable thirst for knowledge. Mr. Adams said he was a profound thinker, and that he had proposed questions to him about the American Revolution, which no other man had ever asked. A few years after Count Vidua visited the United States, he died in the East Indies. Mr. Adams enjoyed the society of these eminent foreigners, and often came to compare opinions with his friends; but the infirmities of age pressed upon him. On the 30th of September, supported by his son John Quincy Adams, who, as President of the United States, had come to visit him, he entered the mansion, long his favorite resort, for the last time. Afterwards he often drove down the avenue, and conversed with Mrs. Quincy and her family, but without leaving his carriage. On the 1st of October, Mr. J. Q. Adams, Judge Davis, Gilbert Stuart the artist, and Mr. I. P. Davis, dinéd with Mr. Quincy. Stuart's attention was attracted by an engraving from West's painting of the "Battle of the Boyne;" and he said, "I was studying with West when he was at work on that picture; and I had to lie on the floor for hours, dressed in armor, for him to paint me, in the foreground of the picture, as the Duke of Schomberg. At last, West said, 'Are you dead, Stuart?'—'Only half, sir,' was my reply: and my answer was true; for the stiffness of the armor almost deprived me of sensation. Then I had to sit for hours, on a horse belonging to King George, to represent King William. After the painting was finished, an Irishman came into West's room, and said, looking at the picture, 'You have the battle-ground there correct enough; but where is the monument? I was in Ireland the other day, and saw it.' He expected to see the memorial of a battle in a representation of its commencement."

At the dinner-table, Mrs. Quincy referred to the happy idea of naming the frigate, which was to carry Lafayette to France, the "Brandywine."*—"Yes," said Mr. Adams: "I believe that gratified

---

* Lafayette was wounded at the battle of the Brandywine, Sept. 11, 1777,—the action in which he first served in the American Army.—*Sparks: Washington's Writings*, vol. v. p. 455.

him very much. The vessel was on the stocks in the Navy Yard at Washington. Commodore Tingey, the superintendent, came to tell me that she would soon be launched, and that they called her the 'Susquehannah.' I said nothing, but asked if she could be ready for sea in six weeks. He replied, 'No: I do not think it possible.' I then told him to inform the Navy Commissioners that the frigate must be ready by the 1st of September, as I intended to send General Lafayette to France in her. Soon after, Tingey came again to inform me that the ship was to be launched the next day. I said, 'I choose to be launched in her,' determined that she should have the name I had selected. Accordingly, when all was ready, and a man, with a bottle fastened to a string, asked me for her name, and I said, 'The Brandywine,' amazement was depicted in every countenance, as it was expected that she was to be called the 'Susquehannah.' One of the lieutenants said to me, 'You intend, sir, to man the ship quickly, I presume. You will find no difficulty: the sailors will think it is grog.' But, when I mentioned my design, the young man sprang into the air, and exclaimed, 'How delighted Lafayette will be! And my father will be delighted too; for he was in that battle.' On the 17th of June I wrote to Lafayette, expressing my regret that I could not be with him on Bunker Hill, and told him I could prove we had been thinking of him at Washington; and then mentioned the name of the frigate, and her destination. His reply was expressive of high gratification."

Mr. Adams then spoke of Lafayette in the most exalted terms, and gave a sketch of his life and his whole political course, which he said had no parallel in history. "Madame Lafayette," continued Mr. Adams, "was a remarkably fine woman. When I was a boy, at school, near Paris, I remember her coming to see me and some other American children. A son of Silas Deane was one of my schoolfellows. I never saw him again till last autumn; when I recognized him on board a steamboat, and introduced him to Lafayette, who said, 'Do you and Deane agree?' I said, 'Yes.'—'That's more than your fathers did before you,' replied the General. Silas Deane," continued Mr. Adams, "was a man of fine talents ; but, like General Arnold, he was not true to his country. After he was dismissed from the service of the United States, he went to England ; lived for a long time on Lord Sheffield's patronage ; and wrote a book, which did more to widen the breach between England and America, and produce unpleasant feelings between the two countries, than any work that had been published. Finally, he determined to return to America ; but, in a fit of remorse and despair, committed suicide before the vessel left the Thames. His character and fate affected those of his son, who has lived in obscurity."

The parting address of Mr. Adams to Lafayette was then mentioned by Mrs. Quincy ; and he said, "Yes : when I bade Lafayette farewell at the President's House at Washington, and he turned from me to depart, his deep emotion, my own, and the excitement of the multitude around us,—all in tears,—presented a scene I never saw equalled. The effect Mrs. Siddons produced on a crowded audience, at the close of a highly wrought tragedy, approached nearest to it ; but this was an event in real life."

In the evening, Mr. Adams noticed the revolving light in Boston Harbor, and said, "There is no evidence of the civilization of a country more striking than the light-houses on its coast. When I see one in the evening, I am reminded of the light Columbus saw the night he discovered the New World, — one of the most interesting moments on the records of history. What must have been his sensations at that instant! He had been sailing and sailing westward ; hope was almost extinct ; when suddenly there was a light, — there was the New World he sought. His enterprise was crowned with success. What a moment for him and for the destinies of the human race ! If I was the owner of this house, the view of that light-house would be worth a thousand dollars a year to me."

During the succeeding months, it was evident that the eventful life of John Adams was rapidly approximating to its close. The following letter of introduction was given by him to Josiah Quincy, jun., who was prevented from extending his tour beyond Washington; and it therefore remained in his possession: —

To Thomas Jefferson, Ex-President of the United States, Monticello.

QUINCY, Jan. 14, 1826.

MY DEAR SIR, — Permit me to introduce to your acquaintance a young lawyer by the name of Josiah Quincy, with the title of Colonel; being aid to our Governor. The name of Colonel Quincy, I believe, has never been extinct for nearly two hundred years. He is a son of our excellent Mayor of the city of Boston, and possesses a character unstained and irreproachable. I applaud his ambition to visit Monticello and its great inhabitant; and, while I have my hand in, I cannot cease without giving you some account of the state of my mind. I am certainly very near the end of my life. . I am very far from trifling with the idea of death, which is a great and solemn event; but I contemplate it without terror or dismay, — *aut transit, aut finit.* If *finit,* which I cannot believe and do not believe, there is then an end of all: but I shall never know it; and why should I dread it? — which I do not. If *transit,* I shall ever be under the same constitution and administration of government in the universe; and I am not afraid to trust and confide in it.

I am, as ever, your friend,   JOHN ADAMS.

In the winter and spring of 1826, Mr. and Mrs. Quincy frequently visited Mr. Adams; and in June, before they returned to their summer residence, he often drove down the avenue to ascertain if they had not arrived. On Friday, the 30th of June, Mrs. Quincy visited Mr. Adams, with her mother Mrs. Morton, and two of her daughters.

He conversed about the railroad (the first in America) then constructing to carry the granite for the Bunker-Hill Monument from Quincy to the Neponset; said he wished he could see it finished; and added, "What wonderful improvements those will see in this country, who live fifty years hence! But I am thankful I have seen those which have taken place during the last fifty." He then spoke of the approaching celebration of the 4th of July, and of the oration Mr. Quincy, as Mayor of Boston, was to deliver in the Old South, on the fiftieth anniversary of that day; said he wished he had strength to go and hear him; and took an affectionate leave of his friends. After they had left the room, he expressed his intention to return their visit the next day. Accordingly, before eight o'clock on the morning of Saturday the 1st of July, in opposition to the entreaties of his family, he was lifted into his carriage by his absolute commands; and, attended by one of his grandsons, once more reached the door of Mr. Quincy's mansion, conversed with his friends as they stood round his carriage, and again said, "Farewell." The effort was too great for his failing strength. After his return, he rapidly declined. Mrs. Quincy was not aware of the change, as, on Monday the 3d of July, she went to Boston to be present at the celebration of the Fourth.

When addressing the multitude assembled in the Old South, on the 4th of July, 1826, the tribute paid by Mr. Quincy to "the Patriarch of American Independence, of all New England's worthies the sole survivor," was highly applauded. "The sounds of a nation's joy were heard by that ancient citizen of Boston; and, when the shades of his evening sky reflected the splendors of his meridian brightness," he joined the great company of the departed.

The death of John Adams on this anniversary seemed an event too remarkable to occur; and the intelligence was at first received with incredulity. On the 5th of July, the event was announced by minute-guns from the Common, the tolling of bells, and the flag

of the United States at half-mast. The one on the flagstaff on the
site of the Liberty Tree, in Washington Street, was especially observed by Mrs. Quincy and her children, as they left Boston amid
these tokens of respect. The sorrow for the removal of a friend, so
long their affectionate associate, was mingled with admiration and
gratitude for so appropriate a termination of his career.

On the 7th of July, a numerous assembly attended the obsequies
of John Adams in his native village, "where his latter days went
down the vale of years."

The excitement of the public, occasioned by the death of John
Adams, was renewed and deepened on the 9th of July, when intelli-
gence arrived that Thomas Jefferson had also died on the fiftieth
anniversary of the Fourth, at half-past twelve o'clock, while the
Declaration of Independence was being read, at Charlottesville, near
Monticello.*

The Declaration of Independence was adopted by Congress on
the 4th of July, 1776, between the hours of twelve and one o'clock,
and publicly proclaimed at five in the afternoon. Thus Mr. Jefferson
died fifty years after its adoption; Mr. Adams, fifty years after its
promulgation.

John Quincy Adams soon arrived from Washington, and passed
Sunday evening, the 17th of July, at Mr. Quincy's house. The
feeling which the recent event had excited at first made his friends
hesitate to dwell on the subject; but he afterwards spoke of his
father as he would have done of any historical character to whom
he held no immediate relation.

The calculation of Mr. Bowditch was mentioned, that the chance
that two of the signers of the Declaration of Independence in 1776

---

* Louisa Smith, the niece and adopted daughter of Mrs. Abigail Adams, who attended Mr.
Adams on that day, informed the Editor, that the last words he distinctly spoke was the name,
"Thomas Jefferson." The rest of the sentence he uttered was so inarticulate, that she could not
catch the meaning. This occurred at one o'clock, — a few moments after Mr. Jefferson had died.

should survive half a century, and die on the 4th of July, was only one in twelve hundred millions. "Yes," said Mr. Adams: "that two men who had been associates in signing that instrument, and who had been rivals for the Presidency of the United States, should renew their friendship, and die on that anniversary, are coincidences unparalleled in the history of the world. Providence seems to have distinguished the American Revolution from all others, in the fate of the principal actors. Take the French Revolution, and the Revolution of 1648 in England: the chief persons concerned all perished in them, or did not long survive. Cromwell, to be sure, died a natural death; but his ashes were soon taken up, and scattered to the winds: while the chief men of our Revolution, and all the signers of the Declaration of Independence, died in peace. John Adams and Thomas Jefferson were the last survivors; and we have seen them living to the extreme of old age, and dying under every circumstance of comfort and alleviation which this world can give."

Mrs. Quincy mentioned Mr. Gwinnett, one of the signers of the Declaration, who was killed in a duel. "Yes," replied Mr. Adams; "but he was from Georgia. A duel is a natural death for a Georgian. Silas Deane, who was a traitor to the American cause, died a violent death; and Arnold lived a violent life: but all the patriotic men of the Revolution were rewarded with peace, — many with long life.

"I remember," continued Mr. Adams, "the day the news of the Declaration of Independence was received in Boston, — the excitement it occasioned; and hearing it read from the balcony of the Town House in King Street. I was then living with my mother in Boston. In the afternoon, I was ill, and was not allowed to go out to see the rejoicings on the Common, — which I thought as great a misfortune as could befall me."

Faneuil Hall, on the 2d of August, was appropriately and richly draped in mourning; and the marble bust of Mr. Adams appeared in high relief above the head of the orator. His portrait, and that of Mr. Jefferson, — both by the pencil of Stuart, — were placed on the side-galleries, opposite to each other.

The coincidences of their death, the union of their eulogy, were rendered yet more remarkable by the fact, that the President of the United States, who then stood on the platform, was the son of Mr. Adams, whom Mr. Jefferson had superseded in that station.

The address by Mr. Webster was eloquent, and appropriate to the characters and events which it commemorated.

After this time, John Quincy Adams sought yet more frequently the society of the friends who participated in his attachment to the memory of his parents, and could appreciate his intellectual acquisitions. As far as his public station permitted, he replaced to them the affectionate associate they had lost in his father. From the turmoil of political life, he delighted to return to the scenes of his childhood, and to revert to his early days. "I remember," said Mr. Adams, "living in the house where I was born, at the foot of Penn's Hill. The day after the battle of Lexington, men came, and took the pewter spoons out of our kitchen to melt them up into bullets. On the day of the battle of Bunker Hill, I heard the cannon, and, with my mother, saw the smoke of Charlestown, from Penn's Hill; and I recollect her distress on receiving intelligence of the death of Warren. During the siege of Boston, I used to go up on that hill every evening to see the shells thrown by the American and British forces; which, at night, had the brilliancy of fire-works. There is no part of the country where there are so few changes. Whenever I drive over Penn's Hill, I see squirrels and wrens running and flying about, whose ancestors' nests I took many a time when I was a boy. A wren's nest was then a great prize to me. There are always nine eggs in a wren's nest, neither more nor less, — always nine. This was known as long ago as the time of Shakspeare. He was an accurate observer of nature; and he makes one of his characters say, 'The youngest wren of nine.' My mother made me learn by heart, when I was a boy, Spence's translation of 'The Choice of Hercules,' by Prodicus; to which I alluded, in my farewell address to Lafayette, as 'the fairest fable of antiquity.'"

He then recited from Plutarch the lines, inscribed on one of the Hermæ, Cimon was permitted to erect as a memorial of his victories : —

> "Let him who, born in distant days,
> Beholds these monuments of praise, —
> These forms that Valor's glory save, —
> And sees how Athens crowns the brave,
> For honor feel the patriot-sigh,
> And for his country learn to die."

The volume was brought, and Mr. Adams read the lines and the following passage : "Though Cimon's name does not appear in any of these inscriptions, yet his contemporaries considered them as the highest pitch of honor; for neither Themistocles nor Miltiades was honored with any thing of that kind. Nay, when the latter asked only for a crown of olive, Lachares, of the ward of Decelea, stood up in the midst of the assembly, and spoke against it in terms that were not candid indeed, but agreeable to the people. He said, 'Miltiades, when you shall fight the Barbarians, and conquer, *alone*, then ask to have honors paid *to you alone.*'"*

"This transaction," continued Mr. Adams, "strikingly illustrates the free spirit and character of the Athenians. Langhorne's 'Plutarch' and Smith's 'Thucydides' I consider the best translations of the ancient writers, in the English language."

When inquiries were made relative to the invasion of the dominions of the Emperor Alexander by Bonaparte during his residence at St. Petersburg, he replied, "Although I was in Russia at the time Moscow was burnt, I never could discover precisely who was

---

* Langhorne's "Plutarch," vol. iii. p. 281.

the cause of that measure. Rostopchin, the Governor of Moscow, was said to have been the person; but he denied it, and the emperor denied having ordered it. They would not have liked to acknowledge being obliged to resort to such a measure for defence. But I believe, that, if Moscow had not been burnt, Bonaparte would have established himself there, and the emperor would have been forced to make a peace with him. If the Russian Government had acknowledged that they caused the fire, they would have been obliged to indemnify the sufferers. Alexander was very generous to them; but still there were many persons who could not be indemnified for their losses. When the French Army was advancing, the Russians were employed for weeks in packing up and carrying away the valuable paintings and ornaments of the Hermitage. The Palace, so called, is not larger than the houses of the nobility usually are in Russia; but, from the style in which it was decorated by the Empress Catherine, it is unequalled in elegance and splendor. It is situated in the midst of the city; and, there being no room for a garden, the empress caused one to be made on its roof, and connected it with the Winter Palace, which extends half a mile on the banks of the Neva, and which is very superb, from the immense size of its halls. One of them, called the Marble Hall, has its walls entirely formed of porphyry; but it was always gloomy. The Emperor Alexander sometimes gave audience in it; and, when it was used in the evening, they would put fifty thousand candles into it, and yet it was dimly lighted. Some one expressed surprise that it was not lighter with so many candles in it. Caulaincourt, the French minister, replied, ' Put the sun into it, and it would not light it.'

" The Empress Catherine had her throne placed in the Marble Hall, and used to give audience there. I never saw Alexander on the throne. He was a man who cared little about thrones; and was one of the most complete republicans, in character and manners, I have ever known. He used to walk the streets of St. Petersburg every day, and stop and talk to any one he met. He was extremely popular, and I do not believe he was carried off by treachery. They employ a quicker process in that case, and he would have died in less time. It is astonishing to observe the coolness with which they talk of assassinating an emperor in Russia, or of applying what they call the constitutional remedy. A nation will bear a despotism for a great length of time ; but, as soon as a man becomes a tyrant, they will get rid of him. The only thing to be regretted is, that they sometimes lose their best men, as well as their worst, in this way. Alexander, during the whole of the war with Bonaparte, exposed himself as much as any of his officers. At the close of that war, he was undoubtedly one of the first generals in Europe. Moreau was killed at his side by a cannon-ball from the walls of Dresden." Mrs. Quincy said, " Moreau's was a hard fate." — " It was so," replied Mr. Adams ; " but I do not think he deserved pity. He was fighting against his country, which no man can ever be justified in doing. A man, if he disapproves a government or a war, may remain quiet and neutral ; but nothing should ever induce him to take up arms *against his country.* I saw Moreau's funeral at St. Petersburg, which was attended with great pomp. His aid Rappertelle, in reply to some expressions of condolence from me on the loss of his general, raised his eyes to heaven, and said, ' Would to God it had been me !' He returned to the army ; and a few weeks after, standing beside the Emperor Alexander, he met precisely the same fate as Moreau, — being killed by a cannon-ball."

Mr. Adams then continued to give minute and valuable information relative to the characters and the relationships of the royal families of Europe.

CHAPTER X.

In 1828, Mrs. Quincy was deprived of a friend, who, from mutual affectionate attachment, deserves a distinguished place in any memorial of herself. Edward Dowse, the son of Jonathan Dowse, Esq., was born at Charlestown, Massachusetts, in 1756. His mother was Margaret, the daughter of Robert Temple of Ten Hills, and sister of Sir John Temple. Without the advantage of a college education, his attainments in literature and in the higher branches of the mathematics were such as are seldom the result of that privilege. In 1792, Mr. Dowse married Sarah, the daughter of William Phillips of Boston, and the sister of Mrs. Abigail Quincy. Being engaged in commerce, he purchased, in 1793, two ships for the trade then opening with China, and sailed for Canton, where he freighted both vessels for the Ostend market. With the one he commanded himself, he made a successful voyage; but his brother Robert Dowse, the captain of the other ship, died at Batavia. His successor in command deviated from the orders he had received; and, instead of following Mr. Dowse to Ostend, brought the vessel to Boston. At the earnest request of Mrs. Dowse and her friends, her nephew Josiah Quincy, then only twenty-two years of age, took possession of the ship; sold part of the cargo, according to the advice of experienced merchants; and stored the residue until the arrival of Mr. Dowse, who entirely approved of the measures he had taken. The plans of Mr. Dowse for this enterprise having been thus defeated, he retired from mercantile pursuits. The widow of his friend Major S. Shaw, the twin-sister of his wife, became a resident in his family; and both ladies received his devoted care and attention. In 1800, he purchased an estate in the town of Dedham, in a commanding situation on the banks of Charles River; and, in 1804, erected a spacious mansion. There he continued to reside, engaged in all the hospitalities and charities of life, in the embellishment of his estate, and in the resources conferred by literature. After a critical investigation of the doctrines of various sects, he rested in those views of Christianity which are denominated Unitarian.

In politics, Mr. Dowse was long a decided Republican, or Democrat, — then synonymous terms. President Monroe, when he visited Massachusetts in 1817, was invited to his mansion at Dedham, and passed there the night preceding his public entrance into Boston. Elected representative in Congress from the county of Norfolk in 1819, a residence at Washington, and a wider and nearer view of the measures of the Administration, changed the opinions which Mr. Dowse had previously held regarding the principles advocated by Mr. Quincy and other leading Federalists. Extracts from his letters to his wife will illustrate his character: —

To Mrs. Dowse, Dedham, Massachusetts.

City of Washington, D.C., Dec. 23, 1819.

There is a learned Jew here, very skilful in teaching Hebrew. With General Smyth of Virginia (just such a book-worm as myself) and several others, I am going to become his scholar. It would divert you to see our school; gray-headed disciples in spectacles poring over lexicons and digging Hebrew roots, and the ruler of the synagogue a young man. It is curious to observe on what different motives and principles men will concur in doing the same thing. I am firmly persuaded, notwithstanding the errors and interpolations which, in the course of thirty-five centuries, have crept into the Hebrew writings, that the mission of Moses was from God. I learn Hebrew with the wish to confirm this opinion. But my friend Smyth, who is openly a Deist, learns Hebrew for a purpose directly opposite, — to detect Moses as an impostor. His prepossessions are so strong, that nothing, I fear, can alter them.

JANUARY 8, 1820.

I am on one of the committees, and have no leisure left, unless I forego the debates in the House, where are displayed such powers, such eloquence, as at least rivals the British Parliament. I confess (and it shows the power of prejudice to beguile the understanding) that I have never properly appreciated our friend Quincy. He is here spoken of with admiration, and his last letter to me on the Missouri question delights all his friends. In political wisdom on this question, he is inferior to no one. Such men as he ought to be in public life.

There is here a great assemblage of talent on the floor of Congress, — some who might emulate the Athenian orator, whose " resistless eloquence wielded at will that fierce democratie." To-morow comes on the great question of the Missouri Territory, the people of which are sufficiently numerous to become a State, and claim to be admitted as such ; and they also claim the right of holding slaves. The question will be productive of much zeal, not to say animosity, on both sides.

I wish you could be present sometimes, and hear John Randolph's wit. It is the most delicate, and, at the same time, the keenest. This is the place to see human nature in great deformity.

JANUARY 26.

Yesterday began a sort of skirmishing on the Missouri business. This preparatory manœuvring will, to-day, probably lead on the shock of battle. The question is undoubtedly of immense importance. On one side, the passions, as well as the present and apparent interests, of the Southern people, are deeply engaged; and, to my sorrow, I perceive that they have drawn over some of our Yankees. The cause of humanity, religion, and sound policy, are the motives, I firmly believe, which influence the other.

FEBRUARY 2, 1820.

From many passages in my letters, you must have perceived that this Missouri question lay upon my mind with a weight almost insupportable. Accordingly, a few days ago, I came to a determination to speak upon it; and yesterday I delivered the speech which I enclose to you. As soon as I had taken my seat this morning, several gentlemen came up, among them Mr. Reid of Georgia, and said many flattering things. As soon as he was gone, Mr. Wood of New York — one of the most learned men in Congress, and with whom I agree on all points — said, " I am afraid, Mr. Dowse, they will make you vain; so many, even on the opposite side, come to bestow praises on your speech."

FEBRUARY 5.

Missouri, Missouri, engages all attention. Scarcely ever was so great a question agitated before a human tribunal. A host of talents is brought into the field. In the Senate, things have gone against us deplorably, owing to the defection of our Yankees: For slavery in Missouri, twenty-seven; against it, sixteen. I am rejoiced that Otis is on our side. The leading members of the Senate are now spectators in our House, where they find themselves surpassed, I suspect, not only in numbers, but in eloquence. I wish Quincy was here to stem the torrent.

That modern Demosthenes, Clay, takes the floor on Monday. In Randolph I have been much disappointed. All he has said on this subject is mere frivolity and small wit. But we have good men of great minds and acquirements on our side. A speech by Hemphill of Pennsylvania affected my delighted imagination like the charms of poetry.

FEBRUARY 11, 1820.

To-day I have enjoyed the feast of reason. Sergeant of Pennsylvania, in favor of restriction, displayed great eloquence.

In a letter I wrote to Mr. Forrest (one of the Pennsylvania delegation), I requested him to tell Hemphill and Sergeant that I thanked them from the bottom of my heart, and fancied myself hearing from the throne of the Eternal, "Servants of God, well done! Well have you fought."

I shall never regret having come to Washington; because it has given me an opportunity to exert my best efforts, however feeble, to prevent the extension of slavery in our country.

FEBRUARY 15.

Monroe will undoubtedly be on the side of the slaveholding States. They would turn him out of the Presidency if he should swerve from what they think is their interest: I mean, they would not elect him for the next four years. Wood in our House, and Rufus King in the Senate, have made great speeches. King lashed severely those who deserted our colors, and went over to the slave side.

This great debate still goes on with unabated zeal and new splendors of oratory; and, I am happy to add, hitherto with suitable deference and gentlemanly demeanor on both sides. The slaveholders, however, put on the boldest front, and talk big about civil war and separation. I myself apprehend that no such consequences would result from the restriction.

FEBRUARY 22.

Young Plummer of New Hampshire has made an excellent speech. When I see such young men, I am proud of my Yankee countrymen. He gave the mighty Clay the severest whipping he has had yet. He ought to be continued in Congress many years. The Southern people keep their public men in, and derive great advantage from the experience they attain in parliamentary business. We in New England change our members of Congress too often.

The great question is drawing to a conclusion. Our House has refused the amendment of the Senate. Their joining Maine and Missouri together has given us anti-slavites great disgust.

Clay and I have become quite sociable, notwithstanding our opposition about Missouri. We board near each other, and frequently walk home together.

MARCH 3, 1820.

At length, the Missouri question is disposed of. The Senate proposed a compromise, which, after strenuous exertions on both sides, was at length carried. I opposed it as long as I could, but am now satisfied *it was the best that could be done.*

Slavery is allowed of as far as thirty-six and a half degrees of latitude. Some people think the Missourians themselves will interdict slavery from their new State. It would be their present glory and permanent happiness if they should do so. I feel most wofully mortified and cast down at the result of our Missouri Bill. Four of our side staid out at the final taking of the question; and four more went over, and joined the slaveholders, which operated as equivalent to eight against us. The whole counted as twelve against us, who ought to have been for us. Whether this proceeded from weakness or treachery, I will not pretend to say. People talk pretty much as if this had been brought about by sly, underhand, Executive influence. I do not pretend to judge, or to form any opinion about it; but, if there were strong reasons to think so, Monroe ought to be turned out the next Presidency. I consider our nation now as disgraced in the eyes of the civilized nations of the earth. We had it in our power to stop the progress of slavery, and *we chose to let it go on.*

I am disgusted with the paragraph in the "Patriot:" it is a project which our Republicans have got up to gratify their own dereliction of principle, and to try to make the public believe that the Missouri question was a party business, in order to get the Federalists into power again.

April 21, 1820.

We are commencing on the new Tariff Bill, the design of which is to protect our own manufactures. I am convinced of its utility, and feel almost as much interest in it as in the Missouri question; but I fear we shall lose this as we did that, and by the same means, — the yielding temper of the Yankees.

I am glad Mr. Lloyd wrote to you. He is an excellent man, and an able one. I wish, with all my heart, he and Quincy were again on this floor. They are competent to the business of Congress. Legislation is a science, and a difficult one too, to be acquired, like all others, by study and practice.

Mr. Dowse resigned his seat in Congress; when he returned home, and left public life. During his later years, he enjoyed the sympathy and friendship of Horace Mann, then a rising lawyer in the town of Dedham; who, in 1825, paid the following tribute to his character: —

" No one could enjoy the society of Mr. Dowse without having his ideas of the compass of attainable excellence enhanced and multiplied. The faculties of his mind would, by themselves, have been conspicuous, had they not been outshone by the qualities of his heart. With him, not honesty, probity, and integrity only, but kindness, generosity, charity, and all the kindred virtues, were duties of perfect obligation. His conversation was furnished from a mind rich in the treasures of knowledge. His studies were various and comprehensive; but they did not result alone in the enlargement of intellect or the improvement of taste, but all tended, through these, to a higher and nobler object, — the object of rendering others happy. Hence that urbanity and condescension which so signally characterized his deportment abroad, and taught the countenance of all who knew him to assume involuntarily the expression of pleasure at his approach; and that man must have been deeply imbued with the spirit of avarice, who, in enjoying his hospitalities, could have coveted the means from which they flowed, rather than the manner of their bestowment. We believe there never was a man who had a higher appreciation of moral excellence, or who was more intensely moved at the recital of an act of generosity or forgiveness. The chords of his sensibility vibrated to the slightest touch; and a stranger would have regarded the keenness of his sympathies at the sight of suffering as a misfortune, until he had witnessed the liveliness of his joy in relieving it. The expression may strike as singular, — we choose it because it is descriptive, — that, in the wide dispensation of his bounties, he was literally furtive and clandestine. Not only, like the good Samaritan, did he bind up the wounds of those whom he accidentally found by the wayside; but, as the common air rushes to fill up a vacuity, he sought for objects of relief wherever affliction was to be consoled or the wants of poverty supplied: and yet, through all this godlike diffusion of benevolence, the injunction of Scripture was strictly obeyed, and the right hand was unknowing of the beneficence of the left. That he might sometimes bestow injudiciously, is only to say that sometimes his generosity triumphed over his judgment, — a triumph we must surely forgive; for, in that contest, it is seldom the victor. When the tendrils of affection spring forth so luxuriantly, they will sometimes fasten upon unworthy objects.

"Mr. Dowse was, in the most comprehensive sense of the word, a Christian: not a *periodical* Christian, at morning or evening, or at church, merely, but at all times and under all circumstances; and evinced the deep sincerity of his faith by the habitual practices of his life; furnishing daily and beautiful illustrations, how much more efficacious are the lessons of the exemplary than the disputations of the polemical."

CHAPTER XI.

AFTER having been elected Mayor of Boston five successive years, Mr. Quincy took final leave of that office on the 3d of January, 1829; and, on the 15th, was chosen President of Harvard University. The acceptance of a station involving such great responsibilities was at first regarded with hesitation by Mrs. Quincy. To relinquish both her favorite abodes, especially her home at Quincy, and remove her family, including her mother Mrs. Morton, then ninety years of age, to a new residence, appeared an arduous enterprise; but when the claims of that ancient seminary, in which she had long taken a great interest, were urged by her friend Dr. Bowditch, then a leading member of the corporation, she consented that Mr. Quincy should accept the appointment. Once determined, her arrangements were prompt and judicious. The estate at Quincy became the summer residence of her eldest son; and in May, 1829, her family was removed to the President's house, which had been repaired and arranged under her direction.

The inauguration of Mr. Quincy, on the 2d of June, was justly characterized as a day of enthusiasm. Surrounded by troops of friends, and received by the officers and students of the University with every testimony of pleasure and welcome, the crowded levee and the brilliant illumination of the evening closed a day of high gratification.

The following letter from Dr. Channing was written at this time : —

To Mrs. Quincy, Cambridge.

Boston, June 2, 1829.

My dear Friend, — I grieve that I am prevented by illness from being at Cambridge to-day; but my heart is with you. I know that *one* will not be missed in such a crowd as will surround you. Still, I should be happy to express by my presence my interest in the occasion, my affectionate respect for Mr. Quincy, and my earnest desire for his happiness and usefulness in the new relations he is about to sustain. I feel that you and yours are to be carried by this event a little farther from me; but I trust a union subsists between us which nothing can dissolve.

Very respectfully and affectionately yours,

W. E. Channing.

Mrs. Craigie (in whose mansion, in 1795, Mrs. Quincy had been received as Miss Morton) and Mr. and Mrs. William Wells, long her valued friends, were among the first who greeted her in her new residence. The hospitalities of Cambridge were cordially reciprocated; and, during the first four years of Mr. Quincy's administration, the President's house was thrown open one evening in the week, in the winter season, to the officers and students of the college, and to the general society of the town and vicinity. During sixteen years, Mrs. Quincy was only once, on any public occasion, prevented by illness from receiving her friends. .

The appointment of Judge Story as Dane Professor of Law, and his consequent removal to Cambridge, in 1829, established a permanent friendship with him and with Mrs. Story. The varied information and colloquial power for which Judge Story was distinguished were highly appreciated. In his evening visits, he often described his experience at the bar, or the great luminaries of the law with whom he corresponded or associated.

At this period, Mrs. Quincy had the pleasure of hearing the celebrated poem entitled "Curiosity" spoken by her friend Charles Sprague, before the Phi Beta Society of Harvard in 1829; and also his Centennial Ode on the 17th of September, 1830, when Mr. Quincy delivered an oration on the two hundredth anniversary of the settlement of Boston, — an occasion to her of high gratification.

In October, 1830, Dr. Holbrook of Milton passed the day with Mr. and Mrs. Quincy, and gave an account of his residence in Cambridge during the siege of Boston in 1775, when he was attached to the medical staff of the American Army. "The President's house was given to the commissary of the army," said Dr. Holbrook; "and I was quartered at the house of Mr. Phips, in the neighborhood. The colleges were much injured by the garrison. The rooms in Harvard Hall, except the one then used as a library, were filled with barrels of salt beef, brought by the country people for the army. One day, during the siege of Boston, a shell thrown by the British from Copp's Hill struck the ground in the square near the President's house. The fuze was yet burning; and a soldier went and stamped it out, at the risk of his life."

Dr. Holbrook regarded with interest the portrait, by Copley, of Josiah Quincy of Braintree; and said, "How proud my old friend would be to see all that I do at this day, and his grandson, whom I remember at his house as a schoolboy, at the head of the University! A few weeks before the death of Colonel Quincy, in conversation with me, he declaimed against the Society of the Cincinnati, with as much vehemence as if he had been speaking in a legislative assembly. He thought it an aristocratic institution, unsuitable to this country."

In 1831, Mrs. Quincy visted Mr. and Mrs. Daniel Wadsworth in Hartford and at Monte Video, Mr. Silliman and Mrs. Salisbury and their families at New Haven, and those of Mrs. Dana and Mr. Pome-roy at Middletown; and enjoyed the society of these favorite friends. The health of her mother, Mrs. Maria Sophia Morton, remained unimpaired until September, 1832. Having passed twelve years in the family of Mr. Quincy, she departed, after a short illness, on the 22d of September, 1832; and it was a remarkable incident, that in closing, in the President's house at Cambridge, a life of ninety-three years commenced on the banks of the Rhine, she was attended, not only by her daughter and her grand-children, but also by her sister Mrs. Jackson (Susan Kemper). Preserving her mind and life-long habits of industry and order, she read her Bible, her German hymn-book, and other religious works; kept a slight diary of daily occurrences; and, though a strict Calvinist, willingly attended the Unitarian church in Cambridge until a fortnight previous to her death.

In January, 1833, Mrs. Quincy was summoned to Dedham by the decease of Mrs. Shaw, at the age of seventy-seven; who, by the excellence and benevolence of her character, commanded the respect of all around her; and, by her affection for her nephew and his family, deserved and received every filial attention. The portrait of Major Shaw, in her apartment, recalled to Mrs. Quincy scenes of her early life in New York, during his engagement to Miss Bowman; and it seemed a singular coincidence, that, in this distant time and place, she should stand toward his widow in the relation of an adopted child.

The Marquis Charles Torrigiani, an intelligent and accomplished young Italian, — who, after his return to Florence, attempted to improve the lower classes in his native city by the establishment of monitorial schools, — brought letters to Mr. Quincy in August. He was accompanied by James Thal of St. Petersburg, who was remarkable for his skill in music and his knowledge of languages; and, by his attainments in mathematics, he had become a corre-spondent of Dr. Bowditch.

Among the visitors of these years were Spurzheim, Audubon, Dr. Julius of Berlin, Washington Irving, and many other eminent men.

On the 4th of September, 1833, the two hundredth anniversary of the landing of Edmund Quincy of England was celebrated, on the estate he purchased of the Indians, by a family meeting of his descendants. Mrs. S. R. Miller, the mother of Mrs. J. Quincy, jun., who then passed the summer months with her daughter at Quincy, took great interest in the occasion, and contributed by her taste to the decoration of the old mansion, and the reception of a party of guests. A parchment, prepared for the purpose, was signed by Mr. and Mrs. Quincy and Mrs. Miller and the rest of the family, as a memorial of the day, to be transmitted to the future representatives of the name.

The course of the Revolution in France, in which Lafayette was engaged, in 1830, was watched by his friends in Cambridge with great interest. The captain of an American ship, who was in France at that time, and who was acquainted with Lafayette, said the General told him, that, the night the Revolution began in Paris, his family, knowing he was regarded as its leader, insisted on his leaving his own mansion. He went to the house of one of his daughters; and, before morning, the royal troops took possession of the lower story. Lafayette saw them from the staircase; but they were unconscious that he was thus accidentally their prisoner. He kept quiet; and, the next morning, a conflict took place in the street before the house. The royalists were defeated, and left the premises; and he was again at liberty.

Lafayette had continued to write every year to Mr. Quincy until this period, when his engagements obliged him to employ a secretary; but he always signed his letters, and sent a message to Mrs. Quincy with his own hand. Her daughter Mrs. B. D. Greene (Margaret M. Quincy), with Mr. Greene, visited La Grange in 1833, and were received with great affection by Lafayette, who spoke with enthusiasm of his visit to America, remembering the most trivial circumstances.

On the 29th of March, 1834, Lafayette cut from a Paris newspaper his last communication to the Chamber of Deputies, and enclosed it to Mr. Quincy with a note written by his secretary. It was received by his friends on the 21st of May, 1834, — the day on which his eventful life was terminated.

After an interval of thirty years, Mrs. Quincy received the following note from her early friend, Mrs. Browne : —

Mrs. E. S. Quincy.

FRANKFORT, KENTUCKY, June 24, 1835.

MY DEAR FRIEND, — My son Mason Browne having determined on a journey eastward, I cannot deny myself the pleasure of introducing him to you and Mr. Quincy. I have forfeited your correspondence by a long silence ; but, I trust, not your friendship.

Though my personal appearance has, of course, much changed since we parted, yet time has kindly spared " whate'er of mental grace was ever mine." And as a proof that, whatever poets say to the contrary, Fancy *does* sometimes live to be old, I spend some most delightful moments in reperusing the letters which passed between " the knot " at Miss Ledyard's school, when you were Amelia Beaumont ; and I, Harriet Villiers : and, while thus employed, how many youthful visions rise before me ! I do not think the present mode of education enjoys all the advantages over that of which we were the subjects, which might be expected from the time and money expended on its attainment. It appears to me like the faint outline of a picture sketched by the hand of a master ; but which, wanting due proportions of light and shade, leaves a large part of the canvas to offend the eye. Revisiting New York after an absence of twelve years, I had heard so much of improvements in education, that I expected to find a generation of De Staëls and Sévignés ; but, with the exception of a decided improvement in orthography and penmanship, nothing was altered for the better. The style of conversation was as uninteresting as I had ever known it, and the knowledge of general literature very superficial. I therefore think that our acquirements, though less varied, were more substantial, and perhaps more intellectual, than those of the present day: I mean, generally. There are glorious exceptions.

I rejoice that you are so fortunate in your domestic relations. Though I may never witness your happiness, fancy often transports me to your fireside.

In vain I try to realize the change which years must have caused. I still see the same youthful and animated features, — the same Miss Morton whom Dr. Miller used to describe as *all intellectuality.*

Ever yours,   MARGARET BROWNE.

To Mrs. Browne.

CAMBRIDGE, July 20, 1835.

MY DEAR FRIEND, — Your pen, like the fabled wand of the magician, with a touch causes past scenes to be represented as in a mirror. What mysterious powers are folded up in our minds! I could not sleep the night after receiving your letter. But I must arrest the tide of recollection; yet it is difficult, when the flood-gates are once raised, to shut them down again. Let this evince that memory and feeling, as well as fancy, can live to be our solace. . . . How differently education is now conducted from that which we received! Yet we did acquire as much solid and useful information as our successors do, with all their advantages. Perhaps, because we had to work it out for ourselves, it became more our own. The beautiful passages from our favorite poets, which I even then admired, remain fixed in my memory.

You have not adverted to our enacting Miss More's " Search after Happiness," and Madame Genlis' " Dove " and " The Milliner," in our schoolroom, the stage ornamented with evergreens, with our parents and friends, Governor Clinton, and several clergymen, for our audience. But my recollections of you go yet farther back, — to visiting you in our house at Baskinridge, which was taken by your father after we removed to Elizabethtown, preparatory to our return to New York.

Have you read the " Memoir and Correspondence " of Miss More? Her biographer is dull; but the book is delightful when she and her friends are allowed to speak for themselves, — her introduction to Dr. Johnson, Garrick, Mr. Montagu, Horace Walpole, and their letters. I have derived the same kind of pleasure from the " Memoir of Dr. Burney," by Madame D'Arblay. Her style is too absurd for criticism. During her long detention in France, she seems to have lost her native tongue : but her letters to Mr. Crisp are charming ; the account of her conversations with Dr. Johnson ; his quotations from " Evelina," &c. This work seemed like a rejuvenescence to me, so sensibly did it recall the exquisite pleasure of first reading " Evelina." These feelings relative to a sterling work of talent will almost answer your question of my opinion of the heterogeneous mass of literature which is now flooding the public. I am almost certain I should agree in your views, be they ever so much at variance with those generally held. Miss Edgeworth has always been a great favorite; and a correspondence we have had with her has resulted in a greater degree of admiration of the qualities of her mind and heart.

Have you read the works of Jane Austen? They are very different from those of Miss Edgeworth ; but, in their own style, most admirable, — presenting perfect pictures of daily, hourly experience of characters and manners in real life. You will derive pleasure from them, if they happen to suit your taste. I say, *if;* for they are not universally appreciated. They were first mentioned to us by Judge Story, to whom they were recommended by Judge Marshall. High authority, certainly. Ever yours,

ELIZA S. QUINCY.

To Mrs. Quincy.

FRANKFORT, March 26, 1836.

MY DEAR FRIEND,—I most cordially agree in your admiration of Miss Edgeworth. Her "To-morrow" has been of more use to me than all the other fictitious writings I ever read ; and all her stories convey striking lessons, which may be introduced into the every-day business of life with the happiest results. I remember acting in the "Search after Happiness," as if it had been last night; and your appearance, as a French milliner, in your mother's dress. I recollect much more of Governor Clinton's kind assistance in fitting up our stage than I do of any act of his administration.

I have read the "Life of Dr. Burney" with great interest, and feel inclined to bury the egotist in the daughter. Madame D'Arblay's own history was so interwoven with that of her father and the other literary personages of the day, that she could not, in justice to herself, omit the circumstances she narrates. How often have I wished that Beattie's "Minstrel" and "Evelina" could be erased from my memory, that I might again revel in the delightful emotions a first perusal occasioned.

As to the effect produced by the present increase and circulation of new books, to judge from my own experience, I should think it deleterious: the mind becomes distracted by variety, and indisposed to systematic study. Do you think that either you or I, if we were fourteen years of age, would now become as conversant as we then were with the English classics and poets, which are now reposing in sullen dignity on our book-shelves, while every table is littered with annuals and monthly and weekly journals? I often feel bewildered like a child with a number of new toys, who knows not which to play with, but looks first at one, then at another, without examining any. . . . But I fear I am trespassing on your patience.

Affectionately yours,

MARGARET BROWNE.

To Mrs. Quincy, Cambridge.

TREMONT HOUSE, BOSTON, June 25, 1836.

MY DEAR FRIEND, — I can scarcely believe the evidence of my
senses when they inform me that I am in Boston, and within a few
miles of your residence ; yet I am determined to act in accordance
with the delightful impression, and inform you that Mr. Browne and
myself arrived yesterday, and intend to pass a few days here. During that time, I hope no impediment will prevent our seeing you
and Mr. Quincy.

Affectionately yours,

MARGARET BROWNE.

Absence from home, on a tour to Stockbridge, prevented Mrs.
Quincy from responding ; but every attention was immediately paid
by Mr. Quincy and his family to Mr. and Mrs. Browne, at Cambridge
and Boston. They extended their tour to Portsmouth, to give time
for Mrs. Quincy to return home ; and, on the 4th of July, the long-
parted friends met at Cambridge, after a separation of almost forty
years, and passed the day together. Extracts from their subsequent
correspondence will evince the pleasure conferred by this interview : —

To Mrs. Quincy.

FRANKFORT, KENTUCKY, Sept. 7, 1836.

MY DEAR FRIEND, — For the first time in my life, I feel some em-
barrassment in addressing you ; for never, until my visit to Boston,
did I suspect that my letters were so carefully preserved : and I now
feel as if I ought to write something worthy of the consequence you
have kindly attached to our correspondence. Hitherto I have written
hastily, for my pen could not keep pace with the sentiments demand-
ing utterance ; and now, with those feelings rendered still more

intense by our recent interview, notwithstanding my wish to write you a *very pretty* letter, I find I must abandon the attempt.

Our journey home was diversified by passing through Virginia, where the roads were bad, the country mountainous, and the stages disagreeably crowded. And then the contrast between the old decayed towns of the Ancient Dominion and the apparently new and flourishing towns of New England was greatly to the disadvantage of the former. I say, *apparently* new; because many of the towns must be old: but they were so neatly painted white, and ornamented with green shutters, that they appeared as if they had all sprung up by enchantment; and, had Lafayette been passing through the country, I should have imagined that they had all put on their holiday dresses in honor of the occasion.

One charm which the Eastern cities possess, consists, in my opinion, in the stationary character of their inhabitants. One generation succeeds another, not only in the course of time, but in the place of their abode. Their successors become identified with the same places, cultivate the same tastes, adopt the same opinions, and perpetuate the same friendships. With us in the Far West, every thing is changing. Here in Frankfort, containing two thousand inhabitants, there are but four families, who were housekeepers thirty-five years ago, who continue to be such. Many have died, but most have gone to seek their fortunes still farther west. The emigration usually commences with the younger members of the family: and then the aged parents practically at last declare, "Where ye go, I will go; and there will I be buried."

Thank Mr. Quincy for his kind and unwearied attentions; which, I fear, interfered with his more important avocations, but which have left as lasting an impression as any he ever bestowed. To Mr. and Mrs. Greene, Mr. and Mrs. J. Quincy, Mr. and Mrs. Edmund Quincy, and those daughters who are inmates of your happy home, I desire to be affectionately remembered. I delight to bring them before me in imagination, and to recall their features beaming with kindness to one so recently known, and manners unequivocally expressive of that kindness.

Ever yours,   MARGARET BROWNE.

To Miss Quincy.

FRANKFORT, Feb. 3, 1837.

MY DEAR FRIEND, — Since the date of your last letter, a new year has opened upon our world; and though the customary period for congratulation has passed away, yet, as there is sufficient time remaining for the enjoyment of much happiness and the suffering of much sorrow, it cannot be too late even now to express my earnest wish that a kind Providence may continue to bestow its richest blessings upon my friends.

Sincerely do I sympathize with your mother on the death of her brother, General Morton. Your reflection, that there was cause for thankfulness on his account, the suddenness of his departure having saved him from the anguish of an anticipated separation from his family, coincides perfectly with my own sentiments.

You told me, when in Cambridge, that you expected a letter from Miss Edgeworth. Has it arrived? or are you in possession of any facts relative to her present employments? If so, be so kind as to communicate them. Tell your mother, that, after several attempts, I have at last procured a copy of "Evelina." I sent first to Philadelphia, but it could not be found; then to Louisville, and was successful. How often do we seek for enjoyments at a distance, only to be found at home! — a trite reflection, but brought to mind by this little circumstance, accompanied at present by a striking exception in my experience. Although I have the usual attachments to home, yet I would cheerfully travel a thousand miles to enjoy one week of uninterrupted intercourse with your father's family. Pre-eminently as I love your mother, she has, since my visit to Boston, acquired an additional claim to my affection, as being the means of introducing me to her husband and children.

Yours affectionately,   MARGARET BROWNE.

The character of the eldest brother of Mrs. Quincy, whose departure is mentioned in the preceding letter, was thus correctly delineated by one of his contemporaries in New York: " General Morton was a zealous and indefatigable public servant. He had held a commission half a century, and was perhaps the oldest militia general in the world, and a beloved and respected chief. He also held many civil appointments; was clerk of the Common Council, through all the dangers of party politics, for twenty-five years; and had been district attorney, alderman, and member of the Legislature. In all these various capacities, he was a conspicuous exemplar of a good citizen and an excellent man. He was at the head of good society in New York, and was a gentleman of the old school, affable and courteous in his deportment, of unbounded hospitality, and generous almost to a fault; full of that pleasant cheerfulness and agreeable repartee which mutually excite kind feelings. He had been in familiar intercourse with all the remarkable personages who have adorned the United States since they became a nation; officiated as aid-marshal at the first inauguration of President Washington, and was intimate with that great man. He was the friend of Hamilton, Jay, Lafayette, and many other eminent men of that day; and was said to resemble Madison in features, manners, and person. On all public occasions, his mansion was the centre of the festivities of the celebration. He was fortunate even in the manner of his departure. At the age of seventy-four, with a friendly salutation on his lips, he passed instantaneously away. Every tribute of honor and respect was paid to his memory by the civil and military authorities and by the bar of New York."

To Mrs. Browne.

" I would cheerfully travel a thousand miles to enjoy one week of uninterrupted intercourse with your father's family."

MY DEAR FRIEND, — Your letter is addressed to my daughter, who claims a right to acknowledge it; but I must be insensible to every endearing recollection, if I were not impelled to answer, in every sense of the word, such an expression of feeling. It is a delightful assurance of the reality of human friendship to meet an instance like yours, not to be diminished or effaced by time or absence. It came at a moment, too, when I was mourning the sudden departure of almost the last of the family circle that surrounded my early days. I have made me new and cherished ties; " have bound congenial spirits to me:" yet I look back with intense interest to those of my youthful affection, and rejoice to find in you *one* still left me, associated with my earliest recollections, and alive to every sentiment of friendship.

I shall leave to my daughter the other parts of your letter; but I must tell you, that, on the occasion of the late beautiful aurora, we expressed a hope that it extended to the Far West, and that you were observing it. Thus we may have annihilated space and time, and met in spirit to admire the wonderful order of the universe, the stars, and all their shining train. I now give the pen to your younger correspondent, happy in having secured for her the privilege of your friendship without resigning my own share.

ELIZA S. QUINCY.

To Mrs. and Miss Quincy.

MY DEAR FRIENDS, — In acknowledging your joint letter, I have a double pleasure before me. If I do not answer each separately, it is because I find such an identity of pursuits and sentiments between you, that, in writing to both, I feel as if addressing *one;* and, in addressing one, you are both equally present to my imagination. How gratifying it is to find myself regarded with the same affection by the daughter as by the mother. This same manifestation of regard affected me most sensibly on my arrival at Boston. I was prepared for an affectionate reception from you, and a kind one from Mr. Quincy; but I was not prepared for the warm and animated welcome I received from your children, upon whom I had no claim but that of being their mother's friend. The manner in which I was received upon that claim afforded a most delightful evidence of filial devotion, which needed no other recommendation; and the unity of sentiment prevailing among all the branches of your family came completely up to my beau-ideal of domestic happiness.

Since I received your communication respecting Mexican antiquities, I have read with deep interest the articles in the "Foreign Quarterly" to which you refer. What a mournful lesson do these researches teach us of our own evanescent existence, not only individually, but as a nation! We, too, must share the fate of our progenitors; and our very existence may become a subject of speculation. How humiliating would be these reflections, were it not that we have that within us which cannot be destroyed by the lapse of ages.

> "The sun itself is but a spark of fire, — a transient meteor in the sky:
> The soul, immortal as its Sire, shall never die."

Your ever-affectionate friend,

MARGARET BROWNE.

This correspondence was sustained until September, 1838; when Mrs. Browne, having survived her husband one year, passed away without a previous illness, highly esteemed by all around her, and deeply regretted by her family and friends.

From the correspondence with Miss Edgeworth, mentioned in the preceding letters as a source of great pleasure to Mrs. Quincy, an extract relative to her friend John Adams is here inserted:—

To Miss Quincy, Cambridge, Massachusetts.

EDGEWORTHTOWN, Aug. 28, 1835.

I was much interested in your account of your "Lord Old-borough,"* as you are so kind to me as to call an incomparably more useful and greater man. The scale of merit, as of nature, in your new world, is far larger and higher than in our old world. You could not have written any page more interesting to me about any one great man of our times than that which you wrote for me on the life and death of John Adams, that true patriot. The circumstances of his death are most striking: "Retaining his intellectual and moral faculties to the age of ninety, and expiring on the anniversary of the day on which he signed the Declaration of American Independence, — the fiftieth anniversary of that day, and at the very hour, the very moment, of the celebration of that event throughout your far-extended Union, of which his own son was at that time President," — is altogether such a sublime, moral coincidence, such a happy close of such a life, as no previous biography, no history, ancient or modern, as far as I can call to mind, has ever before had to record.

One of the most glorious of poetic deaths, as far as mere mortal fame was concerned, was his who was smothered, as it is said, with garlands at the Olympic games; but what are those paltry garlands, compared with the American patriot's obsequies?

The wisest of the ancients, if I recollect rightly, pronounced happiest the death of the two youths who had drawn their mother to the

---

* A character in "Patronage," — a novel by Miss Edgeworth.

Temple of Juno, and who lay down to sleep after that pious action, and never wakened from that sleep; but what is this, compared with the happy death of your venerable President, sinking to sleep amidst his country's celebration of a life of virtue and its most glorious act? Compare his closing hour with the sad, ignoble, pitiful, unpitied end of the Emperor Napoleon.

You may judge by the train of thoughts which have flowed in perhaps too abundantly to my pen, upon this subject, how much your description and the facts you told me interested me. . . .

Gratefully yours,

MARIA EDGEWORTH.

CHAPTER XII.

WHILE sustaining the bonds of early affection, Mrs. Quincy was ever ready to extend the range of her friendships. Having formed an acquaintance with Mrs. Ballestier,* who was soon to embark for Singapore (Mr. Ballestier having been appointed United-States consul at that place), Mrs. Quincy recommended to her notice a " Memoir of Sir Stamford Raffles," which she had then recently read. This incident caused a correspondence, from which the following extracts are given : —

To Mrs. Quincy, Cambridge, Massachusetts.

SINGAPORE, April 13, 1837.

MY DEAR MADAM, — Your just appreciation of the character and the efforts of Sir Stamford Raffles in founding the English colony here, induces me to ask your acceptance of some nutmegs from the garden laid out by his direction, and some specimens of the pitcher-plant, or, as the natives call it, " the monkey-cup." The flowers grow, as you will observe, suspended at the end of the leaves ; and,

---

* A daughter of Paul Revere, whose name is of historical interest from the notice he gave of the movement of British troops by exhibiting lights in the tower of the North Church, the night previous to the 19th of April, 1775.

when brought to me, were half full of water and insects. The smaller specimens were a beautiful green. I have filled them with the Siam cotton, also a curiosity, as it grows on a lofty tree, in large green pods. I also send one of the marine productions of the waters of Singapore, fancifully called Neptune's cup. Beautiful varieties of coral are also found here, but are not so rare as these natural vases, some of which will hold several gallons. They seem of the nature of sponge, but are much harder, and will stand the sun and rains of a tropical climate for months. I have several of them on the portico and in the border of my garden, in which I place my plants.

SINGAPORE, Oct. 29, 1838.

Your very interesting letter of December last reached me in safety after its long voyage; and it gave me great pleasure to hear that the dried plants were in good preservation. I now ask your acceptance of some costumes from Madras, which, although rudely drawn, are faithful; and also of two paintings of fruits peculiar to the Straits of Malacca, — the Mangostein and the Durian. They will have an interest for you, as executed by an old draughtsman of Sir Stamford Raffles, now a cripple; but, though confined to his couch, he supports himself by painting the fruits, flowers, and birds of the Straits. To those who can overcome the odor and first taste of the Durian, it is a delicious fruit. The Mangostein is beautiful to the eye, and delicious to the taste; but, with me, does not bear comparison with the peach. The handkerchief they are wrapped in is of native manufacture, and comes from Collanton, up the coast, — eight miles from Singapore. The Malays wear them on the head, and each tribe has a different manner of tying them. They are worn by the men alone: the women never cover their heads, even when they attain to old age.

I ask your son-in-law Mr. Greene's acceptance, as President of the Natural-History Society, of some birds from the coast of Coromandel, nine in number. They were prepared and given to me by a

French naturalist, and were duplicates. Allow me to thank you for "Van Artevelde," and for the "Life of Washington" by Mr. Sparks, — a great pleasure to us, and a source of pride in showing it to the Europeans here, who know little of the United States, except what they are told by prejudiced travellers. By this opportunity I also send you a Siamese manuscript, and some of the books printed in Siam, for the use of the natives, by the American mission, and also some from China.

You will be gratified to learn that the institution founded by Sir Stamford Raffles is in a flourishing state, and attended by many pupils ; though not as yet, according to his desire, by the children of the rajahs. But it has Portuguese students from Manilla, Macao, and Goa, who reside in the family of one of the head masters, — Mr. Dickenson of Virginia, a most able and efficient person. The building is airy and convenient. They are beginning a library, and have some philosophical instruments. This is also one of the stations for meteorological observations, erected, at the request of the Association for the Diffusion of Science, by the British Government, on a grand scale, and supplied with instruments of every kind.

OCTOBER 18, 1841.

Your letter, and the beautiful volumes of the "History of Harvard University," — a most valuable work, gratifying us in many ways, — arrived after a short voyage. I lately sent you another manuscript, by Hon. Mark Kerr, a young Englishman, the grandson of the Marquis of Lothian, and introduced to us by Mr. James Brooke, who is here, in his own yacht, for scientific purposes, and to whom Mr. Ballestier gave a letter to President Quincy.

I now offer you an illustrated Siamese manuscript, entitled "A Treatise on Fortune-telling," — a missionary friend in Siam had it executed for me ; and also a specimen of the Venus slipper, an orchidaceous plant from the Prince-of-Wales Island. It reminds me of a similar plant I saw, when very young, at Canton, Massachusetts, called by the country people the "whippoorwill shoe." The beautiful color of the leaves is almost destroyed in the drying. With every kind wish for your happiness,

Very sincerely yours,

MARIA REVERE BALLESTIER.

Soon after the date of this letter, Mrs. Ballestier died at Singapore. An extract from a tribute to her memory, in an English journal, is here inserted : —

"Occupying a prominent position in society, Mrs. Ballestier endeared herself to all by every social virtue ; proving that they are not only compatible with, but heightened in their value by being accompanied by, the amenities of life. To obtain her good offices, it was only requisite to need them. A quiet dignity of demeanor, that has passed, we fear, with the old school, gave a pleasing grace to her manners. Her heart was young withal. How often have we seen it go with the little children at their play ! Her sympathies were truly catholic, embracing in the fullest sense the whole human family."

During these years, the Centennial celebration of the foundation of Harvard College, the erection of Gore Hall, the history of the University, and a correspondence and friendship which at this period commenced between Mr. Quincy and James Grahame, the historian of the United States (and which is yet, in 1861, sustained by their children), were sources of great interest to Mrs. Quincy.

In March, 1838, Mr. Quincy visited Dr. Bowditch, whose health had rapidly declined. He found him correcting for the press the last pages of his translation of the "Mécanique Céleste" of La Place. After a most interesting interview, Dr. Bowditch took leave of his friend, and sent an affectionate message to Mrs. Quincy. The death of the great " Practical Navigator," who had guided the ships of all nations over the pathless ocean, was soon announced by their flags at half-mast. In these tributes of sorrow and respect his friends deeply sympathized.

In July, 1839, Mrs. Dowse, the widow of Edward Dowse, and the last survivor of the sisters of Mrs. Abigail Quincy, died at the age of eighty-two years. After the loss of her sister Mrs. Shaw, Anna W. Storer became, through an arrangement by Mrs. Quincy, an inmate in her family. Her companionship and affectionate attentions contributed to the happiness of the last six years of the life of Mrs. Dowse, at whose residence the letter was written from which an extract is here inserted : —

To Hon. Josiah Quincy.

DEDHAM, October, 1839.

. . . I looked with deep interest at your father's monument during my last visit to Quincy, for the first erection of which I was solicitous nearly forty years ago ; and I am now gratified by its repair and renovation. It does not often fall to the lot of a son twice to build the monument of his parents ; but, if ever such a tribute was deserved, that claim is surely theirs. And well has it been answered " by their only surviving child," not only by monumental marble, but by a life worthy of their name and their example. It must now remain with those who are to come after us to continue to preserve the memory and the memorial of those we have honored and loved. But, whether they do or not, the past is secure ; and you may willingly leave to the future the record of your own claims, public and private, to the grateful remembrance of your friends and your children.

I have just returned from visiting the cemetery here, and the monument you have erected to the memory of Mr. and Mrs. Dowse and Mrs. Shaw. I return to their pleasant mansion with a heart full of affectionate remembrance of all their love and kindness to us and our children. In the disposition of their late abode as the residence of our youngest son, they would have been gratified; and I hope our children's children will be taught to whom they owe this goodly heritage, and honor their memory as they deserve.

ELIZA S. QUINCY.

An interesting incident of the summer of 1839 is thus described by Mrs. Quincy : —

"In August, with my daughter A. P. Quincy, and attended by a servant, I crossed the Hudson at New York to Jersey City, went by railroad to Morristown, and there took a carriage to visit Baskinridge. I recollected the whole road as we went on. We passed a handsome house I remembered as the residence of a family of the name of Kemble, and, nearer Baskinridge, that of Mr. Southward; and drove over a tract of ground through which three brooks ran: the last was the one near my father's house. We ascended a little hill; and there was the house, and the spring opposite. It was partly demolished, and stood, as I have described it, on the descent of the hill, one story high on one side, two on the other. I entered the part yet inhabited; and, after an absence of more than half a century, I again tasted the water of the spring around which I had so often played in my childhood. We went up the hill to the village. The view from thence was beautiful; but the old church and schoolhouse were replaced by modern edifices. In the afternoon we drove over to 'the Buildings,' which remain in tolerable repair, having been the property and residence of a respectable family for the last thirty years, and yet bear evidences of having been in former times an elegant establishment. We passed into the court-yard, formerly paved and surrounded with stables, coach-house, and offices, from which it derived the name of 'the Buildings;' stopped at a porch at the back of the house; and went into the great hall, where the beautiful staircase remained, and the great bell yet hung. A fine lawn descended in front of the house to the banks of Black River, which fell into the Great Swamp. We passed the night at Somerville; and then went on, through bad roads but a beautiful country, to New Brunswick, and sent our servant to inform my uncle Daniel Kemper of our arrival, and that we would visit him in the afternoon. Mr. Kemper, then ninety years of age, was one of the most noble-looking old men I ever saw; his sight and hearing perfect. He was delighted to see me; said, 'I see your dear mother in you.' His daughter Jane Kemper, and his grand-daughter, one of the children of his son Bishop Kemper of Wisconsin, were with him; and he had every thing pleasant around his residence. He was always fond of the cultivation of flowers, and took me into his garden, and showed me the stone house in Albany Street where my grandparents had resided, and where he was born in 1749. As a reward for service as Colonel Kemper in the army of the Revolution, he received a lucrative office from General Washington, and is treated by the citizens of New Brunswick with great respect." *

In October, 1839, Mrs. Quincy received a visit from Mr. Gallaudet, who, in 1775, had superintended the transfer of the property of her father, Mr. Morton, from New York to Philadelphia.† Retaining his health and mental power at the age of eighty-four years, he recollected distinctly all the occurrences of that period.‡

The care of a numerous family, which the public duties of Mr. Quincy caused to devolve chiefly on his wife, prevented her from taking an active part in the benevolent societies of Boston; but she was a subscriber to many, and to the Boston Female Asylum for upwards of thirty years. Two of the inmates of that institution were employed in her family until they were eighteen. They married respectable mechanics; and one of them visited the asylum with Mrs.

---

* See Appendix VI.   † See p. 17.   ‡ See Appendix VII.

Quincy, returned her thanks to the managers, and became a subscriber herself to the institution which had shielded her childhood.

In 1843, Mrs. Quincy, with several of her family, made a tour in Canada, and visited Mrs. Sewall, the widow of Chief-Justice Sewall, who, surrounded by her children and grandchildren, was residing at Quebec, and whom, as Harriet Smith, she had met sixty years previous in New York, — in 1783. The next summer, Mr. and Mrs. Quincy visited Niagara and Toronto, where they had an interesting interview with Mrs. Powell, the widow of Judge Powell, who had resided on the shores of Lake Ontario from the time the country was a wilderness, and had seen a city grow up around her. At the mansion of their friend Mr. Justice Hagermann, they formed an acquaintance with Chief-Justice and Mrs. Robinson and the other principal inhabitants of Toronto.

During the last years of her residence in Cambridge, the establishment of the Observatory had been an object of interest to Mrs. Quincy. On the 8th of May, 1845, a transit of Mercury was observed in New England for the first time for sixty years. Mr. J. Q. Adams came to Cambridge to view it; and, in the afternoon, Mrs. Quincy had the pleasure of seeing the planet on the disc of the sun through the telescope, and of watching the observations of Mr. Bond.

When Mr. Quincy attained the age of seventy years, he purchased a house in Boston for the future residence of his family; and in March, 1845, resigned the Presidency of Harvard University. The announcement of his intention to leave the official station he had long held, and remove with his family from Cambridge, was received with a strong and general expression of regret, especially from all those immediately connected with the University. But he never wavered in his decision to retire while his health was unimpaired, and when he could leave the institution in perfect order, prosperous, improved, and enlarged in all its branches during his administration. Although, to Mrs. Quincy and her family, a removal from Cambridge, where they had acquired new friends, passed many happy years, and formed many pleasing associations, was attended with regret, they coincided in the opinion that it was the golden moment for the change to be made.

Among the parting testimonies of respect paid to Mr. Quincy, the request of the four classes of under-graduates for his bust by Crawford, to be placed in Gore Hall, was among the most gratifying. A consequent acquaintance with that accomplished and distinguished artist, who modelled his work in an apartment in the President's house, was a great pleasure to Mrs. Quincy. The closing tributes on Commencement Day in August, 1845, and the crowded levee of the evening, equalled in interest and animation those of the second of June, 1829.

In September, Mr. and Mrs. Quincy took possession of the commodious house they had selected in Bowdoin Place, and were received by their friends in Boston with every attention on their return; and, during the succeeding years, they were constantly visited by those whom they had left in Cambridge.

In the summer of 1846, they resumed their favorite residence in the country; from whence the following letter was written by Mrs. Quincy: —

To Miss Eliza A. Guild, Staten Island.

QUINCY, July 9, 1846.

MY DEAR FRIEND, — Although you have many better correspondents, I cannot refrain from expressing for myself the gratification I received from your interesting letter. There is something in a direct personal appeal to our feelings and affections which gives an assurance of our being loved and remembered beyond all messages conveyed through another medium, however near, and identical with one's self.

You are correct in supposing that we are happily settled in this our ancestral abode, among these dear familiar scenes; but it is hardly possible for you to realize the happiness I feel in returning here, untouched by calamity, after seventeen years of absence. By exertions for the public service, performed, from a sense of duty, with devotion and successful results, Mr. Quincy must be allowed to have earned leisure to pursue other objects of interest and usefulness. The place is in great beauty; the house, in perfect order within and without; and we have retired while we are still able to enjoy domestic pleasures among our children and friends. You, my dear Eliza, with the exception of Mr. Quincy, are the only person whose sympathy can extend with me to the past. You can recollect Mr. Quincy's mother and Mrs. Ann Quincy, to whom, and to many others now departed, these scenes were so endeared. You also remember our family meeting in 1815, — that interesting occasion. I could enumerate every one who was then present; now absent in all but spiritual influences, — and these I feel and recognize in all around me, with the consciousness, that, if those friends witness our daily walks through their former places of abode, they will approve of our filial love and of our gratitude for all they have bequeathed to us.

But I will turn from these scenes to those by which you are now surrounded, — scenes, too, of my early childhood. I am only familiar with Staten Island by sight. I never landed there, but often passed it in my frequent passages to visit friends in Elizabethtown, Newark, and Brunswick. We always sailed by the western shore of Staten Island, through what were then termed " the Kills," — a Dutch name for creeks or rivers; as, Fishkill, &c. The " Kills " derived their name from the three streams which there enter the bay, — the Hackensack, the Passaic, and the Raritan. This piece of geographical information just came into my mind as the answer to my question as to the meaning of the name of that part of the passage, when I was sailing through it.

Those early days! — how difficult it is for me to realize, that I am the same being who then thought no other places or persons could ever be so dear to me, and who have since formed such dearer ties! And yet memory goes back to many kind and tender proofs of love and indulgent gratification obtained for me by those who then formed my circle of family friends, all now removed from the places that once knew them. But the features of nature ever remain the same, to cheer and elevate the mind. I rejoice that you are enjoying at Staten Island all that we are here. To have you with us would add almost the only additional pleasure that could be granted to me.

Ever affectionately yours,

ELIZA S. QUINCY.

The sixth of June, 1847, the fiftieth anniversary of the marriage of Mr. and Mrs. Quincy was celebrated with appropriate testimonies of affection from their family, who met at their mansion in Bowdoin Place, in the evening.

For several years after their return to their former places of residence, Mrs. Quincy retained her power of participating in all the occurrences which interested those around her. The last public occasion at which she was present was on the twenty-fifth of October, 1848, when her eldest son, Josiah Quincy, jun., as Mayor of Boston, presided over the completion of the Cochituate Aqueduct. It was the great festival of the whole people at this period. The order which prevailed among the multitudes who thronged the streets of the city, and the moment when, at the command of the Mayor, the water of the distant lake gushed up in a splendid fountain on the Common, is remembered with pleasure by the many thousands of the citizens who witnessed the scene and enjoyed the celebration.

The health of Mrs. Quincy remained unimpaired until the last year of her life; and the few months of her decline were passed at Quincy, amid the devoted attentions of her family and the tributes of long-tried friendship. Her memory and intellectual powers remained perfect; and the resources of literature, ever her peculiar delight, employed her leisure hours. Her Christian faith was firm, and sustained by "an unfaltering trust." She closed her long and happy life of seventy-seven years, at Quincy, on Sunday morning, the first of September, 1850, in tranquillity and peace, with gratitude for the past, and with confidence and hope for the future.

APPENDIX.

APPENDIX.

No. I. — PAGE 58.

Extract from a Letter from John Morton to Mrs. Jackson, Philadelphia.

ALEXANDRIA, D.C., Dec. 23, 1800.

ON the 19th, I made my visit to Mount Vernon with Mr. Dandridge, and met with a most flattering reception from Mrs. Washington. There were no other visitors, except Colonel Lear and some relatives, who came to dine on Sunday. Mrs. Washington's family at present consists of her granddaughter Mrs. Lewis,* a charming woman still; Mr. Lewis; Miss Henley; and Washington Custis, a good-natured young sportsman, a great favorite with Mrs. Washington, and heir to her estate, though of large fortune in his own right.

Old Frank, the General's mulatto servant, recognized me the moment I entered the house, and tendered the assistance I needed. A stream, called Cameron Run, had been swelled by a heavy rain the preceding night. Dandridge insisted on dashing through it, and took the water above his boots. Being better mounted, I escaped with clothes completely splashed. Frank, seeing our plight, conducted us to our chambers, lighted a brisk fire, and soon put us to rights. Every thing that is good and comfortable abounds in the establishment, and the whole is managed with the same harmonious regularity as in the General's lifetime.

Mrs. Washington, though altered by years, and evidently lost at times in melancholy thought, displays great fortitude, and retains the full strength of

---

* Miss Eleanor P. Custis.

her mental powers. She perfectly recollected our family both during and since the war, made many inquiries regarding them and other families at the northward, and evinced the most minute recollection of events. She conversed freely and cheerfully on public and private affairs; and her whole deportment does infinite honor to herself, and to the memory of the illustrious character to whom she was united. I visited the tomb of Washington with sensations I cannot express.

I had engaged to dine at the President's to-day, on the invitation of Mrs. Adams, whom I saw here at Alexandria on her way to Mount Vernon, but am prevented by indisposition. Yours, &c.

JOHN MORTON.

No. II. — PAGE 87.

THIS mansion in Beacon Street was the birthplace and residence of Edward Bromfield, jun., a youth of high promise, who was graduated at Harvard in 1742, and died in 1745. He constructed microscopes, and the first organ ever made in America. At the early age of twenty-two years, his scientific attainments, and genius for mechanics, rendered him eminent among his contemporaries. In his portrait, he is represented as standing in his library, pointing to his microscope on the table beside him. As it had suffered from time and ill usage, Mrs. Quincy caused it to be brought from Harvard to Boston, and repaired, in the hope that it would be given by his relative, Mrs. M. Blanchard, to the Massachusetts Historical Society, as a memorial of his talents and acquisitions.

The Bromfield Family held extensive possessions in Wales, in the reign of Edward VI.; and became residents of England in that of Elizabeth. Edward Bromfield, who emigrated to America in 1675, was born at Haywood House, their seat in Hampshire, England. He resided in Boston, in the street which bears his name, and on the site of the Bromfield House, then surrounded by fields and shady groves. His son erected the house in Beacon Street, mentioned p. 87. John Bromfield, the last of the family resident in Boston, was distinguished for the excellence of his character, and his munificent bequests to the public and to his relatives.*

In 1847, William Arnold Bromfield, of the Isle of Wight, an eminent botanist, visited Boston, and accidentally became acquainted with Mr. Quincy and his family. Dr. Bromfield and his sister were the last representatives of the name in England, and were descended from an elder branch of the same family with Edward Bromfield. In 1850, Dr. Bromfield visited Egypt and Syria, and died at Damascus in 1851. His sister caused his letters during his journey to be privately printed; and published his " Flora Vectensis, — being a systematic Description of the Plants indigenous to the Isle of Wight," edited by Sir William J. Hooker, London, 1856. Miss Bromfield has thus raised an appropriate and enduring memorial of a brother to whom she was most affectionately attached.

No. III. — PAGE 148.

JOHN HENRY was an Irish adventurer, a naturalized citizen of the United States; at one time, an editor in Philadelphia. Afterwards he resided in Vermont; and, by newspaper essays against republican government, attracted the attention of Sir James Craig, the Governor of Canada, who, during the embargo of 1809, sent him to ascertain whether the Federalists, if they prevailed at the approaching election, would be disposed to separate from the Union, or to enter into any connection with England; and, if any such disposition appeared, the British Government might be communicated with through him. Henry arrived in Boston in March, 1809, and spent three months there, when an apparent settlement of affairs by Erskine put an end

---

* History of the Boston Athenæum, by Josiah Quincy, p. 78.

to his mission. During this time, he addressed seventeen letters to Craig's secretary, describing the discontent arising from existing commercial restrictions, but stating that withdrawal from the Union was an unpopular measure; and the Federalists confined themselves to the ordinary routine of opposition. The source of this conjectural information did not appear. No names were mentioned; and he does not seem to have avowed his diplomatic mission in Boston even to the British consul. He went to England to apply for a reward; but was referred by Wellesley to Craig's successor in Canada, as better qualified to appreciate his services. Not liking this treatment, he landed in Boston with a Frenchman calling himself Count Crillon, who proved to be an impostor; and, obtaining a letter to Madison from Governor Gerry, went to Washington, where he kept secluded, in the daytime, for ten days. President Madison then paid him, out of the secret-service fund, fifty thousand dollars, with which he instantly departed; and on the 3d of March, the day of the President's communication to Congress, sailed from New York for France, in the sloop of war " Wasp," bound to Europe with diplomatic despatches.

His revelations were prefaced by a letter dated Philadelphia, Feb. 20; in which, having already received the money, about which nothing was said to Congress, he offered to make a " voluntary disclosure." They consisted of his correspondence with Craig and Peel. The price Madison paid for these papers, if he knew beforehand how little they contained, is only to be explained by his desire to aid his partisans by exciting suspicions against the Federalists of Massachusetts, and odium against the British Government, charged, in his message, with being engaged, in time of peace, in an intrigue for destroying the Union. As these papers mentioned no names and stated no acts, and as their imputations were wholly conjectural, the excitement, at first very great, speedily died away. The British ministers defended Craig in Parliament; maintaining that, so far from attempting to sever the American Union, he had, in an uncertain state of affairs, merely sent an agent to Boston to obtain information on his own responsibility. The effect on Massachusetts did not answer the expectations of the Administration.*

* Hildreth's History of the United States, second series, vol. iii. p. 284.

No. IV. — Page 160.

THE following letter from the Hon. James Lloyd, senator from Massachusetts, the intimate friend of Mr. Quincy, illustrates the position of the Federal members of Congress at that period : —

To Isaac P. Davis, Esq., Boston.

CITY OF WASHINGTON, 23d June, 1812.

DEAR SIR, — I regret that the State Legislature had risen before the declaration of war could have reached Boston ; as, had it been otherwise, an opportunity would have been given to the House of Representatives at least to have formed and expressed their opinion with regard to it. Here rashness and improvidence are the order of the day. A bill for the issuing letters of marque and reprisal, and commissions for privateers, and another imposing no few additional duties on imports, with a third authorizing an issue of five millions of dollars in Treasury notes, have all passed the House, and are now in different stages before the Senate. They are retarded by objections, but can no more be stayed by the Federal members than they could arrest the progress of a thunderbolt. At this interesting and anxious period, our friends should remember, that, in the Senate, we have no stenographer, nor a reporter of any kind, except the mere transcript of the result from the Journal, which is handed from one of the clerks of the Secretary of the Senate to the printer ; and the composing and writing-out one's own observations frequently is both tedious and invidious. I merely mention this, lest an imputation of neglect should unmeritedly attach to the minority in this branch of the Legislature. We are however, here, literally nobody ; and it is, in some sort, practising a deception upon the community for a Federal man to hold a seat in the Senate from New England, and especially from Massachusetts.

After having laid the commerce of the country a victim on the altar, and applied the knife to its throat, Congress will rise in about ten days or a fortnight, not daring to touch any other of the taxes than the imposts ; and, having declared war, will leave the country nearly as defenceless as they found it ; and will feel very little compunction for the ruin and desolation which that measure will entail on the commercial capital and the navigation of the United States. . . .

Yours very sincerely,   JAMES LLOYD.

No. V. — Page 183.

PROFESSOR KEMPER of Leyden was interested and gratified by the account of the German ancestry of Mrs. Quincy, transmitted by Mr. Vanderkemp ; and requested him to forward to her an engraved likeness of himself, his coat-of-arms, and an extract from his letter, in which he stated that his grandfather Philip Kemper came from Lower Germany ; but that, as he lost his parents at ten years of age, he knew but little of his paternal ancestry, and was uncertain if the arms of his father were brought from Germany, or assumed in Holland.

The engraving enclosed bore such a striking resemblance to Jacob Kemper as to be thought his likeness by the elder relatives of Mrs. Quincy, when it was shown them with the name concealed. His seal, on which the arms were engraved, was lost during his residence in New Jersey ; and no copy was retained. They could not, therefore, be compared with those of Professor Kemper, who, it was inferred from various coincidences, was the grandson of the elder brother of Jacob Kemper, who, on his return from the East Indies, settled in Holland.*

John Melchior Kemper, counsellor of State for Foreign Affairs, member of the States-General, and professor of jurisprudence in the University of Leyden, was one of the most eminent civilians and eloquent lawyers of his time. He was also highly distinguished in political life, and active in driving the French from his country. He accompanied the Prince of Orange on his

---

* See Memoir, p. 1.

entrance into Amsterdam in 1812, and was one of his most influential counsellors. He was beloved for his social virtues; and died in 1824, deeply regretted by his countrymen, and especially by the students of the university.

This tribute to Professor Kemper was translated by Miss Vanderkemp from the Leyden "Courant," July 20, 1824.

Judge Vanderkemp, in 1829, bequeathed to Mrs. Quincy the original manuscripts of his correspondence with Mrs. (Governor) Livingston and Mrs. Abigail Adams. The former were presented to her friend Mrs. Theodore Sedgwick, a grand-daughter of Mrs. Livingston: those of Mrs. Adams remain in the possession of her family.

No. VI. — Page 244.

Colonel Kemper was aid-de-camp to General Washington at the battle of Germantown. He offered to go with a flag of truce to Chew's house; when a younger officer arrived, who was sent, and mortally wounded. His brothers were — Philip Kemper, who went to the West Indies, and returned, and died in Philadelphia; Jacob, who was a captain in the American Army; and John, who entered the naval service of the Colonies, underwent great sufferings in their cause, and died in 1844, at Hudson, N.Y., leaving several children.

Mrs. Jackson (Susan Kemper *), born in New Brunswick, N. J., in 1758, survived all her children, except Mrs. I. P. Davis of Boston, and Mrs. Bernard Henry and Dr. S. Jackson of Philadelphia. The uncommon animation and benevolence of her character rendered her through life a general favorite. Wherever she resided, numerous friends surrounded her: as the elder passed away, the younger pressed forward to serve and attend her. Though remarkable for timidity in her youth, and fearing even the passage of the ferries between New York and Philadelphia, yet her energy in after-life surmounted danger; and, when above sixty years of age, she made several voyages across the Atlantic to visit her daughter Mrs. Henry at Gibraltar, and twice in vessels condemned as unseaworthy the moment they arrived in port.

---

* See Memoir, pp. 28-78.

Mrs. Jackson sought the abodes of poverty, studied the character of their inmates, and the purses of her wealthy friends were ever open to her requests for aid. During her residence in the family of her son-in-law I. P. Davis, Esq., before the establishment of the Ministry-at-Large, no private individual was more efficient in visiting and relieving the indigent classes of the city of Boston. She had the gratification of seeing her eldest son, Samuel Jackson, M.D., of Philadelphia, rise to the highest rank in his profession; passed her last days under his immediate care; and departed in 1846, at the age of eighty-eight. Her brother Colonel Kemper survived her one year, and died at New Brunswick, N.J., August, 1847, at the age of ninety-eight, — the last of the family of Jacob and Maria Regina Kemper, who emigrated from Caub, in Germany, A.D. 1741.

In 1861, the representatives of the name in the United States are the Rev. Jackson Kemper of the Episcopal Church, Bishop of Wisconsin, his sisters and his children.

The eldest grandson of Mrs. Jackson, Thomas Kemper Davis, was a man of uncommon talents and acquisitions. He was born in Boston in 1808, was graduated at Harvard University in 1827, and died at his father's residence in Boston in 1853. The following tribute to his memory is extracted from an obituary notice by Edmund Quincy: —

"After graduating, he commenced the study of the law in the office of Daniel Webster, and was a most indefatigable and constant student. He had read with studious attention every classical author in the entirety of his works. In Greek he especially excelled, and the orators and dramatic authors were his ever-fresh delight. His acquaintance with English literature was perfect and exhaustive; and all that was valuable in his acquisitions he held in the grasp of a prodigious memory, always ready for use. At a somewhat later period, he applied himself more diligently than at first to the studies proper to his profession. He shrunk from no labor that was necessary to his end; and there were not many better read lawyers of his standing than he, when he left the bar. At not unfrequent intervals, during his severest studies, Mr. Davis would seek relaxation in the society of his friends; for he was not one that refrained ' when God sent a cheerful hour.' He was ever a welcome guest at convivial parties and in fashionable circles. With a mind thus disciplined and prepared for the conflicts of the bar and the world, and thus qualified to enjoy and adorn society, he approached the work for which he had been fitting himself with such wise industry. He was just enjoying the beginning of professional success, when he was overtaken by an insidious disorder. Watched over by the tenderest affection, his later years were spent in his father's house, until, suddenly and mercifully, the cloud that had so long darkened his life was lifted for ever."

No. VII. — PAGE 244.

Letter from P. W. Gallaudet, Esq., to Mrs. Quincy.

WASHINGTON, D.C., 8th December, 1840.

DEAR MADAM, — The short interview with you which I had the pleasure of enjoying last October twelvemonth brought back to recollection the days of youth and those I passed in your father's family. The friendship of your parents and of your brother I highly estimated. But those scenes have passed, never to return ; and I am now in my eighty-fifth year. I shall be happy to hear from you, and of your sister also. I remember you both as two little girls, Margaret and Susan. With my respects to Mr. Quincy, with great esteem,

Yours,   P. W. GALLAUDET.

From Mrs. Quincy to Mr. Gallaudet.

CAMBRIDGE, MASS., Jan. 7, 1841.

DEAR SIR, — It gave me great pleasure to receive a proof of your remembrance. Your name was familiar to me in my early youth. My mother always spoke of you as her confidential friend and faithful assistant, and impressed her children with sentiments of high respect for your character. My father, of whom you speak in your letter, I do not recollect. His death took place during the Revolution, when I was too young to retain any distinct remembrance of him. But your allusion to my parents brought back past times to me in a touching manner; and I truly reciprocate all your expressions of feeling.

I have many articles which formerly belonged to my parents, which I think you would recognize. Among these is my father's seal, always used in his counting-house. It is of silver, with an ebony handle. The cipher J. M. is so intertwined as to be somewhat obscure. When you were in business with him, I presume you often used it; and I shall seal this letter with it, as you may like to see the impression once more. With every wish for your happiness,

Your friend,   ELIZA S. QUINCY.

Letter from Mr. Gallaudet to Mrs. E. S. Quincy.

WASHINGTON, D.C., 7th August, 1841.

DEAR MADAM, — I return my best thanks for your letter, and expressions of regard. I was in your father's family from 1771 till July, 1775, when I went into Colonel John Bayard's counting-house in Philadelphia; then being in my twentieth year. The war had then commenced; and your father, apprehending the British would get possession of New York, sent a large part of his stock of goods to Philadelphia, consigned to Colonel Bayard; and I went round also, and attended the sales. I was at his house in Baskinridge, and saw him often in Philadelphia; so that I had frequent personal intercourse with him until his death.

He was above the common size of men, with a ruddy complexion; his whole appearance interesting, and commanding much respect. At that time, a hair-dresser was employed daily. ·Your father wore powder, and his hair dressed in one long curl round the back of the neck, which had a handsome appearance. His importations from England, Scotland, and Ireland, were extensive, and our customers very numerous. His store was unusual, consisting of a great assortment of dry-goods, mirrors, frames, pictures from London, carpets, carpeting, tea in boxes, &c. Besides, he was extensively engaged in shipping flaxseed to Ireland. He also had a storehouse three stories high, with machinery for cleaning and preparing flaxseed for exportation. This work was done in the winter season, and was for some years under my direction. We received the seed from coasting vessels, in a rough state; cleaned and prepared it to be sent abroad; and often turned out, and sent off to different vessels, one hundred hogsheads, or casks, of seven bushels each, in a day, — all in new casks, coopered and marked. In the spring and autumn, I was engaged in the store; yet I found time for reading at night. The seal of which you sent me the impression, I have taken care of. I should have liked to have seen it again, and the other articles you mention. I remained in Colonel Bayard's counting-house two years, and then went into business myself. In the winter of 1776–7, I was with the army in a volunteer corps, — the Washington Guards of Philadelphia. I had the happiness of the friendship of your parents through their lives. I was at their house in Baskinridge a few weeks before your father's death, when I saw him for the last time. I continued in business in Philadelphia until 1800, when I removed to Hartford, Connecticut, where my eldest son commenced the school for the deaf and dumb. With my best respects to Mr. Quincy,

Your sincere friend,

P. W. GALLAUDET.

Mr. Gallaudet died in Washington, D.C., in 1843, aged eighty-eight.

No. VIII.

Extract from a Tribute to the Memory of Mrs. Quincy by Rev. George E. Ellis, D.D., of Charlestown, Massachusetts, published in the "Christian Examiner" for November, 1850.

" So respectful and affectionate are our remembrances of this most excellent woman, that we could scarce refrain from expressing our sense of them after her departure from the earth, even if the many almost public stations which she adorned did not require such a commemoration of her. Her refined and dignified features, her gentle and courteous address, come up impressively before us, and remind us that only a most delicate memorial can befit the graces of her character.

"We recall readily, for we have never forgotten, the impression we received from her benevolent greeting and her friendly words, when as a young guest we were first privileged to see her in her own home at Cambridge. Each subsequent interview or visit, with an increased ability to appreciate excellences of character, and a better instructed estimate of its highest and most difficult virtues, has led us to regard Mrs. Quincy as one of the most admirable examples of her sex in every thing that refines, softens, and elevates the best human sensibility, while natural endowments, and ladylike graces, and true Christian acquirements, completed the engaging whole. Her politeness was uniform and natural, and without a trace of art. Her judgments were always most kind and generous. Her interest in those who were brought into incidental relations with her made friends of those who would not have been slighted if they had been left to be strangers. She was in every respect one of those pure and elevated persons, whose characters and death make it easier for us to believe in such a state beyond the grave as our faith promises to the good. The highest test which we can apply to any character, is to ask ourselves whether its translation from the earth makes heaven nearer and more real to us. That test is tried and commended to us by the decease of Mrs. Quincy.

"Since her marriage in 1797, she has shared the public honors and responsibilities of her distinguished husband, in the succession of eminent offices which he has filled in his long career of services to the nation, the State, the courts of justice, the chief magistracy of the city, and to the college of which he was the President and historian, — all of which he has passed through only to make them more honorable to his successors by his unstained integrity, and by his fidelity. How much aid and strength he must have derived in many arduous and anxious labors from his late companion, her own full sympathy with him can alone afford the estimate. During the sixteen years of Mr. Quincy's Presidency over the College, Mrs. Quincy won the warm esteem and love of the members of the successive classes, and was never named but to be honored."

No. IX.

MARGARET MORTON, born in New York in 1772, the only sister of Mrs. Quincy, resided in her family from 1800 to 1809, when she returned to New York. A woman of great strength and activity of character, she was accomplished, fond of reading, remarkable for industry, and for her skill in embroidery. Her early associates were among the most fashionable women of the day. Mrs. Henderson of New York — to whose daughter Mary, afterwards Mrs. Theodore Lyman of Boston, she stood as godmother — was her intimate and life-long friend.

In 1815, Miss Morton married David Ritzemer Bogert, Esq., of Beekman, Dutchess County, N.Y., who in early life had resided in Broadway, near Mrs. Morton's family, and had been then attached to her daughter. After an absence of twenty years, consequent on his removal in 1795 to Beekman, he returned to New York after the decease of his parents, and renewed his friendship with Miss Morton. They were married in 1815, and resided at Beekman until 1823; when they removed to Malta, near Ballston, N.Y. In both their places of residence, they were much esteemed by all their associates. Mrs. Bogert became as distinguished among the farmers of Dutchess County, as an efficient aid to her husband in his agricultural pursuits, as she had been in her youth in the gay circles of New York and Philadelphia. Mr. Bogert was descended from an ancient Dutch family; and on his decease, at the age of eighty years, he bequeathed the portrait of his maternal ancestor, the Rev. David Ritzemer of Albany, to the Historical Society of that city. A number of valuable books in the Dutch language he gave to President Quincy, who presented them in his name to the Library of Harvard University, and deposited them in Gore Hall. His farm and property he bequeathed to his wife, who passed the last years of her life in the family of her nephew, Charles F. Morton, Esq., at his residence, in the house at New Windsor known as the headquarters of General Knox during the war of the Revolution.* Retaining her mental powers, her correspondence

---

* Lossing's "Field Book of the American Revolution," p. 114.

with her relatives and friends was remarkable for the steadiness and clearness of her handwriting, for piquant expressions of opinion, and for anecdote. By her niece, Mrs. C. F. Morton, Mrs. Bogert was affectionately attended; and died after a short illness, in August, 1859, aged eighty-seven years.

John Morton resided in Philadelphia; and died there in 1835, seventy years of age. Clarke Morton, the youngest brother of Mrs. Quincy, entered into business as a merchant, and died early in life. Washington Morton was a man of uncommon ability and talent; and was also distinguished for his figure and personal appearance, being above six feet in height. His wife Cornelia Schuyler, a sister of Mrs. Alexander Hamilton, was one of the most beautiful women of her day. She was amiable and intelligent; and her death, in 1807, was a great calamity to her family. Her husband survived her but a short time, and died in France.

Washington Morton named his youngest daughter Mary Regina, after his grandmother Mrs. Kemper. As the widow of William Starr Miller of New York, she purchased an estate, which her ancestors in the Schuyler Family inherited, from Mr. Beekman, the first proprietor, at Rhinebeck, where she has erected a Lyceum, and is meritoriously employing her fortune for the benefit of the inhabitants. It is a singular coincidence, that by the mere contingencies of life, without a knowledge of the fact, such a design should, in 1861, be carried into effect by the descendant and namesake of Mrs. Kemper, at the place where her brother Mr. Ernest was first established, and where she passed her first winter in America, in 1741.

No. X.

* *Mrs. Anna C. L. Q. Waterston to Miss Quincy, Quincy, Massachusetts.*

CAUB ON THE RHINE, July 7, 1857.

MY DEAR SUSAN, — The above date will call up many associations to your mind; and many, many arise in mine as I find myself writing to you from this old Rhine town, with which our existence is so strangely interwoven.

---

* Mrs. Quincy named one of her daughters Mary Sophia, after her mother, Mrs. Morton; and the youngest (Mrs. Waterston), after her friend Miss Lowell.

Here are the river, the hills: the old Castle of Guntenfels frowns above, and the Pfalz stands upon the rock in the channel, just as they did when the Kemper Family left Rhineland for what was almost an undiscovered country. Helen and I must be among the first direct descendants who return to the old place, the great and great-great grandchild of those who went to the New World so long ago.

After spending the day at Oberwesel, with its old tower, and the church which contains the tombs of the Schomberg Family, we took one of the sail-boats drawn up on the riverside, and were steered towards Caub, which lay in the distance. As our little boat floated up the Rhine just before sunset, I thought I could truly imagine that spirits " twain had crossed with me." The town is very picturesque and very old; yet it is not dismal or ruined, but looks in good order, and as if the people were thriving. The mountains are covered with vineyards; and the kitchen gardens lie on the river-bank, and seem to have no dividing line. The little inn, or Gausthaus, in which Mr. Waterston, Helen, and myself now are, is neatness itself; and, if grandmamma revisits her birthplace to-night to take a spiritual look at her descendants, even she would be satisfied with the perfect cleanliness of our surroundings. How often have I heard her speak of the castle in the river, and mamma repeat the name while I looked at the view of Caub you copied as the frontispiece to her Memoir, and saw in Margaret's handwriting the account of the Kempers leaving the Rhine, in that interesting story! It is difficult to believe we are actually here, — that I have come to a place so familiar by long association. How strangely are all our destinies linked in with those of other days, — long, long passed away.

INDEX.

THE NUMBERS REFER TO THE PAGES.

Adams, Abigail, Mrs., 58, 77, 86, 187, 254, 259.
Adams, Hannah, 122.
Adams, John, 51, 71, 183, 185, 187, 199, 201, 205, 207, 208, 236.
Adams, John Quincy, 78, 185, 187, 189, 202, 207, 245.
American Revolution, Incidents during the, 17–40.
Alexander, Emperor of Russia, 210, 211.

Ballestier, Mrs., 288.
Baskinridge, Residence at, 18.
Belfast, 19–26.
Bogert, D. R., 185, 265.
Boston, Town of, 60, 87.
Boudinot, Elias, 18, 22, 33, 34, 38.
Bowditch, Nathaniel, 184, 207, 221, 224, 241.
Bowdoin, Governor, 88, 92.
Bowman, Maria, 43, 63, 224.
Braddock, General, 11.
Bromfield, Mrs. Ann, 94.
Bromfield, Edward, 87.
Bromfield Family, Account of, 254.
Bromfield, Henry, 93, 185.
Bromfield, John, 255.
Browne, Mrs., 97, 226, 234.
Buckminster, J. S., 115, 128, 156, 158, 159.

Cabot, George, 59, 60, 62, 63, 74, 78, 111.
Carleton, Sir Guy, 40, 41.
Caldwell, Rev. Mr., 18, 30, 33.
Calhoun, J. C., 153.
Catherine, Empress of Russia, 211.
Caub, Germany, 5, 266.
Channing, William Ellery, 141, 146, 149, 151, 153, 222.
Clay, Henry, 216, 217, 218.
Clinton, George, 47, 51, 228.
Clinton, De Witt, 153, 183.
Cochituate Aqueduct, Completion of, 248.
Cockburn, Admiral, 178, 179.
Copley, J. S. (Lord Lyndhurst), 67, 69.
Craigie, Mr., 61, 74.
Cranch, Richard, 123.
Cranch, William, 102, 105, 132.

Davis, Isaac P., 117, 147, 149, 153, 202.
Deane, Silas, 208.
Dexter, Samuel, 149.
Dickinson, John, 188.

Dowse, Edward, 64, 72, 213.
Dowse, Mrs., 76, 95, 242.
Dwight, Madam, 47.

Eclipse of the Sun, 1806.
Edgeworth, Maria, 228, 229, 236.
Eliot, John, 151, 169.
Ernest, Matthew, 1, 10, 12, 13, 266.

Foster, Augustus J., 140.
Frankfort, Ky., 98.
Franklin, Benjamin, 58, 92.
French Army, Arrival of, 39.
French Exiles, 56.

Gwinnett, Burton, 208.
Gallaudet, P. W., 17, 244, 261.
Gardinier, Barent, 115, 117, 118.
Gates, Horatio, General, 55.
Gerry, Elbridge, 151, 154, 157.
Gore, Christopher, 77, 101, 114, 155.
Grahame, James, 241.
Greene, Benjamin D., 225, 239.
Greene, Nathaniel, General, 81.

Halkett, John, 189.
Hanson, Alexander C., 126.
Hemphill, Joseph, 216, 217.
Henry, John, 147, 148, 149, 225.
Higginson, Stephen, 111.
Hillhouse, James, 103, 113, 130, 139.
Holbrook, Dr., 223.
Holmes, Mr., 128.
Huger, Francis K., 191.

Jackson, Francis J., British Minister, 126.
Jackson, Jonathan, 123.
Jackson, Mrs. Susan, 28, 55, 65, 76, 224, 253, 259.
Jefferson, Thomas, 110, 205, 207, 208, 209.
Johnson, William, 58.
Jones, John Coffin, 153.

Kalb, Baron De, 192.
Kemper, Daniel, 12, 18, 72, 78, 244, 259, 260.
Kemper, Jacob, 5, 18, 19, 38, 39, 44, 45, 78, 186, 258.
Kemper, Maria Regina, 6, 29, 44, 266.
Kemper, Maria Sophia, 6, 9, 13, 16.
King, Rufus, 217.

Kirkland, Rev. J. T., 61, 76, 100, 110, 115, 141, 185.

Lafayette, General, 34, 57, 183, 190, 198, 199, 200, 202, 204, 210, 225, 226, 233.
Ledyard, Miss, 46, 226.
Lee, Charles, General: his Capture, 25.
Lee, Eliza D., 131, 135, 137.
Lewis, Mrs. Eleanor P., 139, 253.
Lincoln, Benjamin, General, 31, 113, 116.
Lloyd, James, 114, 117, 128, 149, 150, 185, 219, 257.
Loan Office, 17, 55.
Lowell, Anna Cabot, 59, 62, 63, 69, 74, 122, 133, 148.

Madison, James, 147, 148, 153, 175, 176, 178, 179, 180, 256.
Madison, Mrs., 105, 129, 130, 132, 176.
Mann, Horace, 219.
Martin, Mr., "the Post," 29.
Mifflin, Thomas, 189.
Missouri Question, Debates on the, 215.
Monroe, James, 110, 185, 214, 217, 218.
Moreau, General, 212.
Morton, Jacob, 38, 54, 55, 57, 64, 72, 187, 232, 233.
Morton, John, 13, 16, 24, 32, 35, 36, 38, 56, 244, 262.
Morton, Margaret, 17, 265.
Morton, Maria Sophia, 13. 17, 28, 32. 38, 40, 45, 72–76, 173, 186, 188, 191, 221, 224, 261.
Morton, Washington, 18, 22, 26, 29, 55, 72, 78, 266.
Mount Vernon, 105, 120, 139, 253.

New York, City of, 40, 64.

Otis, Harrison Gray, 61, 85, 112, 114, 147, 148, 149, 150, 185.

Pahlen, Count, Russian Minister, 137, 140.
Parsons, Theophilus, 87, 113.
Partridge, Dr., 49.
Peace of 1815, 181.
Pennsylvania Line, Revolt of, 35.
Perkins, James, 112, 114, 147, 148, 153.
Perkins, Thomas Handyside, 77, 87, 112, 131.
Peter, Martha, Mrs., 58, 105, 131, 139, 145, 174.
Phillips, William, sen., 85, 87, 95, 213.
Phillips, William, 88, 95, 147, 156, 169, 171, 185, 188.
Pickering, Timothy, 58, 103, 130, 136, 139, 163, 170, 199.
Plummer, William, jun., 217.
Poinsett, J. R., 125, 128.
Putnam, Colonel, 200.

Quincy, Abigail, Mrs., 72, 85, 213, 242, 247.
Quincy, Josiah, of Braintree, 90, 92, 95, 123, 183, 223.
Quincy, Town of, 92.

Raffles, Sir Stamford, 239, 240.
Rogers, Commodore, 125.

Savage, James, 147.
Saxe Weimar, Duke of, 201.
Sergeant, J., 217.
Shaw, Samuel, Major, 43, 63, 86, 224.
Shaw, Mrs., 72, 76, 95, 123, 214, 224.
Shaw, William S., 114, 147.
Silliman, Benjamin, 223.
Sitgreaves, S., 65, 68.
Smith, Chief-Justice, 40, 42, 57.
Smith, Harriet, 42, 245.
Smith, John Cotton, 103, 104.
Smith, Samuel S., President, 58, 60, 67, 78.
Sprague, Charles, 223.
Springfield, N.J., Burning of, 31, 32.
Stirling, Lord, 28, 42.
Storer, Ebenezer, 89.
Story, Joseph, 222, 228.
Strong, Caleb, Governor, 149, 151, 155, 157, 160, 171.
Stuart, Gilbert, 53, 202.
Sullivan, William, 62, 65, 66, 185.
Sumner, W. H., 117, 185.

Tallmadge, Benjamin, 103, 118.
Teackle, J., 131, 133, 188.
Teackle, Henrietta, 131, 137.
Torrigiani, Charles, Count, 224.
Tracy, Ann, Mrs., 94.
Trumbull, J., Governor, 102.

Vanderkemp, F. A., 183, 258, 259.
Van Schaick, 48.
Vane, Sir Henry, 88.
Vidus, Count Charles, 201, 202.

Wadsworth, Daniel, 102, 187, 223.
War of 1812, 159, 160, 173, 257.
Warren, J. C., 199.
Washington, Bushrod, Judge, 105, 120.
Washington, George, General, 18, 25, 50; Inauguration as President, 51, 58, 62, 139, 188, 233, 244, 254, 259.
Washington, Mrs., 58, 58, 253.
Waterston, Robert C., 267.
Webster, Daniel, 189, 198, 209.
Wells, William, 222.
Wolcott, Eliza, 53, 54, 70, 186.
Wolcott, Oliver, 58, 78, 86.